WHAT PEOPLE ARE SAYING ABOUT

THE HIGH HEELED GUIDE TO SPIRITUAL LIVING

The High Heeled Guide to Spiritual Living *is the perfect up-to-date resource for the modern reader. Intimately written with warmth, intelligence and humor, it guides the reader through the chaos of everyday life. A real candle in the darkness.*
Jacky Newcomb, Best selling author of *An Angel Saved My Life*

Alice Grist has done it again. This sassy, spiritual adventurer is back with a witty and personable guide to bringing living, breathing spirituality into your everyday life.

Whilst some writers seem to encourage you to live a monastic life - aloof from the real world, Grist gives us 21st century advice complete with inner Goddesses, chocolate cake and of course, fabulous shoes. If you haven't met Grist before, welcome to your new best friend: get home from work, kick off those high heels and allow her to demystify spiritual living for the modern woman.
Dr Manjir Samanta-Laughton MBBS, Author of *Punk Science* and *The Genius Groove*

Alice has her finger on the pulse of the Universe and her insight into modern culture and tips for avoiding the traps of a consumer world are golden. Alice is an amazing role model for women who just know there is something more to life than what we are being sold. A must-read book for a new switched on generation of women tired of leading passive lives.
Sharni Montgomery, Author of www.sharnanigans.com

After a delightful taste of her own experiences shared through the pages of The High Heeled Guide to Spiritual Enlightenment, *Alice Grist is back to introduce the reader to her best work yet, offering needed tips and wise advice on how to recognize our lives for the spiritual journeys they are.*

The High Heeled Guide to Spiritual Living *is an impressive collection of lessons focused on finding the sacred in the ordinary.*
Sandra Carrington-Smith, Award-winning author of *The Book of Obeah* and *Housekeeping for the Soul: A Practical Guide to Restoring Your Inner Sanctuary.*

This book is a must read: fun and fabulous. Alice, who is feisty, fabulous and kick-ass, shares her own spiritual secrets and experiences, busts mystical myths and speaks directly to any girl (or guy) who need to spiritualize their life in the 21st Century. You'll find lots of inspirations and insights into your own spirituality, the mechanisms of your thoughts and the magic of being in the moment - love it!
Lisa Clark, Author and creatrix of www.thesassysorceress.com

The High Heeled Guide To Spiritual Living *is a super guide to beginning and navigating the endless path of spiritual living. Shot through with comedy and twinned with personal experience – this book is filled with not only the 'how to' but also the all important 'how not to' make spirituality achievable and life changing.*

A great read for spiritual seekers - especially lipstick loving ladies who are not afraid to do what it takes to find their soul.
Cher Chevalier, Spiritual advisor and author of *The Hidden Secrets of a Modern Seer*

Alice Grist has written an incredible book for all of 'us' confused people. Within this she teaches what is truly important in life and how to seek joy and appreciation for every moment of every day. A really beautiful book, one that you will want to share with everyone you know'.'
Anna Rodgers, Miss Eco Glam – Eco-friendly journalist www.blog.missecoglam.com

Brilliant! I could read it over and over again. The High Heeled Guide to Spiritual Living *is a feast for your soul! Whether this is your first*

look into spirituality or if you are a longtime student Alice covers all you need to know. Alice has delicious ways of serving up the perfect words to feed ours soul's spiritual needs. Guiding us through the sometimes-bumpy road of faith, love, body-mind connection and life's reality checks. Alice, thank you for sharing your talented spirit with us through this incredible guide!
Amy Schuber, Success coach for women and teen girls, founder of Be Inspired by You www.beinspiredbyyou.com

Grab life by the antlers with Alice Grist as she takes you on a journey through the joys and pitfalls of a spiritual path. Alice makes countless important points for living a truly spiritual life. Alice manages to find the balance between daily life and the greater reality beyond, she weaves them together to show the reader how to live in a new and exciting way.
Gabriel Morris, Author of *Kundalini and the Art of Being*

Alice Grist offers an honest, witty and detailed account of her spiritual journey and how, whether we realize it or not, each of us is already on a spiritual path. Through her own personal insights, Alice challenges you to free your mind of perfection, embrace the idea there is no coincidence and experience the messages the natural world is offering you. Your next steps along the path are only yours to take but Alice's book will definitely help you along the way.
Delphi Ellis, Specialist in dream and nightmare analysis, This Morning TV show dream expert

In her new book, The High Heeled Guide to Spiritual Living, *author, Alice Grist reveals the necessary tools for spiritualizing modern life, offering up a digestible platform for today's spiritual seekers. This is a fiery book covering many areas of human experience upon which contemporary spirituality can be based. If you are ready to reignite your inner spark this is the book for you.*
Gabrielle Bernstein, Speaker and author of *Add More –ing To Your Life*

Alice is a woman on a mission: she is determined to make 'spiritual living' accessible for everyone! She is not afraid of jumping in at the deep end and reporting her discoveries with blunt self-honesty and a delicious sense of humor.

Alice's book manages to be both entertaining and thought provoking at the same time. If she can do it – you can do it! Her story promises extraordinary encounters, coincidences and adventures along the way. Buy a copy of Alice's book but don't expect to be exactly the same person by the time you reach the final page. Fasten your seatbelt and enjoy the ride!!!

Imelda Almqvist, Painter and shamanic practitioner

Alice steps deeper into her truth and teaches us by sharing her experiences. We hear the wisdom of her Higher Self speak through the beautiful human being that she is. As we follow her journey through the landscape of her spiritual awakening, we learn the central lesson of the Age of Aquarius: to use our own discernment, to follow our own teacher within, instead of some external authority. Be ready to be entertained, challenged and inspired!

Judith Bogner, TV presenter, event moderator, spiritual healer

The High Heeled Guide to Spiritual Living

The High Heeled Guide to Spiritual Living

Alice Grist

Winchester, UK
Washington, USA

First published by Soul Rocks Books, 2011
Soul Rocks Books is an imprint of John Hunt Publishing Ltd., Laurel House, Station Approach,
Alresford, Hants, SO24 9JH, UK
office1@o-books.net
www.o-books.com

For distributor details and how to order please visit the 'Ordering' section on our website.

A CIP catalogue record for this book is available from the British Library.

Cover Artwork: Sarah Craven

Design: Stuart Davies

Printed in the UK by CPI Antony Rowe
Printed in the USA by Offset Paperback Mfrs, Inc

We operate a distinctive and ethical publishing philosophy in all
areas of our business, from our global network of authors to
production and worldwide distribution.

CONTENTS

Thanks and love to…

My husband James for his constant support, love and being the
very best kind of soulmate.

My parents for their guidance, love and always being there.
Rebecca Coakley and Karen Mc Bride. Tony and Aileen Grist.
The Brothers Joseph and Michael. My Grandparents and family
in the UK, USA and in heaven – big, huge love.
Patricia Laurie.

Sarah Craven for the stunning artwork.
Good Friends; Roisin, Reina, Clare L, Shireece, Claire S, Sharni,
Gaynor, Gary, Natalie, Neil. Little friends; Lainey & Jacie.
Cat kisses to Jimi & Molly.

John Hunt and everyone at O-Books for letting me loose a
second time and helping to make dreams come true!

Finally to everyone who has stumbled upon my path and has
ended up affecting the pages of this book (and of my life) in
some fantastic way. I believe we are all intrinsically linked, as
energy and as souls, so my sincerest thank you to all those
sparkling lights who have come my way for better or for worse.
We all help each other become who we are, the sooner we are
grateful for it, the happier this world will be. So thank you!

About the Author

Alice Grist is the author of The High Heeled Guide to Enlightenment, the book that charts Alice's journey from party girl to sassy spiritual woman. Her second book The High Heeled Guide to Spiritual Living has come hot on its heels and follows Alice as she progresses on her journey. Alice contributes to various publications as a freelance writer and is regularly a specialist guest on numerous radio and TV shows.

Alice is the founder and managing editor of Soul-Cafe, an online network dedicated to 'women (and men) who know there is more to life than lipstick'. On Soul-Cafe Alice regularly interviews and features the spiritual advice and writings of experts and authors. Soul-Cafe provides a safe, happy space for all spiritual seekers. Soul-café.net

Alice lives happily with her musician husband James who is the singer and guitarist with SuperEvolver. They have two cats and veer very nicely between the quiet life and a little bit of rock 'n' roll.

www.alicegrist.co.uk

A Note from the Author…

Yesterday my husband, James and I were clearing out the house looking for a lost passport. Somewhere in the mêlée of drawers, boxes and paperwork he came across my diary from nine years ago. The diary began just a few weeks before I met him. It documented my arrival in the town of Leicester, our meeting and my general life around that time.

It was like being confronted with a total stranger. Even James remarked that I am now a totally different woman from the lost, self conscious, slightly conceited girl that I had been then.

It made for hard reading. I was horrified by some of my small-minded comments and throwaway asides. I felt sorry for the child inside me who had been very confused about the world, about relationships and about where on earth her life was headed. It was the diary of someone consumed by her own messy life, and was desperately trying to fathom a way out, but without having to make too much effort. It was Bridget Jones but with soft drugs, hard rock and a boyfriend.

What scares me now when reading back through my diary, is how unconscious I was to anything. These days I am stringently aware of myself, of others, of the world, the planet, animals and all of our spiritual places within it. Back then, I could not see past my own bed, work and another rampaging night out. I was living the fantastical young woman's life. I was exploring all that life had to offer when living in a two up two down on the hard side of town.

I was making friends, meeting people, shopping with the funds from my first proper job, misbehaving and apparently having massive amounts of fun.

But my thoughts never drifted beyond all of this. The only inner seeking I did, was to harp back to my life just before Leicester and wonder where it all went wrong.

This may sound like a familiar scenario to you. Many of us have a tendency to live shallow, self-seeking lives, not because we are bad people, but because there are few other options apparent to us. We earn money, we buy things, we feather our nest and we believe that this gives our lives meaning. At weekends we pour this money into a social account that sees us through another week with a few funny memories. The lucky few of us have great careers, or wonderful children to focus on. But still... we are not thinking outside of the four walls of our own lives.

I believe there is more to our lives than we currently realize. We are not simply little human consumption machines, we are powerful spiritual beings and it is time we started to explore this. Accessing this knowledge and empowering ourselves with it is the aim of this book.

The High Heeled Guide to Spiritual Living will help take you from the shallow side to a deeper and more fulfilling existence.

I intend to show you that beyond our little lives, you are connected to infinity. You are in cahoots with all other people and things on this planet, and when you know this you can begin living above and beyond your current, somewhat limited, potential. I want you to know that you are a spiritual being, having a human experience. To explore this you do not need to wait until you die. You are spiritual now, this is your life now. The two things can be merged to great effect and all things can become more meaningful than you ever anticipated.

Whilst we didn't find James's passport during our clear out, it became clear to me that somewhere along the line I had found my passport to a crazily fulfilling life. By realizing my spirituality and the life force and energy of all things, I too had realized who I am. I have found my purpose and flown to greater, happier heights.

I will say no more, save for the fact that this book is written for you. My last book, if I am honest was written for me, it was a kind of therapy that prepared me for my spiritual path.

Instead now I devote this book to you in your high heels, your biker boots, your sandals and your bare feet. I devote it to women, and to men, and to children should they feel that way inclined.

All I want to do is help change the world and if I can get your consciousness to budge one tiny little millimeter, then I am smiling.

Peace and Love

Alice

Introduction

"I believe that we are so unenlightened in our ever distracting world that simply opening ourselves gently to the notion of enlightenment is a small enlightenment in itself. It is an achievement simply to choose to believe and to let the faith that follows become a life guide."
Alice's Diary March 2010

If you learn one thing whilst reading this, then let it be this, you are already spiritual; you must be, because you are spirit. This is one spiritual truth that is often overlooked and lost in the complexities and varied opinions that inform you how to become a spiritual person.

The premise of this book is that your spirituality is entirely individual to you. *The High Heeled Guide to Spiritual Living* aims to show you that the true discovery of your spirituality can only ever come from your own personal existence. Gurus, books and mantras aside, I believe that your spirituality is innately and unequivocally yours, it already exists, it is you, and I hope to help you scratch the surface and set it free.

I started learning about spirituality through consulting the wisdom of ancient faiths, as is depicted in my book *The High Heeled Guide to Enlightenment*. That was hugely profitable in beginning to understand a global view of what spirituality is, and how I could bring it into my modern life. After finishing my explorations of faith, I found myself at a loose end, and it was within this loose end and the resulting year or so of living that my own spirituality truly found me.

In writing *The High Heeled Guide to Enlightenment* I had opened myself up to a spiritual life. At the beginning of my trip towards enlightenment I may well have believed spiritual life to be all fairies, angels and wishing upon a star. However as my divine trip progressed I soon came to see that spirituality is found more powerfully in the things that you see and experience every day.

There is spirituality in your work, in your arguments, in your debt and in your grievances. There is spirituality in your bad hair days, your best friend's pony and the way your sister always borrows your clothes without asking. There is spirituality in your heart, your mind, your flesh, your bones, in your walk and in your talk.

Let me assure you of this, a bus ride home from work can be as spiritually enlightening as a private dinner with the Dalai Lama. Your life is your spiritual teacher, and *The High Heeled Guide to Spiritual Living* is your personal road map to your own version of spiritual freedom and enlightenment.

Through the pages of this book I wish to show you that spiritual living is not the sole remit of a far-flung journey to the mystical corners of the planet. It is not a guru chanting mysteries of the universe into your ever-willing ear, whilst you pay by the hour. It is not found solely in a spirituality class, through meditations or via a strict cleansing, fasting and praying regime.

Spirituality is found through your every day life. It is discovered through the highs, the lows, the boredoms and the barmy! Any guru worth their robes and title should tell you that fact. A good guru should tell you that what you are seeking is yourself, and they should tell you to look inside yourself for answers. But that is a bit vague isn't it? Yes a few meditations may help, but what about when the boiler breaks and the tires burst or your best friend runs off with your husband? What about real life? How are you supposed to get spiritualized when life gets in the way?

Well I have lived through that dilemma and I am now finding my way to the other side of it. I am beginning to understand that spirituality will find me no matter what, but I will not see this unless I alter my way of understanding the world.

This far along in my spiritual path I have been forced to

examine a number of areas in my life in minute spiritual detail. I have had to open up my heart and soul to really get to grips with what is true and real to me. I have had to decide for myself what I believe in and what I do not.

I am not only talking about spiritual subjects, I am talking about topics like the environment, and beauty, shopping, my body, diet, my liking of alcohol and my tendency of feeling sorry for myself sometimes. I have held a spiritual mirror up to all of that and more, and the results of this are reflected back in the pages of this book.

The High Heeled Guide to Spiritual Living sets out my spiritual experience, as an example. My life is one that is lived very normally. I do not hang out with writers, spiritual gurus, psychics or celebrities. I do not have Oprah on speed dial. I work full time, I see my friends, I have minor car crashes, I have pets, I love to eat and I moan when my jeans get too tight. I too have seriously bad hair days.

Within this book I do not attest to tell you The Truth. I can only tell you my truth. If that rocks something deep inside of you, then jump on it and experience it for yourself. I intend to help you to understand the intrinsic spirituality that is already inside you.

It is my mission to assist you to find your personal spirituality. I intend to show you how to find it through the familiar, through the ups and the downs of your everyday existence. 'Is this possible?' I hear you shrill and shriek. 'How can little old me, up to my eyeballs in business, bills, nappies, shoe choices and housework, possibly find the spiritual divine in my own life?' 'Surely a trip to India is needed?' I hear you cry! 'Maybe a trip to the local meditation retreat at the least?'

Well maybe... but then again, I really do not think any of those are necessary. The reason they are not necessary, and the fact that we all tend to gloss over, is, as I stated before, that you are already spiritual. You are a spiritual being hacking it out in a human body. I believe that part of our purpose in life is to somehow fuse the two.

Nobody owns spirituality, they can tell it to you all day long, they may even try to sell it to you, but it is not a product, it is not something you can purchase. Spirituality must be lived. Spirituality is what you are. You simply need to realize that fact. When you have realized it, then it is your job to find a way to live it.

Unlike my first book, the only person's advice I have taken on writing this is my own. I have had one or two dealings with potential gurus, but they have had their own set of complications and unexpected spiritual lessons. Instead of following someone else's lead I have trusted my personal connection to the spiritual divine, as I will encourage you to trust yours.

I am not trained, or attuned in anything (other than a dose of Reiki). I am not your guru. I am a woman who has learned thorough the mayhem that is life, and who has a better idea about how to understand and interpret her own very special spirituality. It is my aim now, to help you to do the same. No trips to India required!

The adventures and mishaps that are contained within these pages are fresh and steaming from the annals of my own life. Seriously, I went through the mill on this one for you! I aim to show you how it is the every day events, and our spiritual interpretation of them that make each of us our own Guru. I hope that through the everyday enlightenment of my daily occurrences, you will see similarities in your own life.

I have set the book out in 'lessons'. Each of the lessons covered is something that I have had to plough through to get myself a little closer to the genuine spiritual being that lays inside of this human woman's body. I believe each 'lesson' will address aspects of your life that are similar to mine, and some that I believe to be the sicknesses of our society and generations. Each lesson will help you to knock down blocks that are barring you from your own spiritual self. Each lesson will assist you to see life a little more spiritually and in turn help you to forge a stronger link to your true, higher, divine self.

As well as setting out lessons, I have proposed many fun and easy exercises to help you get stuck into fast track spiritualization! From there onward you can start to get to know your own personal and highly individual version of spirituality and enlightenment.

You are here to learn your spiritual lessons, as I am here to learn mine, I am sure that our paths are quite different. It is the similarities within our lives through which we might both find some solidarity and some spiritualization. I hope that this little offering, *The High Heeled Guide to Spiritual Living*, helps us both on our way!

A brief aside first: I will use the term spirituality frequently in this book, but I will also use other terms. I do not feel the term spirituality does justice to any of what I have written about. Having wrangled with other words, none, on their own, quite fit the bill. So instead I will use a variety of language, because it is colorful, I like it, and it fits into the realm of spirituality as I see it.

When I use terms such as divine, mystical, higher self, angels, guides, helpers, energy, vibration, please know that these all mean the same thing to me, more or less. These terms mean, the force, the energy, the spirit and the soul that makes up everything. They are spirituality spoken in a myriad of ways and so to reflect the dynamic, exciting and mysterious nature of spirituality, I have chosen to use them all.

So let's begin.

Having sat more deeply within my own spirituality for a few years since writing *The High Heeled Guide to Enlightenment* there are a few things I would like to share. This book represents my real life learning about what spirituality is to me. I hope *The High*

Heeled Guide to Spiritual Living will kick-start your journey into the world of all things divine, mystical and spiritually exciting.

This book is here to help show you, that in fact, everything is sacred, and every action, movement and thought you undergo can easily be done with spirituality as its starting point and center point. As a society we have swayed too far from this path and it is for that reason that I believe our society is somewhat confused. We have in essence forgotten our essence! I believe that everything is spiritual, and that if we all lived that way our society would be a truly wonderful place.

The High Heeled Guide to Spiritual Living will help you to look at your own spirituality in a universal context. I want to show you how to keep your own spiritual self-true and then how to expand that beyond yourself so that you increase your own spiritual flow and assist others to find theirs too. This book is about peace, harmony and love; it is about finding it, keeping it and about beginning to live at your spiritual peak. It's simple, come join me.

Lesson 1 – What is Spirituality?

What exactly do you mean when you say you are spiritual? What do I mean by spiritual? Are we thinking the same thing? Probably not, well, not exactly the same, but we might have a similar enough idea that we can get our heads together and work out a compromise. Spirituality is as individual as the person.

Following my dabbling with a number of faiths in *The High Heeled Guide to Enlightenment* and the living that followed I have come to a few of my own conclusions and I offer them up here. I intend in this lesson to give you my insights so that you might find and reinforce your own.

On any path of spiritual living it is a good idea to have a rough idea of what you are seeking. I can only tell you what spirituality represents to me, and what it does not. I hope my idea of spirituality roughly tallies with yours, but if something rubs, or does not quite fit, then don't worry, we are simply unique spiritual beings living differently. What's true is that we are both still learning.

So for your delectation, I have set out what spirituality is and what spirituality is not. I have started with the 'is not' so they can be ruled out quickly and we can move swiftly onto the wondrousness of 'what is'. This is spirituality according to Alice Grist (not a guru, sage or saint) but more a high-heeled occasional sinner who is determined to get fully enlightened one of these fine days!

Spirituality is not religion...

I believe it is important to set my stall out and to explain why I find religion to be very different from my personal version of spirituality. In doing this I hope I can help you come to terms for yourself with the difference, hopefully engendering in your own mind and soul a more whole reason as to why you feel spiritually drawn as opposed to religiously defined.

To me religion, any religion is essentially talking about the same thing that spirituality is. The general gist of all beliefs, be they Hindu, Catholic or Tribal is that there is more to human life and that life goes on beyond death in some kind of spiritual context. This is of course a rather generalizing and minimizing comment. I am sure I will be criticized for saying this, indeed I already have been. In spite of that criticism I won't apologize, because I truly believe that at the heart of all religion, no matter what dogma or stance that religion has become embroiled in, lays the very stark belief in goodness, love and life beyond our current conception.

At one of my very first book signings I had a gentleman start a perfectly civil conversation with me about spirituality. He said that he had experimented with a number of alternative spiritualities and credited them with saving his life. He said that he had recently become a born again Christian. I commented that my belief was that whatever religion or faith we had, they were likely all different human interpretations of the one same thing. He looked at me and flatly stated that it was very interesting how the devil made me believe that. He then turned his tail and left, leaving me with his self-righteous attack stinging in my ears.

In retrospect this event was quite amusing, though at the time it was most unnerving. I felt frustrated at this man's lack of respect and insight. It was as though he had started a friendly conversation with me purposefully and was simply waiting for the right moment to put his Jesus touting boot in it.

This exemplifies my first reason why spirituality is not religion. Many religions teach that their way is the only way. Everybody else is going straight to hell. I think that this is very sad and lacks any perspective of the forgiving nature of their religion, never mind of faith as a whole!

So whilst I believe that all faiths have that one thing in

common, not everyone is keen to be so open and giving. I believe that the problem lies in the fact that formalized, institutionalized religion is dictated to us; it was set out thousands of years ago and has been interpreted over the ages, at first by prophets and preachers and more recently by kings, queens, politicians and governments. As a result religion has become prescribed and dogmatic. Religion is taught and comes pre-packaged, ready to assemble, often according to strict instructions. It is hugely unfortunate that most modern day religions proclaim themselves to the true purveyors of God's word. When everyone thinks they are right, it becomes a big fight and nobody will ever win.

Most world religions have blood on their hands. Religion has been (and still is) drastically abused to promote various people's agendas. As a result, any underlying message of peace, love, respect and learning has been lost in a mêlée of opinion, direction, orders and severe discipline.

My faith, my spirituality will never cause another person, or people to bleed. I don't buy into the bloodthirsty power games of religious politics. Spirituality is never about politics. No... I'm wrong in fact it probably is about politics. But it is more about the dissolution of politics and the return to a faith led existence, rather than a controlling, agenda lived existence... that however is a whole other book!

Spirituality is inherent to religion, although for me, religious spirituality is somewhat trampled on by centuries of human interpretation, bloodied history and the political power games I mentioned previously. Religion informs you how to feel spiritually, and how to exist spiritually as per the instructions of the relevant book. Religion is a how-to manual, and it is presumed that you are not capable of acting spiritually or indeed feeling spiritually on your own accord. Religion therefore gives you a structure, a lineage, a power base and a leader. Religion makes you its subject and the guy at the front of the room is your purported savior, your leader, your emperor and the word of

God comes solely through him.

Another contention I have with religion is the massive reliance on the ancient texts and preaching for our understanding of spirit. I believe it is dangerous ground to be basing our personal beliefs on something that was written in a time so hugely dissimilar to our own. Particularly as the latter interpretation of the texts that govern religion is something that has been subject to change so very often, has been the job of males in a patriarchal society and renders your personal interpretation null and void.

As you will discover throughout this book I feel strongly that it is time we started to interpret our spiritual beliefs through our own personal experiences instead. It is my thought that religion disempowers your spiritual insight, it creates your faith through a set text. Whereas I feel in my heart and soul that spirituality is free flowing and internal, of course some structure may help, but spirituality is to be lived and experienced. Spirituality allows for us to get personal and practical, whereas religion seems concerned in the main with adherence to theory.

Spirituality is not religion because Westernized religion is inherently sexist. There is no equilibrium, there is no balance, religion gives us a God figurehead, but we have no Goddess. My interpretation of mainstream religion is that it is essentially a male faith. There is a whole feminist agenda behind this brief paragraph so I will be brief and summarize! In religion women make great whores. When not prostituting ourselves, we are sufficient to take on the role of mother. Women are condemned or idolized by religion, beyond this we simply do not feature very much.

No wonder society is in the mess it is and that women sway wildly between vampish sex bomb and nurturing momma. We have no in-between space. We are one version of sexuality, or the other. Female nature has been slammed into two definitive jars and religion is partially, if not wholly responsible. We have spent the last few millennia worshipping the male and have forgotten all about his equal counterpart, except for in terms of what she does for the guy. Religion does not give the female breathing space.

For me this is one of the most striking reasons why spirituality is not religion. Religion gives my vagina and me no credit, no space, no truth. As I write this I have learned that the Vatican has just ruled the ordination of women priests to be akin to sexual perversity and should be punished the same way. I have nothing polite to say about this. I know that many Catholic priests know a thing or two about sexual perversity, but I think what they know about women is bombastically wrong. Women can vote and work and raise the next generation all at the same time and so this stance is quite clearly ridiculous. The death cries of a dying breed.

My five-year-old friend Lainey recently took me to one side and imparted me this wisdom: "Girls are the best". But shush, apparently we are not supposed to tell the boys, and it is clear that nobody has yet told the pope! But even if girls are not the best, and are in fact equal to boys, this is not reflected in any Western traditional organized faith that I know of. Hence the fact I cannot get on with religion. I am a feminist – so sue me.

Since starting my spiritual journey I have realized that spirit, God, Goddess, angels, guides and divinity all touch and affect my life every day in every way. This does not make me a messiah or a prophet or even a mystic. It simply makes me a spiritual being acknowledging my divine self and enjoying the experience of it, whilst continuing to learn more about it daily. I see spirituality in every single thing that I view or that I experience. I much prefer the familiarity of my own spiritual faith. The formality of religion holds no water for me. Let the religious masses think that the devil has visited me if they want to! I know that is far from the truth.

I prefer my faith to be visited in a dream, a passing butterfly or an insightful moment. If that is considered a little bit pagan or heathen, then I really do not care because I reject the labeling and criminalizing of religious zealotry. I would much rather be a part of the creative spiritual process. I am a spiritual process, and honey, I will not be told!

Let me be direct, I simply do not need religion. It holds no interest for me. It cannot give me anything I cannot find existing already inside my own heart.

I believe that divine consciousness expands far beyond the realms of any particular interpretation and it is with due respect to the loving heart of all major religions that I have walked swiftly away from that path and onto my own.

Spirituality is not Salvation...

Spirituality is not your personal savior. It cannot rescue you from the irksome and grim side of life. Becoming a spiritual person does not stop bad things happening to you.

I say this because people tend to think that once they embrace a faith they should be immune from darkness, disease and disaster. I know this because I have been guilty of this way of thinking myself.

I personally blame the curse of Santa Claus! We are raised to believe that if we have been good all year long then we deserve our goodies. As children it is constantly reinforced to us that being good, in any arena of life, will bring rewards.

Well on a spiritual level, that does have so much truth, and in many respects life is better once you start to uncover your soul. In spite of this you must know that you are not especially protected. You are not a 'chosen' person; you are not the Goddesses' golden girl. We are all equal in the eyes of the divine and no matter how much you meditate, pray or chant, you are as liable to break your leg in a skiing accident as the next man.

I have been on the receiving end of bad news and felt astonished. Part of me wondered, why me? I may even have got slightly grouchy and asked the powers that be, "but don't you know who I am!"

I've had moments when I thought that because I was 'spiritual' I was above all the bad news days. It seems that there is some strange natural urge to see spirituality as a form of protection racket. You are on the side of the big guys and gals, and therefore, bad stuff happens to other people and never to you. But the annoying truth is that spirituality is a path of growth, and nobody can grow without all the good and the bad happening to them. So no matter how cozy you are with your personal faith, you are always just as vulnerable as the next person.

Life can be excruciatingly hard, no matter what you do or who you are. Spirituality will not stop your hair going grey, your loved ones dying or the bills mounting up. Spirituality is an understanding; it is not, in any shape or form, your very own prince charming or knight in shining armor coming to rescue you from the wicked things.

Once you embrace spirituality, your life will continue in very much the same way as it did before you encountered your spiritual path. Spirituality is not a miracle cure. Yes, it can make wonderful things happen in your life, and it will transform the way you see life, as this book will go onto describe. But if you are looking for a shield, you have come to the wrong place.

Hardships happen to us all, and I'd go so far as to say, I believe that this is the point of our existence. Alongside the happy times we are here to weather the storms, to grow older, bolder and better. It is how you handle the darker side of life that helps make you spiritual, and that is what truly counts. So no, spirituality will not make your life a fairy playground of perfection.

But do not worry because this book will help you to spiritually embrace the harder times in life for your highest personal benefit. On a positive note, whilst faith may not always save your skin from scrapes and your heart from hurt, it can help ensure your sanity, and guide you through the hard times in a way that strengthens and spiritualizes your soul!

Spirituality is not a business...

One thing that gives mainstream religion credibility over spiritual enlightenment is that religion is free and to an extent it is regulated. To get your soul saved by Christ, Buddha, Mohammad or Abraham, all you need to do is pay with your loyalty and commitment. It is unfortunate that some people offering 'spiritual salvation' are doing so at a steep price. That price may not solely be to your bank account.

Of course there are plenty of great, honest, loving, giving and well priced spiritual people out there. But there are also charlatans. When I wrote *The High Heeled Guide to Enlightenment* I did not realize how many charlatans there actually were. I know this now because half of them have tried to contact me, tried to work with me and/or tried to con me. It has been a steady theme in my life that I am absolutely finished with. It is one of the reasons why I wholeheartedly advocate you getting to know your spirituality on your own terms, rather than employing somebody to show you how to find it.

My issue is not all about money. I understand that spiritual teachers, mystics, healers and psychics are not backed by institutions in the same way that organized religions are. As such they often cannot offer their services for free. In spite of this any truly spiritual person will be doing their work for the love of spirit and they will charge you a reasonable, affordable, thoughtful price. They will not add on any surcharges toward fairy dust or angelic consultation fees!

If you require a third party in your spiritual path, then do be careful. I cannot stress this enough. Spiritual fakes and frauds will not be obvious to you, just as they have not been obvious to me. They come across as nice, kind, caring and well... spiritual. If you feel a situation is wrong, then trust your intuition and be strong enough to know that it is wrong. Back out, take your money and go to the library, to a respected teacher, or do some meditation instead.

Spirituality's modern presentation as a business is utterly disheartening to me. Many spiritual people describe themselves as business people. Indeed I have been described as a business-woman, which I am not. Business to me means money. Spirituality is not, and never has been to me about cash. If I can pay my mortgage and keep myself in the normal lifestyle I already have, then I am a happy woman. If I cannot and I need to continue working elsewhere for a wage, then fair's fair, I will do that. I do not want to be a guru sat on a stash of gold.

Spirituality should never be commercial, not if it is going to truly mean anything. We have the power here. We can get to the heart of spirituality, or we can misunderstand it entirely and make a bucket load of cash. I believe we should take a leaf out of Jesus' book and upturn the traders in the temple, for they spoil spirituality for the rest of us.

If spirituality is any kind of business it is the business of the soul, and of life beyond this life. Money has little place in spiritual circles. You would not go to a church and expect to pay the vicar for the privilege of praying would you? Yet recently I was offered an exclusive deal, I could pay £150 for a spiritual man to pray for me. Clearly I was flabbergasted. When I refused he tried to haggle with me! No...in my mind prayers are free, they go with the territory.

Another example of my frustration with this stems from a great love of mine, reiki. I have recently become a little disillu-sioned with the high price of learning reiki. In my opinion reiki has been divided up and formalized in a way that means it can be sold in parts. It has been set out in stages of development that I am not sure I truly believe in any more. The power seems to lie in privileged information and a higher price to pay to get that information.

Essentially I feel that reiki is identical to the spiritual healing techniques I was taught aged 13, by my father, for free. The results are the same too. Try as I might I cannot see or feel the difference. I love reiki, I am not sure I love the structure and formality and the overall cost and politics that are involved in attuning to that modality of healing. Healing is part of your life and your spiritual heart; you cannot simply stump up some cash and qualify. You are already qualified; you just need to be shown how.

Recently some lovely new friends of mine attuned me to Seichem Reiki, for free. It was a kind and generous offer made all the more wonderful by them giving me an attunement gift at the end of it all – a statue of an Egyptian cat. This is the true nature of spirituality, the generous, heartfelt, unexpected and loving development of oneself and others. This was done with no money involved and performed for no other reason than simply because they could.

Because of this I am making it my mission to teach all my friends spiritual healing for free, because to me healing is a natural gift. My hope is that they will be empowered to go home and offer warm, loving healing energy to their dog, their kids or their partner's headache. Healing, reiki, or energy work is only a matter of harnessing a universal power that is everybody's birthright. I am simply sharing the healing love around and I'm doing it because I can.

Spirituality is not fortunetelling

Spirituality will never be found in the bottom of a cup full of tea leaves. I have mistakenly believed that a psychic can give me spiritual advice on how to live my spiritual path. Of course it is intriguing to have someone predict things in your life, and it is mind-blowing to have a medium connect to your deceased loved ones. Psychics and mediums can offer up a wonderful affirmation of a spiritual life beyond human life. Indeed they can help open your eyes to a whole other side of existence. But this on its own is not spirituality; it is merely a teensy tiny peek behind the curtain.

I have seen a good number of psychics and very few have been any good. Often they overlook the very fundamentals of my life. They usually do not even touch on the stuff that is important to me. I generally leave with the feeling that I have been ripped off. Of course some psychics have an apparent gift, but this does not make them instantly spiritual, nor does it make them gurus. Psychic abilities are not necessarily akin to wisdom or spirituality.

So it is my definitive opinion that Spirituality is not found in predictive phenomena. Psychics, mediums and even tarot (my specialty) are at best a fun, practical and interesting sidetrack from spiritual beliefs. They give you a brief window to glimpse your own life, but get this, they are rarely anything more, and often they are far, far less. Please do enjoy what they offer, but realize that your path as a great spiritual being is essentially your business alone. This is your life and you have to learn from it on your own accord.

It is also my belief that in embracing your own spirituality you will not have any real need for other people to tell you about your life. As you become spiritual you will naturally open to your intuition and even your own psychic sense. This book will help to show you how, and then the rest will be down to you.

My dear friend Roisin recently went to the best psychic I have ever heard of! The psychic sat there, looked at her and told her that she really ought to be doing this for herself, as she was perfectly capable.

I wholeheartedly agree and I extend that message to you dear reader. Embrace your spirituality and the knowledge that comes with that can be profound. You are a powerful soul and you do not need anybody to tell you anything. Believe it.

Spirituality is not all karma, blame and judgment...

It is vitally important that you understand that spirituality is yours and that the person most fit to interpret it, is you. Other people's interpretations of what has happened to you are only as valid as you allow them to be. You know you, and you know your life. I have felt critiqued, judged and blamed by even some of the most spiritual people in my life. As a result I have withdrawn my life from their grasps and I will be the boss of me.

I want to make you aware of this, because in the early stages of your spiritual path it is all too easy to put your life in the hands of another seemingly more experienced person. In spite of our spiritual tendencies, as in all realms of life, spiritual people are still human. On occasion a spiritual human can be a real nasty piece of work. So if you find yourself in a place where you believe that people are putting judgment and blame onto you, and making you feel bad about yourself, I advise that you walk away.

When I was researching *The High Heeled Guide to Enlightenment* I had a tendency to put myself into other people's hands to learn about my spirituality. This is a dangerous game because it immediately sets up a power structure whereby I am the student and they are the teacher. This can work out quite well sometimes, and as my book attests I met some wonderful, talented people. But I have seen a darker side to this, and one that worries me. I have seen very human opinions passed off as message and guidance from spirit, I have seen vulnerable people become quite frighteningly reliant on their 'spiritual guru'. I have been aware of blame and judgment being cast down as loving caring advice.

I do not adhere to being judged very well. None of us do. But when it comes from a person who claims not to be judging, then it is simply hypocritical. This is the problem of a spiritual path sometimes. You will come up against people whose idea of spirituality is different from yours, or whose behavior, whilst overtly spiritual, may challenge you in other respects. It was through a series of situations like this that I decided to withdraw myself from anybody's guidance and to become a mainly solitary spiritual seeker.

Nobody comes to spiritual realization more quickly by being told off. In my experience we must do that learning for ourselves and not because another person tells us what they perceive to be the problem with our life or our actions. Spirituality is for sharing; it is not a tool with which to whip people.

We must learn to look at our own lives kindly too. We should not expect others to judge us, and we should not then judge ourselves harshly either. Recently I had two car crashes, both times a driver went into the back of my car whilst I was stationary. After the first incident I went through my life mentally with a fine toothcomb and totally refocused myself. As a result I felt hugely happier, on track and ready for more of life. Then bam! I was rear-ended again!

My initial thought was...oh dear... what have I missed? What have I not changed in my life that needs changing? Why has this happened to me again? Of course I had an outpouring of sympathy from concerned friends and this was lovely. But then out of the blue a stranger sent me a message on Facebook that was entirely unsympathetic. The message was "Hmmm......
Maybe you need to rethink your life path, usually this has something to do with it." No sympathy, no, 'hope you feel better soon'. Instead the message laid the blame clearly at my feet for my apparently faulty life path. I sat and sulked about this. I did not know what more I could do for other people, as a friend, as a good wife, or as a spiritual writer, that would improve or better my life path at that moment.

This judgmental comment got me thinking. I started wondering about other people's faith, and how their faith is assimilated into their mind in a way that makes them judgmental, cynical, self-righteous, and in this instance thoughtless. This event reminded me of the school of thought that 'blames' people for their own circumstances. The kind of spiritual thought that believes disabled people deserve their disability because it is punishment for their wrongdoings in a past life. Well, excuse my French but that is just merde de chien!

To me every event contains learning. It is an education. In my mind Spirituality is not a blame culture. We are not punished by a wicked God until we are whiter than white. Events occur, and if we possibly can, we learn from them and we grow from them. They are not punishments. I believe in Karma, but I see Karma as an opportunity for growth, to learn about oneself and to change your ways. It is not a slap on the wrist from a vengeful deity determined to make you suffer.

I say all this because I want you to know that if something bad happens in your life, it is not automatically your fault, spiritually or otherwise. I believe that occasions like my second car crash happen so that we can learn something. Maybe part of my learning was so that I could move away from the situations I was in where I felt I was being judged. Indeed the original crash gave me time and space to get my head together, it was a blessing not a curse. The second crash helped me to have some time to think even further. I was not being given punishment, I was gifted growth, learning and time to think.

Punishment, blame and judgment on others and their life paths are a human matter, not a spiritual one. I do not believe that a spiritual existence bothers much with retribution. Life is hard enough on this planet without adding more guilt and blame on our own doorsteps. Yes, I believe Karma can come back to you for your naughtiness, but it is only ever for your good in the long run.

As I discussed in my first book, love, unconditional love is the key to all enlightenment, I still firmly believe that. Passing judgment is never an act of love, whether you pass judgment upon yourself or onto other people. And if the words or opinions of another make you feel judged, then please do disregard them and move on.

To summarize... spirituality is not religion, it is not a business, it is not judgment and it is not fortune telling. I am sure that there are a lot of other things that spirituality is not, these are simply the ones I have tripped over on my path, and so I wanted to signpost them to you.

Having gotten the above 'is not' points off my chest, let us now move onto the life affirming and wondrous description of what Spirituality is...

What Spirituality is...

I have chosen to keep my description of spirituality loose because nobody should dictate to you what your spirituality is, or how it should look. Having said that it can be helpful, especially in your early spiritual years, to find out what spirituality means to other people. That way you can take what works, dress it up in your clothes and accessorize as per your specific requirements.

Here is a little on how my spirituality manifests into my daily life. This is my spiritual wardrobe laid bare.

I am an utterly modern spiritual girl, my modern life is where I need to be and it is where my spiritual lessons lie. So as I sit here, cat on lap, blue nail varnish, tapping away, and lip gloss sloppily applied on a sunny Sunday afternoon, know that your spirituality can be you, it is you, you are spirit and there is no need to dress up a certain way, or become a stereotyped role. Honey, you are as spiritual as they come.

I have found that spirituality has been a wild trip into getting to know myself. It beats a few dozen counseling sessions hands down. Spirituality has saved my soul and at the same time rendered me utterly sane (most of the time). My eyes are clear, my mind is astute and I do not worry, daydream or wish for a better life, well, not in the way that I did before my spiritual yearnings kicked in. I know myself, which is so amazing, because before embarking on my spiritual trip, I did not even realize that I did not know myself! Knowing myself is one of the top side effects and ongoing lessons of a spiritual life.

In my life spirituality is something that has originated organically. It is an inner knowing, and it arose into my consciousness naturally and when I was in dire need of it. Quite often people will recall spirituality coming to them in their darkest moments, following death, depression or personal darkness. Of course some lucky ones simply have spirituality visited on them when things are calm and smooth, perhaps whilst gazing at the stars or exploring the pyramids!

Spirituality may feel so familiar as it begins to bubble within you, like a wisdom that you once forgot but that is now seeping back into your excited heart. Spirituality will find you because it is you, it emanates from you, and it is already within you. There are no entry requirements and it is not a competition. You cannot be more or less spiritual than anyone else, because we are all spiritual. Some of us may just not know that yet. Spirituality is what you already are, do you realize that? Welcome to the ride!

Spirituality is freedom. It is freedom to believe in a way that suits us. Spirituality allows us to make our own minds up about what our beliefs mean to us, and gives us space to interpret these beliefs in our daily lives. Spirituality gives you room to interpret for yourself. Spirituality recognizes the innate spirit and soul in all people and all things. You are divine, I am divine, the Archbishop of Canterbury is divine, as is the homeless person you pass on the street. We are all divine and I believe that each of us is able to access that divinity should we wish to.

My personal spirituality is influenced by my life and its events, not that of long dead prophets. Spirituality to me is freedom to believe and to interpret as I see fit. Some people may feel uncomfortable with this; perhaps a lifetime of religious teachings makes you concerned that I am dabbling with the unknown or the occult. Of course I would disagree with that. There is nothing occult about love, light and choosing to interpret my life through my own eyes and with trust in a spiritual grace to serve, help and protect me. Nor is it so hugely different from religion, it's just that in my version of spirituality I choose to be my own priestess.

You may be drawn to established paths to help you to understand what is arising inside of you, as I was drawn to explore a number of faiths as I described in *The High Heeled Guide to Enlightenment*. Such faiths provide marvelous guidance, but I could not commit myself to the full-on incorporation of those faiths into my life. Instead I cheekily took the wonderful philosophies, applied them as I saw fit, and moved on. I am a spiritual hermit. I find my spirituality inside my own private shell, and only occasionally borrow a little from pre-existing temples.

Spirituality gives you a blank book and allows you to fill it in. Whilst religion might be easier to follow, because it gives you the answers in the form of an already written book, your own story is not accounted for there. Spirituality is a living, breathing, transforming experience that wraps you up and assists you through life in a way that the preachings from a pulpit cannot do.

Everybody's experience of enlightenment will be different and this will arise within individual lives in unique and fascinating ways. Your interpretation, whilst similar to mine, will never be the same. This makes neither of us wrong, indeed we are both correct. We have our own life purposes and individual lessons to learn, and so adherence by everyone to one particular belief is not our chosen route.

Spirituality may be a lone and personal pursuit in the first instance, but being social creatures it is inevitable that our spirituality is taken into society, our relationships and even the workplace. I have introduced my colleagues at work to angel cards and they are fully enjoying the benefits of this freely accessible tool for affirmation, encouragement, guidance and a boost that feels as good as a new lip gloss used to do.

Spirituality is about recognizing that we are all connected, not only to one another, but also to the living planet, and to the elements, plants and animals.

Every thought or deed committed in your name reverberates and echoes its way around the lives of thousands of people. Your choices and your actions ripple out to cause a tsunami of possible happiness or grief to everyone they touch and affect.

Spirituality fills you with love, and as you become happier in your own beliefs, you may find you are drawn to help other people, either with their spirituality, or just because, as a spiritual being, you can not help but help.

It sounds trite but my spirituality has made me a better person, I am kinder, more considerate and a lot more empathetic. I feel so deeply for all humanity. Show me a tragic human life and I will show you my tears. The same goes for animals and the environment, I am just a big blubbering love machine, and I do what I can to help people, situations and good causes. I am now officially a real spiritualized softie.

Spirituality is about being in love with life, even though on occasion, that life kicks you when you are down. It is about making efforts to see things from a spiritual perspective when all you really want to do is run away and hide in a large glass of Chardonnay.

It is about learning to understand the wonder of symbols, messages and signs from spirit, guides, angels and the natural spiritual universe whilst applying those signs into your everyday existence and to your decisions big and small.

Spirituality is about sharing your love and learning in a modest, caring and generous manner. It is about treating all others as you would treat your most cherished child, and then some. It is about knowing that we are all connected, so that if you hurt your neighbor, you hurt yourself.

Spirituality is about getting to know the real you inside and out. This is the version of you that is unencumbered by fashion, make-up, cash flow problems or a nice new handbag.

What sits beneath your flesh, in a part of you no scientist can pinpoint, is your soul. Your soul is the everlasting, astute and divine part of you. She is poking you right now; she wants you to know that you are she, and that you are so much more than you previously thought. You are life beyond death, you are reincarnation, you are raw energy here to explore, laugh and to be set free. That means now – in your body. Not once you've departed the world of flesh.

Spirituality is the root to your own power. Intuitive guidance has been with you since the day of your birth, perhaps it is only now that you are starting to distinguish it. Your intuition is precious and far wiser than all the other mess cluttering up your thoughts. Spiritual thoughts and guidance are deep within you, perhaps whispered into your ears by angels, or beamed into your mind from your higher spiritual consciousness. Intuition, inspiration and psychic moments are your already existing divine higher self making herself known.

I am by no means perfect, but if I ignore my intuition things fail to work out. Intuition is one of my favorite spiritual tools and it really helps make decision-making easier too. As an indecisive Libran, anything that helps with decision-making is a winner in my opinion!

When you listen to your intuition and follow your gut instinct, it can ultimately change your life. Your intuition and gut instinct are inherent to your spirituality because in accessing them you are accessing your wondrous higher self and your age-old natural wisdom.

I believe that we are all given the chance, time and time again to access our own higher spiritual selves. I believe that we all have access to spiritual delights that come to us in the form of dreams, intuition, visions, angels, spirits, signs, thoughts, books and the timely comments of friends and strangers. It is these seemingly magical happenings that grasp at our attention and make us think a little more deeply about our lives and our existence here. In *The High Heeled Guide to Enlightenment* I talked about the fact that these coincidences are meaningful, and that they can transform your life if you allow them to. I choose now to call them non-coincidences, because there is nothing coincidental whatsoever about them.

Today I have lost my phone, I have not left the house and I have been nowhere. The phone has vanished. I interpret this non-coincidence to mean that my higher self, my angels and the spiritual source to which I am connected wants me to sit down, shut up and write this book. And so here I am, and there you are. Hello.

Spirituality can help you start to find some freedom from worry. It promotes an inner faith, that no matter how bad life gets you always know that there is a good reason for it. Life becomes a lesson, and I have become a willing pupil. Occasionally that lesson is damned hard, but if it has got to be learned then who am I to argue!

Spirituality is about finding something educational, eye-opening and even wondrous in every event. It is about realizing that all events good and bad are sent to help us to learn, to grow and eventually to become wiser souls.

I believe that as you become more spiritual, your abilities to cope with life increase, as does your ability to access your spiritual knowledge. You will become more intuitive and better at listening to your gut instinct. If you listen to the kind and loving voices in your mind then your life can improve inordinately.

In fact spirituality is about transforming your dualistic way of looking at the world. Spirituality shows us over time that life is not black and white, good or bad. Such stringent distinctions and categories are muddied and muddled when looking through spiritualized eyes. As you become more familiar with mindfully watching over your own life, you will see that there is good in the bad, and bad in the good. You will come to an acceptance that life is not always as it seems and that the greatest happiness can directly stem from the most heart wrenching tragedy. Somewhere down the line you will not only accept this, you may too embrace it.

Spirituality is my saving grace. It is a wonderland of amazing stuff, mixed with the fun, frolics and occasional nightmares that every day life holds. My spirituality is a human based, nature-loving exploration of all things divine within myself and in all that surrounds me. It is finding the phenomenon in everything that happens and everyone I meet. It is knowing that no matter what adversity is thrown at me, I will learn from it and I will grow.

Spirituality is fun and it is fearless. It is something I highly recommend. Whilst I cannot confirm or deny that a heaven full of angels, fluffy clouds and mesmerizing music exists, I can tell you I do believe that there is something utterly mind-blowing beyond this life. I believe there is a place that is our true home, and that place fosters us, repairs us, teaches us and then sends us back to earth for another go at living this crazy up and down life.

I do love this crazy human life. Yes I want to pump as much spirituality into that as I can, but I do not want to be floating round on a cloud ushering pixies to my side to sugar coat my experience, my living and my reactions.

What I do want is to explore my spirituality from a human perspective. It is easy to be spiritual when you remember one key fact; you are spiritual, because you are spirit. Spirituality is, in fact, everything.

The more we acknowledge our spiritual selves, the better access we have to our source, to its wisdom, love and knowledge. This however cannot be done overnight, it is a life long journey, and it takes commitment, self-awareness and a passion. Once you embark on this path, though, it changes your life and completely alters the way you see the world. A taste of enlightenment is addictive, and in my opinion, it's the only thing worthy of becoming healthily addicted to.

You are spirit, you are here to experience humanity, but inside that humanity you are a perfect little shining soul. Believe it! It is not our time to float away into the ether quite yet, so let us explore what spirit is. We will explore it through the unique eyes of somebody who is real, solid, prone to crying at life's cruelties and ready to face real life with a large dose of spirit always in their heart!

Lesson 2: Faith

Faith is our starting point, it is our bridge and it is the foundation that forms our spiritual lives. Very simply faith to me, means to believe in something beyond our more obvious human existence. It is to know wholeheartedly that there is more to life, death and the mysterious in-between than you, I or even the Dalai Lama will ever know. Faith is a fervently held knowing that there most certainly is 'something more'.

I do not believe that we need to pinpoint the exact form and nature of this something more, I think we can simply acknowledge it's existence and trust that it is relevant to us and that it is a part of us. I like to believe that in my faith I open myself to a loving consciousness that shapes everything, and that in turn this loving consciousness can help guide and shape even my little life.

Faith is the knowing that we are an important part of a greater scheme of things, it is believing that a grand consciousness exists and that this remarkable energy believes in us right back. In having faith in 'something more', I find I must also have faith in myself as a powerful ray of spiritual soul. Faith like trust must go both ways.

I believe that to have faith is natural to the human soul. Although sometimes the act of having and holding that faith is the most difficult thing in the world. Many people wish to see proof of their faith. The cynical amongst us would like to see their faith evidenced on a daily basis and several times an hour. But then what would be the point of faith?

I believe that you have to have the faith first before it can be proven correct. Yes, sure, you have the occasional convert who was shown something miraculous, and as a result they now have faith. But most of us trudging on in our daily lives are not about to be saved from a burning building by an angel, or escorted back to our bodies by a host of glorious beings following an out of body experience on an operating table. Most of us only just have time to hang the washing out, take the kids to school and get to work on time.

We do not have the time or opportunity for a massive enlightening experience. Besides… that would be cheating. For the majority of people enlightenment is a long slow trek. Faith is the sustenance we need to help us to get to where we are going.

To have faith we must throw ourselves head first into believing despite a lack of scientific evidence. It is only when we do this that the magic starts to occur. Of course you will have your own personal reasons and your own evidence which got you here in the first place, this 'evidence' may not stand up in a court of law, but if it stands up in your heart then you are ready. I assure you that your faith will be proven, but it may not be by burning bushes or flocks of doves or plagues upon your enemies.

Your faith will be proven through you, through your internal feelings, your thoughts and your inner guidance. Follow this inner guidance sincerely and wondrous things will happen. Look out for magical non-coincidences and they will occur. External signs are likely too as you tap into the energy of the universe.

You are a small part of a whole mass of existence, and if you believe, then the world we live in will show you that you are right. Keep to this belief and life will ebb and flow toward you rather than away from you.

Sometimes the ebb and flow means we have to think outside of the box, and things that seem unfair, or that appear to be going 'against us' may require special thought. For example, I am sat here typing these words two days into an ongoing flight cancellation; I should instead be on my Grandparent's porch swing in Kentucky. So, you see, things do not always go to plan.

But my faith does let me know that I wasn't supposed to be on the plane. Fate or spirit, or my hungry soul wanted me to go to

Glastonbury instead on a mini spiritual pilgrimage. I did as I was told, and I am now reinvigorated, happy and positive. Life is not always how we plan it, or envisage it, sometimes there is an even bigger vision, and what comes up instead by way of the turn of events can be different, and it can be better.

Faith allows us to give up our expectations and give over to a higher force. Faith relaxes our tight grip on controlling our lives and helps us to heed what happens.

Sadly, in this day and age faith has been replaced by control. We love to think we are in control of everything and anything. Often we are shown that we are not in control. But we quickly gather up our gadgets and gizmos, we marshal and delegate, we make plans, presentations and schedules, we fill out our calendars and we assume that we have got it all under our thumbs. We do not of course, life does not go according to our schedule, however hard we try to plan ahead and appear to be 'organized'. Mother Nature might step in at any moment, hence volcanoes explode and your country's flight system flops over and collapses. People fall ill, or they die, no one ever plans for that, and it always seems to be too soon. Your car might be crashed into, perhaps twice in a month. Anything can come along to upset our planned and ordered world.

Faith helps us to see the natural order behind this.

As well as believing in the mirage that we are in control many people believe that our human minds and makings are the pinnacle of existence. We are surrounded by natural miracles every day, and yet so many of us think that we know better. Corporate society tends to view nature as unintelligent and dismisses it as a thoughtless happening, a coincidence of circumstance. Or something wild to be brought under control and harnessed for productivity.

By thinking in this way, human experience becomes the top and bottom of everything. Humans have taken the power of enlightenment and replaced it with the power of a thousand television channels and an ever more powerful mobile phone. We have closed down our spiritual inclinations and we wonder why the whole of society is down, low and lonely.

I wish we all had a little more faith. Faith takes us some way beyond all this. It takes us to a place where none of these human accomplishments matter any more. It takes us back to our spirit. When faith is proven, as I will show you it can be, miracles can start to happen. The world is transformed and our spiritual path of everyday living can truly take off. We can start to see the patterns, we see the intelligence and design of the world around us.

In our faith, nature is no longer a dirty word, it is part of a grand design, and we start to see our human minds as part of a greater global intelligence.

When our faith is proven we begin to understand that our minds are only a tiny piece of a greater energy. This energy exists in all things, from the chair you sit on to the birds flying overhead. When we have faith we plug directly into this and that chair or those birds can conspire to give you a sign to help buoy up your faith even more. Maybe this sounds wacky, but somewhere down the line I have faith that your faith will show you exactly what I mean.

Faith in spirituality comes blessed with a thousand little perks. But it also means that you must accept things will not always go your way. Some people may expect that having faith will create miracles, cure our diseases or bring our loved ones back to life. Faith is scorned when this does not occur and we take this failing as proof that no Higher Power, Divinity, God or Goddess exists.

We are under the confused belief that if a higher power did exist then they would not allow bad things to happen that make us feel so unhappy.

The task here, and it is not an easy one, is to have faith that this horrific event occurred for a reason, that lessons might be learned and that your loved one still exists and is no doubt close by you right now, as you are reading this.

Faith is a challenging topic, but it is essential to your spiritual journey. I believe we are all here for a purpose. And, I believe that the things that happen to us always happen for a reason.

Earth is a harsh existence for our little sweet souls, but it is an existence where we learn a great deal should we choose to be open to learning the lesson. My spiritual path is one of continual learning. Whenever I think I am sufficiently enlightened for the time being, thank you very much, something new is sent to test me and quite often this sends me reeling. But that's ok; I have accepted that life can be hard, but that lessons can be learned from every foul event that occurs. Of course I sometimes wish that was not the case, but whilst I am a spiritual being like the rest of you, I am also human, like the rest of you, and like all good humans before me, I sometimes feel sorry for myself! Happily, though, my spirituality helps prevent that stage of feeling sorry for myself from spiraling into anything deeper, darker or depressing.

God, Goddess or the angels cannot bring back your much beloved granny, nor can they change world problems overnight. However they can whisper in your ear, give you signs and help you out in infinite ways. And yes, occasionally they will help you out in ways that you do not like or that feel painful at the time.

In whatever way that help comes, and whatever signs, intuitions and inspirations you are gifted, you firstly need to have faith. You must learn to recognize that faith being played out when it happens. Until you believe and recognize that a greater mysticism enshrouds your little human life, then all that spiritual help and all of the miraculous moments will pass you by unnoticed.

So are you capable of faith? Have you got it in you, or do you need proof?

I propose a little exercise that will give you some small proof.

I tend to dislike exercises in books. I always skip them. But don't worry. This does not involve you writing anything down, or doing anything other than thinking. So…get your attention span fired up and let's test your faith!

An Exercise in Faith

Faith is essential to your spiritual progress (and your progress as a human being). If you are going to believe another word I say then you need to embrace some level of faith. Many of you will already have it; others of you might be teetering on the edge of cynicism and uncertainty. So let us get straight down to it. Let's test your faith.

I presume that you want to believe in spirituality, that you feel it calling you and that you would like to incorporate it into your life. So here is a test for your faith, to try to show you that a little faith goes a long way, and that if you choose to believe, then all kinds of incredible spiritual happenings can come your way.

So for this week only, I want you to have faith. For a full seven days I want you to make huge efforts to believe in your own innate spirituality and in your connection to the divine. I know that you might need a little bit of proof, just something small. So I want you to ask for it. Yes, that's right, just go ahead and ask for it. Ask out loud or don't make a sound. You can choose to pray, or meditate or just ask in your head. But make sure you do ask. Then I want you to believe that your faith will be proven correct, and in the next seven days I believe that it will. Simple.

So how do you know when your faith has been proven? Well honey, I cannot tell you that, only you will know. It is entirely up to you to believe it when you see it. It is likely that a little sign or message from your higher self and the heavens above, will confirm your faith. You may see or hear something meaningful to you; you might turn the radio on only to hear George Michael wailing out *'you gotta have faith, faith, faith.'* You may open a book to find a picture that resonates with you, or a car number plate in front of you may near enough spell out the word 'faith' or believe or something particular to you. You may have a conversation with a friend or a stranger that triggers something in you and you will know that this is your sign.

If nothing specific happens straight away, keep on waiting and carry on believing. It is likely that your sign will come when you are not really expecting it. Spirit tends to like the element of surprise; divine beings have a penchant for cosmic jokes and dramatic gestures! Try not to double guess what it is that you will see, hear or feel, because it is unlikely that you can imagine what your 'sign' will be. Just trust that a sign will come, and that you will know it when it happens. It really is true that you'll know it when it comes.

I want you to enjoy this challenge, and I want you to really truly believe. I hope this will show you how your own personal faith can bring about minor miracles in your life. All you need to do is to be open and willing to accept these signs and mini miracles when they show up.

Enjoy this little experiment because it will make the reading of this book all the more meaningful. It will show you how on the simplest levels, having a little faith can bring about your personal belief in spiritual living.

To help elaborate and demonstrate I have tried this test and it worked for me. My own seven-day faith test has opened up a whole new series of events in my life that is still ongoing. I love it! I renewed my faith and my spirituality came back in with a roar! Everything else that you read in this book now stems from this roar.

Since undertaking this test of faith and looking for a sign, my life has catapulted into a whole new spiritual sphere. So in what way did this happen? Well firstly I will start with the small things that happened. The first sign occurred when I asked two friends, Hannah and Shireece to join me on the seven-day test of faith. I asked them individually, and when I asked them, they both said how funny it was because Shireece had chosen that very morning to have faith and for her faith to be proven. Hannah's timely non-coincidence was that earlier that very day she had caught herself singing and dancing to a cheesy dance track called '*I believe*'. Within a day of me proposing this seven-day task to test our faith, Hannah went on to have a whole catalog of signs and messages occur.

As for me, on the second day of the task I was randomly thinking about how pleasant it would be to have a feather float toward me. Then later as I went out into my garden, a perfect fluffy white feather did just that. When I went to collect it, it was no longer there. How mysterious! It just disappeared into thin air. As I returned to the house there was another one by the back door, so I collected that one instead as 'proof' of my little experiment.

Feathers are definitely something you should look out for in your seven-day test of faith. Also flowers, animals and the appearance of other natural phenomena such as leaves, petals and shells can all be taken as significant signs if they find their way to you, or show up where they are not expected. For example a butterfly trailing you down the street when you live in New York, or opening your back door to find petals or a shell awaiting you, could all be valid signs from the powers that be. Perhaps your favorite bird will follow you twittering its song or it's presence will appear for you repeatedly and in a number of ways, such as an overheard conversation, or a picture on the back of a bus.

Of course your sign need not be one that is a natural phenomena. You could pass by a billboard that is emblazoned with a few words that fit your life perfectly. Signs and messages will crop up in objects, in images, in songs, on television, the newspaper and in your dreams. And you will know your sign when it appears. Just trust it and go with it.

The outstanding sign I had during the seven days test of faith, and continually since then, is the occurrence of the number 22 and 222 in my life. Interestingly when I was writing my first book I constantly saw the numbers 111 everywhere. It seems I have moved up a number! Whenever I happen to glance at a clock it is 2.22. More exciting than this is when I glance at the timer on the microwave and it is precisely 2.22 minutes left, or as happened recently a car pulled out in front of me with a personalized number plate reading 222. Or my change in the shop, or the cost of my goods comes to £2.22. Or I pick up a random document at work and the number 222 is stamped on it, or a letter is dated 22nd of February. All of these and more have happened to me in just one week. When I investigated the spiritual meaning of 222 I found that it meant to 'have faith'. How very apt.

Following the influx of 222's in my life, things appeared to take a turn for the worse, to the point that I was feeling a distinct lack of faith. I was having a 'why, God, why????' kind of week. Things had been going horribly wrong, I was strung out, stressed and tired. My chicken was ill and then it died, then the first of my two car crashes occurred, leaving me sobbing and hysterical on the Junction 22 turn-off on the motorway.

Aha! Junction 22. Even through my hysteria I could see the funny side of it. As I said before, they love a cosmic joke.

When this crash occurred I had been driving to work, and I allowed myself to do something I had not allowed myself in a very long time. I had started to think negative thoughts. I had started to worry about all the, what ifs…? I have not done that for a good few years. But I did it then. And within a few minutes – BANG, the car felt like it had exploded. In that second I knew it was a wake up call. And when I saw where the crash occurred I could not help but giggle through my sobs. To add insult to injury, I noted a sign to my left, which stated that roadwork started on the 22nd of that month.

I called my friend, who later reported that the phone call was received at 8.22. When I told another friend about this strange occurrence, she left my house, only to find herself stuck behind a number 22 bus that was clogging up her route! Though she soon understood the message and called me to report back!

That number is still happily haunting me, but I understand it now, I get what it means. I hope the universe gets that I get it, because what with the whiplash, I have had enough of lousy stuff for a little while.

It is true that the 22's have coincided with things going drastically wrong in my life. But I don't see this as a reflection of the number itself. Rather the number has become a shining beacon of hope, letting me know that I am on the right path. In spite of the occasional negative thought, the shock and upset of the crash and the resulting painful neck, the 222s remind me that all is well.

With this in mind the assault of 222 continues…since writing all this, a young lady I met offered to do me a numerology report. It was returned to me swiftly and my life path number is… yep, you guessed it, 22. Some people might be entirely freaked out by this, or even fear that the number 22 was causing the troubles in their lives. I do not believe this to be the case. The 22 for me is a constant reminder of what I have achieved, where I am going and the fact that my life, whilst somewhat chaotic, is well and truly going in the right direction. The number 22 is a thread pulling me through all the difficulties and reminding me of my own faith. It is a sign, it is a symbol, and given the quantity and quality of its crazy appearances it is a powerful guiding light.

To add a little more to my 22 stories, I have just returned from my trip to Glastonbury. I went there to help restore my mojo after the two car crashes (2 car crashes is a little sign too of course!). Whilst I was there, of course my guiding number 22 showed up at the most opportune times. The house right opposite my bed and breakfast guesthouse was number 22. The bar I discovered that was suitable for a lone female with a laptop was adorned with a larger than life number 22 on the door. The stone I chose at a jeweler for my wedding ring resonated at 22. The metal that I chose was also found to resonate at number 2. Which of course means that the resonation of my wedding ring is 222!

My story of 2's is a jolly good example of how innocuous signs and symbols can find their way through and light your path to help to lead you out of the darkness. As you can see, when you ask for signs, you get them in bundles, all you need do is sit back and have faith so that you recognize and appreciate them when they happen, which they will.

I hope you have an amazing experience on your seven-day test of faith; and I am sure that this experience will snowball into bigger and even more meaningful events as your life spirals into a more spiritual way of being.

I hope that within your week something has happened that you know in your heart to be true and totally personal to you. If you do not feel that you are sure, then all I can ask you to do is try again and just be determined to have faith and to believe it when you see it. Maybe rope a friend in to do the seven-day test of faith with you so that you can compare notes, and so that you can notice signs for each other if they are whizzing over your head. Sometimes other people can see a blazing sign that we have ignored, misunderstood, blocked out of our mind, or logically tried to explain away.

This experiment will help you to open up to the divine energy and spiritual significance that can come out of mundane everyday life. It will set you off on a path of other non-coincidences and amazing little occurrences, and as your faith grows so will you. Slowly your intuition and natural psychic knowledge will assert itself. You will begin to live in tune with your soul, as a multi-dimensional being rather than simply as a three-dimensional human being. Think of your spirituality as the fourth dimension, and the fifth and the sixth!

Sharni's Faith

Little did I know that following the completion of my first draft of this book I would be asked to test its propositions. Nor did I believe I would be writing about it within that same book. But with three weeks to go until my deadline date, that is precisely what I am doing. Oh how the divine works in mysterious ways, and oh how it loves to keep us on our toes!

A few days after completing what I thought was the whole of this book I had an email from a friend who was in crisis. Sharni is an Internet friend, but one I feel very close to. I think we both see each other as soul sisters. She lives in Australia, whilst I am literally on the other side of the world in the UK.

She emailed me almost as a last resort. She was feeling very low and people were suggesting she go to the doctor and get herself medicated with anti-depressants. Nobody knew what to do with her, and I believe she did not know what to do with herself. So she decided to give me a shout and see if I could help turn her life around.

At first she asked if I could help her bless her home, but immediately I knew it was not her home that was the problem. Sharni, as a talented writer and blogger was becoming a little reliant on the Internet for her self-esteem. She was truly exhausting herself, and not attending sufficiently to her own needs, or that of the people around her. Her rut was deep and wide and I hoped that a little bit of spiritualization could help lift her out of it.

So I happily volunteered to be her spiritual soul coach and see what we could do. Having just written this book I knew I had some great tips and pointers to hand, and I was curious to see how they worked in the real world. I know they have worked for me, but could that be conveyed to someone on the other side of the world via email? The cosmic forces were now putting what I'd just written to the test!

I asked Sharni to have faith and to look for signs. Knowing how powerful this had been in my life, I wanted to see if the magic of it could be summoned up over on the other side of the world.

Sharni said she was willing to give it a go and almost immediately the spiritual miracles kicked in.

Following some recommended meditation Sharni started to get some signs to support her faith, these came into her life strong, fast, and without a moment's hesitation. She chose to have faith and her faith was quickly rewarded.

"Did a little prayer to my guides and asked for a sign...

As I was doing the dishes - I kid you not a sparrow landed at the sink. I of course screamed and freaked out and ran out of the house, the sparrow was crashing into walls trying to find its way out (I don't even know how it got in as all doors were shut). It was definitely a sign. In fact, I saw the meaning in it straight away - the bird represented me - a bird needs to be free to roam and fly about the world - if a bird is contained in a room it starts crashing into walls and panics trying to find the opening to the whole world. I feel that I have been like a bird stuck in a house — —- I need to find the light and fly out into it! Truly amazing.

Alice — wow, one DAY and I feel like a new woman, I feel reinvigorated with the world and I am so glad that I did the meditation thing - I am very receptive and ready for this spiritualization and cannot wait to see what tomorrow holds."

As time went by Sharni continued to get better and better and one of my favorite signs occurred just when she was struggling a little bit with her new spiritual life plan. One of the key points of the plan was to get her away from living online, so the next event could not have been more apt. Indeed it truly shows that the spiritual powers have a wicked sense of humor too!

"I do not know how these sparrows are getting in the house but today another one got in... and wait for it... it SHAT on the computer!!!!! Ok I get the message!"

A few days after the pooping sparrow I recorded a tarot and animal card reading for Sharni and sent it over to her. I hoped this would give her the boost she needed to get her through the second week. Again this catalyzed some more events of wonderful spiritual signage and significance. Her reading included her receiving an animal card, which was a Bear. The Bear brought her the message that she should spend some time in introspection to help her move forward with her life.

"I loved that video it was so good and personalized!! I am writing this from my parents' computer because guess what - after I watched it, my Internet won't work!!!! ANOTHER SIGN!

I love that so much and afterwards Monte came running out of his bedroom with a book and he had it turned to a page with a bear on it and said "Mama Mama" and I said "It's a bear" and he said "Bear" then he kept saying Bear, Bear - and he had never said that before!!!!

Too many non-coincidences ;-)"

The spiritual signs that occurred when Sharni decided to have faith are more proof that in the big scheme of things we really, truly matter. Often we go about in our lives completely closed off to asking for any kind of divine help. Many of us refuse even to ask for help from friends and family. We are too proud, or too afraid to admit we need a little something to help us to cope or to find meaning to our lives. Pride, however, is well known to come before a fall. Asking for help from the wondrous, loving cosmos can be fruitful and glorious. There is no shame in asking for a mini miracle in your life. You are loved and guided by a higher power, do not be afraid to let them in.

Indeed you are a part of that higher power, that higher power is our parent, our sister and a part of our own soul. Don't be anxious to ask for help and for signs, in fact I highly recommend that you do it today. Spiritual love and help is abundant – all you need to do is make the decision and then simply ask...

Your Faith

So by now I hope you have had some incredible experiences and had your faith restored or kick started. There is sometimes a little downside when this starts happening. I will deal a little with how your faith might set you apart from your peers, your family and those judgmental folk I warned you about earlier.

I realize that faith can make you feel isolated at times. It may even make you feel like the odd one out and you could encounter resistance from people you know, some of them will be people who have known you for a long time who weren't really expecting you to change. That is all right, we have all been there. I assure you that at some point down the road, those who are resisting you at the moment could very well come to you for advice. Even those who dismiss it all and tease you as a way of distancing themselves, will at some point be in need of your spiritual opinion.

This has happened to me many, many times. If the naysayers do come to you for some spiritual guidance, some time in the future, then be sure to give it.

I act as my heart tells me, I do not hold back because someone held back with me. If someone is brave enough to ask for my help, after ridiculing me, then I am brave enough to give it. Never hold back and never sway to opinion. Be your best self ever, and if people do not like it, then that is none of your business.

Your faith is going to be very different from anyone else's that you ever meet. You may find that some people criticize you, or lean on you and expect you to have all the answers. But then, that is why it is called faith and not fact. Those atheists among your friends and family may take some patronizing pleasure in denouncing you as a crazy hippy. Let them. I find the easiest path to take with these people is one of little resistance. Smile and move on. Do not get involved. Overlook a great deal. It is not an especially proactive stance, but it causes least harm to all, and so it is a spiritual stance. Reactions cause nothing but fracturing and unpleasantness. Your power can be in your peace!

You may find that people surprise you. My husband James is in no way overtly spiritual. However fairly often he comes out with something so profound, and in my mind spiritually enlightening, that I think I must have married a secret guru. He supports what I do, but he does not get hugely involved. He likes what I do, but he does not spend time with me while I'm doing it. This is all fine by me. We are different people. Relationships of all kinds can work just fine across the spiritual borderline.

Respect is the key to this, and an understanding that spiritual enlightenment need not have a title. James writes awesome music, meaningful lyrics and sometimes he says things that become my mantras. He may say he is spiritual, or he may not. That's his business and I do not need to marry a fellow spiritual believer to fulfill my own spiritual potential. I can do that quite nicely by myself.

Indeed it is often the least spiritual things in life that show us the divine. My brother Michael has in the past been spoiling for a debate on the matter. I believe that he is frustrated by my answers because they are based on faith, and on my personal experiences. However when I have directed him to books about the scientific nature of spirit, even he has budged a little in his stoic attitude. He is by no means spiritually inclined, but the hard edge is slowly softening. I will keep chipping away at him, and if worst comes to the worst I'll see him in heaven and we can have a giggle about it. Gosh he will hate this paragraph – love you Mikey!

The fact that some of your friends and family are not spiritually aware does not make them any less precious, nor does it mean they will drag you backwards. Perhaps they will change their views over time, and you being in their life will give them the strength and support they need. That said it might be their role in your life to keep your feet on the ground, or to help you understand what it is you truly do believe in. Their awkwardness might have a real purpose, so embrace it and do not try to change them. Their spiritual path is their own business.

The more you progress on your spiritual journey, the less other people's opinions will matter. Not because you are 'above' other people, but because you will understand those people a little more. As a empathetic spiritual being you may come to realize why certain people are unable to believe, and why they cannot open themselves to something that to them seems radical or plain crazy. As you progress you will be OK with their reasons and their limitations. You will not feel fear or frustration toward them, you won't sit in judgment of their mental and spiritual processes, but instead love and compassion will color your view.

Happily I think that times are changing. I believe that more and more people are opening their minds to something else, something beyond their usual life. Many strangers I meet will say how pleased they are to have met someone who is not going to think them mad or judge them for what they believe. That is all I can ask for. And it's also all we can ask of ourselves – not to judge other people for what they do or do not believe in.

Faith, my dears, is only the starting point. Once you have had yours proven a little bit, and you are open to all things spiritual, consider yourself a little bit enlightened. We can now move on.

Lesson 3 – The Goddess

"The Goddess is rocking my world. She is everywhere I go. I believe she is going to save us all from ourselves."
Alice's Diary April 2010

So vital is the Goddess's input to this book that she more or less told me I had to write about her. What she has to teach us helps to underpin many of the lessons within this book. I believe that the Goddess, and female energy is vitally important to our future.

Never one to ignore a passionate deity, here is my Goddess related learning. My recent trip to Glastonbury set my whole new Goddess vibe off. Glastonbury was Goddess Central, but I expected no less. This theme has continued in my life since I left. Most recently at work I was consumed with thoughts about Goddess energy, she would not leave my mind. Later that day I chose an angel card for myself, it was a card I had not seen before, it was aptly named, Goddess.

Not only did this reflect my thoughts but also when I looked up to my pin board, there in front of me was a note from my friend Shireece. This was written out weeks before on personalized notepaper that had the image of Shireece and her sister at the top, lounging about in true divine Goddess style!

The note contained the lyrics to a song. These lyrics stated clearly that I must embrace my Goddess energy to help heal the world. Ok, ok, ok, enough already. I hear you loud and clear! Goddess I got your message and here I am, let's do this thing.

I am a feminist, innately and unequivocally. No matter what has happened in my life, and whatever else I have bluffed about (seriously I really am a natural blonde, more or less, the sun just brings out these highlights) I have never lied, denied or bluffed about my feminist beliefs.

So many people think that feminism is no longer even worth a mention. For some reason it seems that lots of women and men think we have equality, that we have won that particular battle. I'm afraid that this is not the case.

We are in a manmade cage, a pretty and gilded one with the semblance of freedom about it, but it is a cage nonetheless. This is why having a female deity, or a female energy, as part of my spiritual belief, is essential.

Sadly feminism is viewed by many as a nasty and negative stereotype. People pigeonhole feminists as short haired, butch dykes. Yeah... and... So what if they are? Why the hell does that scare women so much?

The reason we see this as a negative thing, is because we are trying to appeal to our male counterparts and simper to them in the manner to which they have grown accustomed. The manner they've become accustomed to often means surgically modified breasts, surgically uplifted arse, surgically inflated pouts, socially engineered giggles and an ultra girly giddiness (so that we don't seem too 'threatening').

Many of us play into the, 'I'm not a feminist because I'm straight, or high heeled, or girly, or I'm married, or I'm a man,' but no my sisters and brothers, that does not wash. Detaching ourselves from feminism due to negative discrimination against lesbians has done nobody any favors. Detaching ourselves from it because we believe it makes us look ugly, hard or sour-faced is ludicrous. Men detaching themselves from it, because it is the domain of 'crazed super women' is laughable. Feminism, surely, is about finding and maintaining some longed for equality, respect and recognition, there is nothing scary about that.

As a result of our fears of feminism what we have been left with is a society full of females who are "empowered" through the gratuitous sexualization of their physical bodies but still disempowered by the gratuitous limitation of them selves into sexual stereotypes. It's the token girlie sidekick presenter on TV.

It's the giggling girl band. It's everywhere, it has been me, and it may well have been you. It's the tolerance of pornography, the casual asides about a person's intelligence based on the height of her heels or color of her hair. Little girls want to be wives and girlfriends of sporting legends and grow up wanting to look like somebody, rather than actually being somebody in their own right.

On a more serious note women are still frequently victims of domestic violence, domestic murder, rape, sex trafficking, sexual harassment and the list goes on. So the job is not quite done yet sisters.

It is true that many women have good jobs, better wages and multiple choices. But when you look across the board at the poorer women in our towns and cities, who may be working all hours to bring home the minimum wage, or those who don't have the independence that earning their own income provides, or the ones with a tragic secret of abuse or victimization, it is not such a pretty picture. The fear of feminism has become an epidemic, and it is making society a very sick place.

So how does Goddess spirituality come into feminism or vice versa? I believe that spirituality is a huge empowerment tool for women. It takes us out of our cultural frame of reference and forces us to look inside ourselves.

In getting to know ourselves we meet up with our souls and our higher selves and we start to look a little further at ways of fulfilling our potential. With spirituality at our side we can begin to see this material life as temporary and the 'must-have' and 'must-buy' gender oriented facets of it to be fake.

Women are currently living under a false economy; we truly believe that what we look like, and our possessions are what make us unique. Wrong. What makes us unique is deeper than the flesh, the fabulous shoes and the quirky pink lipstick. No, it's not even our perceived achievements. What makes us ourselves is ancient, wise, feminine, knowing, and divine.

That is correct ladies, you are divine. The men are divine too, of course, but mostly they have lost their way as much as we have. Women have grown used to embracing male energy, we have had to do that to help us to get anywhere in the past fifty years. Yet it is still quite taboo for men to embrace their female sides. This is changing of course, men push swings in the park on Saturday and Sunday, but the legacy of a male dominated past still resides in our cultural commentary. Just look at any barbecue near you and you'll know it's true – we have divided and split, it is a war of the sexes, and no one is winning. I think perhaps both sides have given up exhausted!

I believe that spirituality and inner soul seeking can help us to mend this split. I believe that embracing a divine female energy, as well as the traditional male energy, is the way forward. Western Society has been skewed for too long, focusing on godlike achievements and godlike goals.

The Goddess and the feminine aspects in our society have become lost to us, female energy has been denigrated as primal, irksome and pagan. But the female essence is fertility, life and rebirth. She is creation from the inside, instead of from the outer trappings of achievement, attainment, and materialization. She is nature and nurture and she is at one with the winds of this planet. For too long 'nature' and 'nurture' have been steamrollered over by the masculine 'progress'. It is time to reintroduce them as both valid and valuable.

The female is naturally environmentally aware because her body echoes the cycles of nature. In male dominated society the environment has been dashed and deserted. Nature has been made into a dirty word. Science is God. Which is all well and good (we love the convenience of our domestic appliances) but this means females are somehow akin to that less civilized perception of humanity. Yet we are being forced now to embrace female qualities before it's too late, because without an innate understanding of nature, nurture, and abundance, we as a society are on the brink of becoming lost and desperate.

Canny business people are catching onto this and you can see the evidence apparent in the new eco businesses and caring capitalists cropping up.

There is much damage yet to be resolved, but in bringing back a love of all things female related, we are helping to rebalance the planet. This, I believe will help to free us all. Women will be freed from the gilded cage that says they are not good enough unless they look good enough, and men will be free to explore the natural parts of themselves that they have locked away and repressed for fear of criticism. The Goddess is finding her way back into our lives, so if she knocks at your door let her in!

Having rejected formal religions I was not too keen on the idea of deities. But today it dawned on me just how important deities are to our understanding of our own spirituality. Indeed it occurred to me how important female deities are to society as a whole.

For centuries and centuries the human belief in spirituality has been based upon a higher power that is intrinsically male. But prior to that, in the classical era of civilization – let's not forget, the ancient Greeks who developed philosophy and mathematics, as well as their predecessors and parallel cultures around the world, had a religion that embraced a pantheon of Gods and Goddesses, each representing different themes, traits and specialisms. There was a Goddess of the hearth, a Goddess of wisdom and learning, a Goddess of poetry and music, a Goddess of healing, a Goddess of childbirth and a Goddess of the moon and therefore the planting cycles and harvests. There was even a Goddess to represent the power behind the throne.

In Africa, Asia, the Americas and Australia, there were Goddesses of rain and wind, fruit and flowers, Goddesses of the seasons and the animal kingdom.

But suddenly the pantheon of God and Goddess characters, who each had a role to play that mirrored our own human frailties, and awkward negotiations through life, were banished to the heavens as no more than constellations in the night sky. Since then our projected image of God has been a grizzled old bachelor, a single father (who can be quite exacting and who doesn't always understand), who grimly manages us all down here on earth. Kindly or punitive, however you view this God of the west, he is invariably seen as a man's man. Eve's role was carnal knowledge, and Mary's role was as a virginal mother or remorseful ex-harlot.

We have been living in a world whose social and cultural roots stem from a patriarchal religion, where male traits are worshipped and viewed as the most important. We have had a male dominated society that has emulated 'godly' traits. We have dissected God's creations and replaced them with a genetically modified and technological version. Now Mankind has become the new God, and in our culture the God status is reserved for the rich and successful only, however vacuous their outlook on life or their achievements may be.

We no longer look to our souls for truthful guidance and leadership; we look to celebrities, politicians and newsreaders, newspaper gossip columns, makeover magazines, the promise and allure of advertising images. We blindly play follow the leader and we put no trust in our own senses.

These powerful and incredibly influential people dictate life to us, and we often forget that their agenda is to become more powerful and more godlike in our secular culture. This is messed up and crazy.

What we all need right now is the love of a good woman. That and the dissolution of the mediocrity that we all adhere to under the belief that working nine to five, spending up a credit card debt, and constantly watching television, is a normal and acceptable way to live our lives.

The myth of a higher power being male has led to destruction and oppression of anything feminine. Females have had to embrace this essentially masculine and godlike energy, to pull themselves to a different level where men would be able to view us as equals. Even now we still struggle to bring a feminine perspective to old male institutions, like politics and law.

I believe it is time for the feminine to be appreciated in its own right and for our own innate Goddess to come out to play.

Women are stepping up now. We are breaking out of our backseat role and taking a major part in society. A feminine influence is being brought into the workplace and into society and that feminine influence is being valued, respected and listened to.

Motherhood too is taking a central place in society. It is no longer a 'behind closed doors' necessity, women are talking about it and newspapers are talking about it.

The world at large is open to women and to our nature. It is fascinating stuff. But we are still mid flux. On one page we have a girl baring her breasts, and the next page hosts a piece on maternity leave, we are not there yet. We are, however, on our way. At the same time Mother Earth herself is playing up no end, wreaking havoc and reminding all those powerful male energy people, that she will always have the final say.

It is time for women to step out of the shadows of a too masculine society to become total equals. It is so time. Any society that swings too far in one direction will always lose its balance, become unstrung and fall foul of itself. I see that happening to us now. I see it in our power structures, in our big man politics presiding over all us little people. I see it in the propaganda of other countries – which no doubt reflects the propaganda of our own. I see it in a nanny state that is not nurturing, but that is becoming manipulative, materialistic and hugely controlling.

The male energy of this planet has us all in his grasp. We are pawns in a very big game and it is my belief that in order to be able to counteract this we need to usher the feminine energy back in. The feminine will free us from the need to play power games, it will allow us to sit in compassion rather than yearning for more dollars, bigger contracts, higher sales and an unlimited supply of oil to fuel our big cars.

Nature has been denigrated and femininity has been lampooned and locked away. The balance has tipped too far. Forget about the tipping point of global warming; instead think about the tipping point of yin and yang. Instead worry about the over stimulation of testosterone in our planet's culture, because this has brought a lot of misery to a lot of people. It has helped to destroy the environment, render species extinct, caused countless wars and it has made us all wage slaves addicted to the weekend.

I believe there is another way. I believe that power is an optical illusion and that much of the structures of your life are pretend. Money does not really exist, but in buying in to it, we make some people very, very rich and powerfully happy. To make more people happy and better fed, we ought to start believing in something other than the creation of wealth and success.

Male and female are two aspects of a higher spiritual power. Do I believe there are actually a God and a Goddess up in the sky? No I do not, but I do believe that divinity, energy, mysticism, spirituality is both male and female in equal parts. But both these parts must be embraced, not just one. Embracing just one causes misery to the other part. This cannot happen any longer.

I believe that our world is becoming more evolved, more spiritual, more conscious. Within that consciousness we must acknowledge what we have previously failed to acknowledge. We must worship and revere it, just as we do its other half.

The female divine is in us all, and part of everything. It is not lesser. It is the same, but different. She needs ushering in to balance out the damage done by an off-kilter world that was only concerned with manly ways.

The Goddess is hugely important to me. She is a symbol of feminine freedom but also of male and female empowerment.

The majority of people on this planet are enslaved to the financial systems that rule over every detail of our lives. We are all captured by a belief that things cannot be any different. Sadly those at the top of this big money pile are so afraid of losing their power and their money that they are willing to do anything they need to do in order to keep us under their control.

By embracing our female energy, the whole money / power dynamic loses its importance. We do not need to have an uprising; we can slowly slip out from under that control and seek out another way of life for ourselves. We can refocus our lives around the things that matter, the people we love, the children we look after, our animal companions, our potential for creativity, compassion, our passion for the planet and our love for one another. We can stop pillaging each other's pockets and we can work together in communion.

We all need each other, spiritually speaking we are part of one another. Without each other there would be nothing. The Goddess energy will help to show us how to live with each other, rather than living off each other.

Embrace your inner Goddess; embrace the Goddess in your brother, your husband or your dad. Embrace your inner God, it is not his fault that his energy has been abused and blown out of all proportion! Know that now is a time of great changes. Acknowledging that femininity is precious, beautiful, powerful and to be celebrated, is the starting point of a spiritual revolution in our global consciousness.

Feminine divinity is powerful beyond measure. We have, up until this point in recent history, not really known it existed or not cared. We have certainly not given it much thought. But I have today, and in one day I can see why it is vital to my future existence. I always knew that women were special, I always knew that God must be a girl, now I see how this can transform everything!

After writing this small section I felt a deep urge to channel the Goddess. For those who are not familiar with channelling it means that I allowed the Goddess to speak through me. I sat still with a blank page on my computer and I allowed my hands to type the words that flowed out. I believe that what I wrote is a spiritual message from a feminine divinity, or from the feminine side of spirit. Her message is beautiful and I'm going to share it with you now...

"I am the Goddess and the Goddess is God and God is the Goddess. It is all the same. As an energy as a deity as a being and as you. We are all the same. We are part of each other.

Your faiths have seen my only one aspect for too long. In that aspect you created great things but you forgot your own creation. You forgot that my and your nature is an equal to what you had made.

Your Godhead made you self-righteous in your abilities. But you did do so well. You really did. Look what you have! But your Godhead made you more callous. You became accepting of destruction and you misused the God energy, claiming it your own, structuring it, justifying your decisions through it. What an interesting lesson for you all.

The Goddess mind is coming in now. I never left, I just watched you play and you could barely see me. You have been like teenagers for some time, so full of your own answers! I was always here. I am in your mother and in your own baby soul, I am in nature and even in your merciful God. For as I say, we are all the same.

Reclaim me now. Not over and above your God, but as him and her too. As together we make all that is. Neither superior nor inferior. We are accompanying each other as loving escorts. But really I and he are a he/she. I know you laugh, it is not all so serious you know! We are perfection and we love you as you love us. We are us. All of us.

As a constructive way to understand me, I hope you will look inside and realize your own Goddessness. See that too in the men, women and children all around you, in your animals and plants. I am more powerful than all your human made creations, which of course means that you are more powerful than all that too.

I wish you to remember that I am your child and your mother. I wish you peace. Find me and you will find peace. I love you and you love me. We are one. Welcome to our world, baby child."

When the Goddess speaks she says it well, does she not! I do not intend to channel any more. That is quite enough for one book. I will say though that the Goddess is such a friendly energy, so non-judgmental and so nourishing, that when I read that back it makes me want to weep with joy.

After channeling the Goddess energy I felt so serene, happy and wiser. I am so honored to pass on such a kind and loving message.

The Goddess rocks my world. So build her an altar, see her in your mirror, be her incarnation. I am convinced she is on a mission and her energy is here to stay. I look forward to the future with her in it.

Lesson 4 - Free your mind

"Last night my friend stood in a dog poop and managed to walk it through her house. If this was not bad enough she threw a total and utter hissy fit about it. I was witness to her anger and it felt like a blow to the stomach, a psychic attack on me, though of course that's not what she intended. Ten minutes later the mess on the floor was all cleared up but the anger in the air was still quite apparent. She was so mixed up in her anxiety over this that it didn't occur to her that it was not a big deal. She became a slave to her own reaction, and everybody watching was dragged into the drama too. Ouch I feel it in my gut just remembering..." Alice's Diary October 2009

Lesson four is about examining the bad habits of a lifetime and extracting yourself from them so that you can start to see the world differently... spiritually. My voyage into living a spiritual life has done one incredible thing for me. It has spiritualized my sanity and freed my mind. I believe that our minds are enslaved to a great many situations, stresses and ways of thinking in this modern life. Before you can even begin to unhook your thinking from the pressures of society, and retrieve your mind from the unhealthy aspects of mass consciousness, you must first rescue your mind from yourself.

Prior to undertaking my spiritual life, I had become a victim to a number of nasty interlopers of my character, such as an unhealthy ego, negativity, bitchiness and over-analyzing. All of these added together meant my mind was not in a very healthy state. I was overcome with a variety of unhealthy thoughts that spiraled into further states of confusion. I totally lost track of who I was, what I wanted in life and what my opinion was. The craziest thing about it was that for a long time I did not even realize there was anything particularly wrong with me!

Spirituality charged in and forced me to examine my own mind. This in turn obliged me to take a good hard look at myself, at my wants, my needs, my desires, and indeed, how many of my own problems were arising from my own thoughts.

It turned out that the majority (if not all) of my personal issues were very much a product of my own thinking and mental patterns. Now this came as a shock and a relief. A shock because I had spent a long time blaming everyone and anything else for my problems. It was a relief because the power lay firmly in my hands to change my mind and to take control of my life.

Embracing a spiritual way of life cut through all my mental nonsense like a sharp and feisty meat cleaver. I am now left with a cleaner, more focused mind that avoids the drama of life, rather than creating the drama of life as it did before. My spiritual development has made a huge and substantial difference to my everyday existence.

My path toward enlightenment has shed a thousand bulb chandelier of light onto who I am as a person. It has been a giant dose of self-help and self-esteem coaching. Spiritual living has shown me a new way to view the world and my place within it. I have learned that self-discovery is beyond doubt the most important and ongoing part of your spiritual path. My life is very different now to my pre-spirituality days, and I cannot deny that I am far happier as a result. Allow me to elaborate...

As I have alluded, I have gone from a slightly crazy minded Alice, to a far more serene and sanitized version of my self. To help you understand your own mind, I have laid mine bare here....

I believe that my current spiritual journey began when I was born, I am sure of that. I will tell you why. Because I am spirit living in a human body, therefore I believe that I am spiritual inherently, deeply and always. Spirituality is my thing, because how can it not be, it is literally, metaphysically, in my soul! I am sure that it is in your soul too.

If we choose to go further back, then yes I believe that I was therefore spiritual before birth too. I believe that each of our souls pre-date our current body, and will go on to outlive it.

But let me confirm this; we are spirit, therefore we are infinite and our existence precludes the human body you sit in right now. I believe that each human body we incarnate into poses its own problems. One of those problems is the troublesome aspect of our minds. Part of our life on earth is to overcome the human aspects somewhat and to find a way to exist in a more peaceful, spiritual way. We may not transcend the human body entirely whilst it is housing us, but we can allow our spirit to take a greater control and to overrule the less healthy quirks and habits of thought that a human body and human experiences presents us with.

So we all start somewhere, and the most obvious place, and the one we all know happened for a fact was our birth. We are born to parents who give us a set of values and problems that we often spend the rest of our lives trying to reconcile.

In my case I was born straight into a form of spirituality. My father was a Church of England vicar, who later became a Wiccan. My mother and her partner Patricia brought my brothers and me up in a pointedly feminist environment, and with a great deal of love. At weekends I stayed with my father, his wife Aileen and their household of visiting pagans, and resident cats, budgerigars and gerbils. Life was always interesting and colorful!

My spiritual sanity was not a problem when I was a child. When I was young I was way too deep. I prayed like a crazy thing, and I believed in powers beyond what I could see. Something within me knew that there was more to the world than meets the eye. I was a philosophical little thing. I spent my time pondering the meaning of my life, convinced that some higher power was guiding and watching me.

Then along came boys, parties, booze, a silly modeling career and a taste for all things vacuous to throw me off course! Upon the descent of hormones, I got overwhelmed by a love of mankind, literally, and spent several years in a state of harboring different crushes and wearing skirts that were too short.

After university I went on to meet my husband and spent a good deal of time trying to get life right. I was always on a mission to do something other than what I was doing. I guess I was ambitious, but with no real outlet or focus for it. I did not understand myself, and I also struggled to understand anyone else. As a result I was trusting yet suspicious, naïve yet too brave, I was a contradiction, I was moral and fair but with a skewed and messed up approach! I was in a true muddle, lost in the shallow end of a murky puddle!

In my teens and twenties the only higher power I answered to was the god of temporary highs and a whole range of hard spirits. It was fun for a while; I certainly racked up some worthwhile and interesting experiences. I lived it up and let go for longer than I probably should have. The result being that I swam myself right up to the shallow end, nah let's be honest, I got out of the pool and was hanging out in the changing rooms with a bag of cosmetics and a wry smile!

As is life, my husband James and I had a series of ups and downs. He had a hell of time with his bands breaking up, which if you have ever experienced it, is akin to a divorce. We spent a lot of time in our twenties picking each other up, dusting each other off, and then flinging headlong into another project or party. I also did a lot of stuff I didn't necessarily like that much, or even enjoy. I drank a lot. I was obsessed by my weight, hair, nails, blah, blah, blah. My main concern towards the end of my twenties was what I would wear at the weekend. I was bored and the only outlet was physical over-indulgence, and over-thinking to the point of true anxiety.

I got to a place where I was miserable. Something was dramatically missing from my life and no matter how much I thought about it I was making no progress. Besides, I had weekends and parties to plan! What I really needed was action, and action that helped show me how to stop thinking so goddamn much and start living. I required action that dealt with my unhealthy ego and kicked it to the curb. I needed to find my true self, not the made up girl in the mirror or the crazy Saturday night girl in the photos.

It was in this cringeworthy mess that I began to seek out my inner spirituality and self. Wholly inappropriate as some of the activities may have been, it was a fair start. I began drunkenly reading tarot cards or attempting to summon up my old spiritual healing skills to cure my drunk and drugged friends. I look back on it now and I see it was all totally wrong. But it was also totally right, because I needed to start somewhere. If drunken tarot cards were my way in, then I guess I can thank the Goddess for that intro!

Of course drunken tarot and high healing will only get you so far. I began to realize I was borderline depressed. I was annoying myself. I was lost. My head was not in a good place.

Of course all that misery and the many facets of it were a major catalyst to getting me onto my spiritual path. I am sure you have a similar story, many of the spiritual seekers I meet do. We push ourselves to the brink of something nasty, the next obvious step is oblivion, depression, and abject nothingness. Yet at this point something swoops in and hands us our spirituality. In our darkest hours we find a chink of light. That light if we choose to see it, can be our savior. Then everything has to change... including, of course, our minds.

I first found reiki and from there I was catapulted into a spiritual world and this was my saving grace. Almost overnight reiki opened me up to a better place to start to know who I was, and what I wanted. It calmed me, and it somehow cut through all the clutter and crap and sought out a more genuine version of myself. For the first time in a long time, I began to feel happy. No, it was more than that, I began to feel at home.

From here on I entertained the teachings of many spiritual faiths, as can be seen in *The High Heeled Guide to Enlightenment*. I have lived with my spirituality for a few years now, and I am becoming increasingly saner. Much of this has come about through continued self-discovery and getting to know my mind; my true, divine mind.

The past few years have been a roller coaster of becoming self-aware and admittedly on occasions failing, and then repeating the process. It has been one of the hardest things I have ever had to do, but at the same time, it has been one of the most wondrous, life changing, soul shaping expeditions I have ever set out upon. It is worth doing, it is boot camp for the brain, but it has been well worth the effort.

Though of course it is never ending and I do not kid myself that I am now suddenly enlightened, because I am not. I am a work in progress as I will be until the moment I step off this planet. Spiritual sanitization is a pleasure and there is always something new to know about yourself and fresh adventures to oversee. I am in it for the long haul and I hope you will join me.

One of the first steps towards spiritualizing your sanity is to get some control over your mind. Many of us do not even realize quite how rampant and scattered our minds are. We are living in a society where peace and quiet equates to a few hours' sleep.

While we're awake there are always a million distractions to keep us from looking too deeply at our thoughts. As a result we tend to lose track of who we truly are. With all the noise in our brains we have very little chance of being in contact with our spiritual higher self. Our true self is easily overruled by the opinion of our friends, television presenters and what the magazines say.

Our minds are constantly filled with a clutter of random thoughts. Many of these thoughts are unhelpful and some of these are the effects of a wounded or rampaging ego. A good majority of them are simply thoughts that are based around our immediate physical needs. These various vapor like thinkings bash up against one another, leading us to inner conflicts, confusion and at times unhappiness. This turmoil is reflected in how we act and in turn this affects other people and our communities. We too easily create our own drama and trauma from the craziness that is flying around in our busy brains.

The most important thoughts we have, the insights, the intuitions, the voices of our higher selves, are lost in this chattering mêlée. It becomes increasingly difficult to distinguish the helpful sounds in our heads, from the harmful ones.

I believe that we must retrieve our meaningful thoughts from this stressful soup and find a way to keep ourselves from losing them again in the roundabout that is our daily life. It is my heartfelt belief that when we open to a spiritual path we can calm this rage of inner talkies.

Our minds are gifts that are not always well used. We abuse them, tire them out and we rarely stop to smell the flowers or give our busy brains a break. Mind control (by yourself and not the government) is your first important step to a spiritual life. By seeking out your higher, wiser and divine spiritual self, you help to defeat the nonsense in your mind that drags you downward.

Spiritual Insanity and Ego

Most of us have thoughts rambling across the grooves and furrows of our grey matter continuously. What I did not realize before I started out on my spiritual adventures was that my mind was out of control, and was in fact making me miserable. My thoughts were careless and my ego was like a benevolent dictator. I believe that many of us are victims of our busy and over-analyzing mind. The result being that we have a stressed outlook and an inability to focus on life beyond our immediate thought. When you cannot see beyond your thoughts you have no chance of deepening your connection to your higher self or indeed with angels, spirit, Goddess, guides and the divine.

Spiritual insanity can be summarized as being a mind that is not truly your own. But what does a mind like this look like? When you have lived with a busy mind for most of your life, then its habits and patterns become normal. All of the following represent examples of thoughts you may have if your mind is a little spiritually insane! Do not be too concerned; everyone you know will suffer from a good few of these. By the end of this book it is my intention to help you get your control back and set you off on a happier and more conscious way of living.

1. You are consumed by your most current choice. For me it was always something like, what should I wear? Should I go to the gym? What shall I eat? What will I do on Saturday night? Where can I buy false eyelashes? How will I do my makeup? Have I put on weight? Shall I go to the gym? And on and on and on.

2. You are stuck in a place of over-analyzing... conversations about the meaning of the tone of a text message could go on with your best friend for weeks. You go over somebody's actions or reactions towards you with a fine toothcomb, possibly for weeks, months or even years.

3. You talk a lot about other people. You love these conversations, you feel as though something is buzzing inside you, and the gossip is too good to resist.

4. You set the world to rights, and you make little judgments about others, perhaps believing that you are in some senses a little bit superior.

5. Perhaps you are shunning thinking about anything at all

as you throw yourself into mad routines, regimes, work, partying, parenting or something else that distracts you from getting to know the real you.

6. For those of us with difficult life issues to contend with, you may be consumed with thinking about the past. Worrying about regrets, guilt, things you wish you had done differently. Life for you cannot go on as usual because you are always stuck in some era many moons ago wishing the world could change.

7. Do you worry fanatically about things that have not yet happened? On occasion constructing events, fantasies and conversations in your head about imaginary events, whilst planning what you will say or do if that thing does happen. This might be about sad or happy events. It might be about meeting a movie star or being chatted up by the guy at the bus stop. It could be morose, such as what you would say at a funeral, or it may even be an imaginary fight with someone who you feel is against you.

8. Do you replay real life events in your head time and time again? Perhaps for the thrill they give you, or to try to figure out what went wrong.

9. You ask the advice of several different people before making a decision, and you do this often, not just about big decisions like whether to follow your boyfriend with his career move, not just medium decisions like where to go on holiday, you do it over really trivial decisions. I used to ask everyone I worked with whether or not I should go to the gym. I used to ask them this every single day. It grew tiresome even to me.

10. You desire and need the next...handbag, car, I-pod, boyfriend, fashion trend, house, fabulous red shoes or pocket Chihuahua to make you feel happy. When you get this you want something else. Your life becomes a cycle of purchasing and attaining, but never quite being happy despite having all these attainments.

If any of these sound familiar, then you are living in a mentally crazy landscape. I have been guilty of all of the above, and on some days I still have to reign myself in.

Becoming spiritually sane involves putting yourself under a microscope. It involves becoming conscious of your thoughts, rather than just letting them control you. The chances are that in the mad marketplace that is your life, you have sold yourself short. The girl you once were is drowning in perfume, and not so sure about anything beyond her next holiday, or plans for supper. It is a comfortable and easy rut, my dear friend, and it is time to wiggle yourself out of it. Consider me your water wings; let us venture to the deep end!

One of the first steps to getting deep into your own spirituality is getting control of your chaotic mind and discovering a better way to exist. The mind is one of your best tools, but can also be one of your biggest stumbling blocks on the way to a spiritual existence.

We are easily mired in ways of thinking that are essentially just bad habits. Such ways of thought lead us into our own destruction, time and time again. Yet, we often cannot see that, we often believe we are right to think as we do, or other people are wrong to think and act as they do. The fact is we are all probably thinking too much.

As well as over thinking and unhealthy thinking we all have an ego which if overzealous or unhealthy can add dramatically to our spiritual insanity! The ego from a spiritual perspective can be hugely destructive. The ego puts itself first and tends to thrive on fear, ambition, selfishness and desperation. The ego itself is something we will never entirely overcome, and I believe that ego, to an extent is a necessary piece of mental equipment. But when the ego expands and takes over your whole mind - that is when you have problems!

We all have a general knowledge idea of what an ego is and usually it is reserved for referring to someone who you dislike. Having a 'big ego' is not a compliment and usually espouses the fact that somebody is vain, cocky and overly pleased with himself or herself. Whilst it is a great descriptive term for that stubborn ex-partner of yours, it is something else too. It is you.

We all have a touch of the egocentric about us. I believe that ego is a natural defense mechanism that the human physical body employs to get ahead. It is a primitive throwback to harder, less evolved times. The problem being that we live in a society where survival of the fittest is no longer about who can till the fields for longest, or who can run away the quickest from a marauding band of Vikings. Ego's traditional 'survival' uses have been replaced by a desire to simply be better than everybody else.

When it's not prompting us to survive, our ego helps us to understand our individuality, and can lead to the construction of great things for all humanity. Many helpful and kind people are performing their kindnesses out of a sense of ego and self-importance. Is this a bad thing? Yes and no. It is great that they wish to help, and that they make a difference. But pushed too far that ego can become twisted, judgmental and self-righteous. Ego is essential for survival but it is also something we need to keep in check if we intend to live a genuine spiritual life.

The ego is the physical you, it is the part of you that consists of needs and wants and desires. It starts off as being simply hungry, you feed your ego and it wants a desert, then it wants a coffee with a mint, and before you know it, it is demanding a ten course banquet, with hog roast and champagne. It knows no bounds and there is the danger that it will never ever be happy.

When it gets greedy it will always want more, no matter how good your life is, how handsome your husband is, how rich you are, it will never be enough.

When you cannot give your unhealthy ego more it will whisper in your ear and tell you that you are not good enough. Buy your ego a Mercedes and it will be most pleased with you, but it will soon want a Ferrari, or a formula one driver husband, or a yacht. Your ego is cruel. It tells you that you should have exactly what you want, and it makes you believe you should get it anyway you can. When you cannot get what it wants it bitches about you, in your very own head. How rude!

The collective ego of society may tell you that spiritual needs are irrelevant and that your need for moisturizer is far superior, but again the ego is focused on the shallow, the easily achievable, the vacuous, instant gratification.

Ego is fake and it wants you to be fake because it cannot cope with the deep, spiritual, higher self of you. It cannot cope with the fact that you do not need it, and that you could, if you really thought about it, be happy on your own terms, without purchasing another goddamn lipstick for the rest of your life. You could be happy in your own skin, moisturizer or no moisturizer. You could be happy to simply be yourself.

On a very simple level, an unhealthy and insane ego is about our desire to be stronger, faster, richer, thinner, glossier, prettier, cleverer, funnier, wiser, sexier, most popular and more successful. Ego is our need to win, and to beat everybody else, and to have everybody else applaud us and tell us how great we truly are. It is also about the desire to make everyone else a little bit jealous, and to make him or her want to be us, to desire us, to envy us. Ego is all about me, me, me. When extremely twisted ego is happy to see others fail and suffer.

When you are spiritually imbalanced, your mind and body is effectively in a jail cell separate and unconnected to all the other little souls that surround us. An unhealthy mind is lonely, and its day is filled with material objects and cheap talk. All this stops us from realizing our true and divine state. Our society raises us to put ourselves at the centre of the universe and to constantly think about our own needs. It has become entirely normal in our materialistic world that we are the main focal point of our thoughts, actions and efforts.

Often this tips into utter unreasonableness and I believe it is a type of madness. We can be self-centered to the point of craziness and more often than not our ego helps us to believe that we are right to be so.

Whilst those are obvious symptoms of ego, ego is a tricky foe that sneaks into everything we do.

Ego can even show up in seemingly good acts, when we are being kind, generous, caring and loving. Ego is rarely obvious and it may take a lot of soul searching to even realize that your own kindnesses might be based on purely selfish goals. Some examples of ego led behavior might be:

1. Do you give to charity because you believe in the cause, or because it makes you a better person?

2. Do you tell a friend when you hand a homeless person money, or do you go about your business and forget about it?

    If you tell someone you did it, why did you tell them? Is it because you want them to think you are kind? If you are kind then why tell somebody that?

3. When you do someone a favor do you tell other people about it?

4. Do you criticize somebody you helped, but who does not help you in return?

5. Do you name drop? Do you associate yourself with good things and people so that you can bask in their successful light and look better?

6. Do you give to receive?

7. Are you ever two faced, kind to a person and then not so kind when their back is turned?

8. Do you think you are above other people and therefore pass judgments in the form of kindness and advice to them?

9. Do you enjoy the small failings of friends or family? Does this make you feel better about yourself?

10. When you purchase something fancy and new, do you tell others about it and point it out if they don't notice?

11. Do you measure yours and other success by possessions or appearance?

12. Do you have friends or colleagues you feel embarrassed to be seen with, or who you would not want others to know about?

BMW (Bitching, Moaning and Whining)

As you can see, ego is a multi-faceted nightmare! It expresses itself through what we own, how we feel and how we treat and react to others. For many people ego exhibits itself not through having a flash car and fancy handbag or fabulous charity credentials, but through something altogether less obvious, but entirely more damaging to everyone involved, by bitching, moaning and whining. These concepts are all signs of your ego, bitching, moaning, whining – BMW, as I will choose to refer to it from now on.

I have been guilty of all these, and I still am on occasion. The saying 'old habits die hard' has never been truer!

It is my sincere belief that the majority of people on this planet are essentially good people, one way or another. Most people commit random acts of kindness, are helpful to their friends and will raise a smile if you grin at them in the street. Most people are polite, friendly and will give you directions when they're asked. But to defeat ego and regain your spiritual sanity you must be better than simply being a 'good person'.

Being a good guy is conditioned into you from birth. You are taught to be polite, to share, to offer kindness to your brothers, sisters and classmates. However, I bet most of the good people you know, including yourself, have done something undesirable this week. I know I have.

I do not mean you have gone out and mugged an old lady or dealt drugs to a minor. I refer to the fact that you have committed BMW. It is a serious offence and, my dear, you are the biggest victim. My guilty sin this week was to snap at a friend. She made me feel embarrassed in front of other acquaintances in what I took to be a patronizing dig on my character disguised as helpful advice. For all I know it was probably just helpful advice. But I made a comment back and probably we both walked away from that conversation feeling a little bit smaller. Her comment to me, whether purposeful or not, challenged my ego. And my ego strode in and rose to the occasion. As a result I bitched at her, then I felt awful afterwards. I drove home from that event feeling so guilty and bad about myself.

This really was quite a minor event but in reaching to soothe my ego, I battered my better self. I allowed that darker side of me to step up and take control for a split second. The result was both out of character and probably quite hurtful to the other party.

Many of us do this all the time. Sometimes it is direct to a person's face, but more often it is a sneaky dig behind their back. The B of BMW is not the only thing at fault. The M and the W are equally damaging. If we moan and whine then we are wallowing in our perceived sense of unfairness or inadequacy, our idea that our life should be better, and essentially buying into the idea that we deserve more. We might also mourn over past failings or mistakes. Whenever we are BMW'ing we are not being spiritual in the slightest, we are letting negativity rule over us. We allow darkness into our lives, and that is always damaging. We become victims to our own thoughts. When all three elements are combined, then misery reigns.

Whilst on the surface we are good people who hand out sweets, make cups of tea for everyone and listen to our friend's problems, we all have a tendency to this sort of darkness. BMW'ing exacerbates this tendency and kills spiritual learning dead.

It is difficult to admit to our BMW tendencies because as pretty little females we are not supposed to have a 'dark' side. Those of us that do are pigeon holed as vamps, sexual mysteries or freaks.

I have many friends who are open with me and as a tarot reader people confide in me, I believe I can say without doubt, that even the pinkest, most feminine, frilly, glossy lipped beings have a dark side.

We have a tendency to gloom. We are likely to sink into melancholy, depression or feel sorry for ourselves for prolonged periods of time. Many of us do not admit it. We step into our three-inch heels and cosmetic facades and go about the day pretending to be pretty rays of light and joy.

But on the whole, it is not true. You are a woman and hell do you have a dark side. It is ok to admit it, I won't tell anyone.

The thing with the BMW and the 'dark side' is that these elements of our existence all stem from our unchecked minds and our greedy ego.

The BMW and the dark side make us indulge in shallow, unspiritual pursuits to alleviate our feelings of sadness, our fear or our general disempowerment. It is a recipe for spiritual insanity and it's time we all got wise to it.

My own personal answer has been spirituality and the lessons that I have encountered on a spiritual path. There are plenty of temporary salves for the BWM darkness, such as chocolate, a girls' night out or in, wine and even exercise. But they are not enough on their own. Indeed taken in excess some of those options are liable to lead to only more darkness in the form of guilt and hangovers. It is a horrendous hamster wheel but as luck would have it, spiritualizing your life can help you to get off.

My Ego battles...

So to help you understand the ego I am willing to bare my soul (again) and tell you all about a few of my ego situations. I am no guru, I am an ordinary Lancashire lass, trying her best to get spiritualized, so it would not be right for me to simply tell you what it is, it is far more effective for me to show you what I mean. Here are my recent ego confessions...

Having written *The High Heeled Guide to Enlightenment* I found myself with time on my hands. I lived this spare time in a very human manner. I got married, I partied, I celebrated birthdays, I saw my friends and let the new spiritual me take a back burner. Which was fine, however it was one weekend in February 2009 that I realized I had let it all slip a little too far.

Whilst trying to be useful and promote *The High Heeled Guide to Enlightenment* I had become inadvertently obsessed by it. I was looking to my book, or the idea of my book, to be the cause of true, lasting happiness and I was projecting everything I had in my heart, soul and mind onto that one achievement. In the same way that many a good woman before me has projected her entire life onto a knight in shining armor, only to later realize, that he, like us all, is not entirely perfect.

In allowing myself to become wholeheartedly frantic about the success of my book I had cast aside most of my fundamental spiritual learnings.

I had decided earlier in the year that I was handing my life over to spirit, the universe and the angels. I trusted that they would take my book and me wherever we needed to go. I allowed them that power.

However, I soon forgot that and allowed my lustful ego to take over my thoughts and actions. I felt an incredible need to spend hours in front of the computer promoting myself to the world, telling them about my book and trying to get people to review it. I was exhausting myself and I was not happy. My actions in constant promotion and thinking about the book were in effect me trying to wrestle control away from the divine powers that I had entrusted with my care. I was undermining the essential trust I had initially put in them to look after my career and me.

As a side effect of all this I was getting ever so stressed. I was checking my emails like a demented woman hoping that God herself would pop out of my inbox. Indeed I soon found that I was growing increasingly concerned with things that were far less than spiritual; my hair, my make up, my weight, my boyfriend. My ego was trying to make my life fit into an imagined new role. I was allowing the lust for achievement to take over my mind. My ego had been allowed full reign of my mind and I was suffering her slings and arrows.

My ego had sneaked into my life and had started to dictate to me what I should do to become happier. In fact my mind was doing a darned fine job of telling me how miserable I was and how I needed to do A, B and C to improve things. The lust for success was making me unhappy and it was rubbing off with an increasing effect on my wellbeing and the people in my life.

My spiritual side was reclining and my ego was slowly edging its way into the driving seat.

It was during the general malaise that resulted that I heard warning bells. I began to notice that I had forgotten all the amazing spiritual things that had happened to and for me, and instead I was greedily focusing on how I could amplify them, make them bigger and bolder and more impressive.

Luckily I realized what was happening and I am sure the divine stepped in to help me see and understand. I soon got control over my ego again and life cheered up immensely. In this case simply releasing my life to spirit (again) defeated my ego. The ego is very controlling, and by dropping my ego's need for control, whilst also having faith in fate and in the divine I successfully re-spiritualized my mind.

Be sure to recognize that your ego will make you feel sad so that it can take control and present ideas of things that will make you happy. The fact is that none of these things will make you happy. They are, as Buddhists would call them, 'delusions'. Delusions make you temporarily happy, but they will leave you thirsting for more. If you follow the route of the ego you are following a false route. You will never be happy. Delusions are what prompt you to 'keep up with the Joneses' or see the grass as being greener. Ego gives you a negative mentality and puts your needs and your desires first. This never ends happily.

I discovered this through my obsession with my email inbox and the fact that my happiness became sadly dependent upon it. If I had an email I would buzz. Depending on what that email said I would be either exhilarated and jubilant for a brief moment or deeply saddened. Even when my emails made me happy I would soon be sad again when I re-checked five minutes later and my inbox was empty. My ego was feeding off the attention of other people; it was a sad state of affairs.

Ego crops up in my life all the time in many ways. Today it cropped up because James wanted to stay in and I wanted to go out. I had to fight back against a potential surge of self-right-eousness. I could hear my little mind chirruping about who deserved what, and how he did not understand me. But I ignored this. I mentally tried all the usual routes ranging from feeling sorry for myself through to possible divorce! All of these fleeted through my head. I gave credit to none of them. I found something more constructive to do instead.

All is now well. My ego tried to doubt me and doubt my relationship; a few years ago this might have led to an argument or something more destructive. Now I check her back in, acknowledge her existence, acknowledge she is not being helpful and act from my soul instead.

I know that you are familiar with what I am talking about. We all do it. It happens all the time, your ego is constantly bothering your thoughts, like the devil on your shoulder. It is your ego that makes you say nothing about it, in case you look silly. Well there you go, I look silly and I guess I am ok with that. It is also possible that your ego has tricked you into thinking that she is a helpful and meaningful part of your thought patterns. I know she chirrups away at the back of your head too; telling you how you deserve better and making you feel hurt feelings and wounded.

An unhealthy mind is easily achieved. But with a little consciousness and an awareness of spiritual teachings and thoughts, we can turn that around. I am sure that everyone reading this has some small battles to fight with their minds, and it is my aim to help you do this. We must get clever to our thought patterns and learn how to let our true self be in control. Self understanding and improvement is the first step to a spiritual life, so here is some advice on how to achieve that...

Spiritual Sanity

All of the behaviors I have talked about so far in this chapter, and the ego with all its sneaky ways, are the result of an unconscious mind. If you relate to any of the above, then your mind is like an untended garden, full of weeds. These weeds choke the life out of the true, beautiful spirit that resides within you. You become focused on the shallow side of life far too easily and you begin to forget who you are. As a replacement you become obsessed by purchases, other people, gossiping and anything but your true self. You may also become a bit of a cranky person to be around, because you are allowing your mind to feel sorry for itself constantly. Living on the brink of disaster and potential ego collapse is not a good place to be.

Spiritual insanity is the enemy of your divinity and of your happiness. An unchecked mind can totally destroy all your spiritual intentions and ruin you in so many ways. Being a spiritually inclined person does not a Buddha make. Once you have taken your initial steps toward spiritual enlightenment you will no doubt find you are becoming a happier, more productive and kinder person. However life, ego and everyday reality has a habit of tripping you up and always when you least expect it.

Life is happy to throw a zillion curveballs and it is our own responses to these curveballs that define who we are. Complete awareness of our mind and our actions is the answer to our spiritual insanity.

We must pay vast amounts of attention to what is going on in our minds and start to get stricter. We must tweak our thoughts and actions on a daily basis. For one good spiritual day, can easily roll into a less than spiritual night. Life will naturally test your resolve, so complete attention to your mind is required.

By consciously dropping our ego based practices and controlling how we think, we come to understand that our needs are not hugely important in the bigger scheme of things. We learn that our needs are best served by inner peace, love and self-understanding, than they are by cosmetics, BMW'ing and a new car. By calming our minds we make space for new and wondrous ways to be happy and fulfilled, ways that are far longer lasting and more life changing than a fancy new pair of shoes or a gossip session will ever be.

When we embrace a place of spiritual sanity we remember that we are connected to everything and that our actions ripple out and affect the well-being and happiness of the planet and all of the people upon it.

When we understand this we are opening ourselves to the helpful, loving energy that is spirituality and the divine. If we release the human pretensions and desire to be the centre of everything, then we can begin to deal with everything as it actually is, rather than what we think it is through our ego tinted glasses.

There is a wiser power than your ego. It is your higher self. When you calm and sanitize your mind then you enable yourself to hear your higher self. This rarely comes as a voice in your ear; instead it is a sensible voice in your mind. It comes as intuition, feelings and gut instinct. The higher self will guide you and protect you in a way that your busy ego filled mind never, ever could.

So how do we – modern people, with our many hundreds of distractions – get into contact with our spiritual side and our higher self? Well I have devised a very simplified three-step formula. A little further on in the chapter I will develop on this. But for now, the answer is simple and easy. There is no need to over-complicate or over-think our access to the spiritual side of our being. So here it is. The three-step mind control program:

1. Accept your life as it is and live in the moment.

2. Trust that what is happening in your life is right. Know that all things happen for some higher reason, even if you cannot see what that is.

3. Surrender the fight. Hand over your life to your divine purpose - whatever that may be - and have faith that you will be guided.

Obviously that is a very simple way of looking at something that may at first be difficult to do. Trust me though, spiritual thinking does get easier. If a true commitment to a spiritual life is present, then our minds are worth exploring. You have the power to live consciously, you simply have to decide, and then do it. Accept, Trust, Surrender.

This lesson is not here to inform you how to become psychiatrically well, or to counsel you on your life's problems. Spirituality is not always a replacement for such services. Spirituality is however a gift that focuses your attention on your life in a way that is transformative, revealing, and above all happy making! Overcoming a problematic mind is about finding and feeding your true inner self, as well as capturing a faith and a link to the divine spirit that you are. Only you can know your mind well enough to have a significant effect upon it.

In living spiritually you will constantly be fine-tuning your life, your reactions, your thoughts. When you go wrong, then simply learn from it and start afresh. It is about stopping the BMW'ing, it is about acting from the heart sometimes instead of the head, it is about giving your life over to divinity and not looking back. Spirituality is about not trying to control everything and everyone. It is about stopping the worry and stress, because worry and stress does not solve anything. It is about being content in your own skin and not spending your life wishing for something else. As my friend Sharni declares on her wonderful life affirming website, it is about knowing that the grass is greener where you water it!

Spiritual sanity is to be conscious, to be present, to want for nothing, to feel love and compassion all round. It will take time to get there. Even when you get there, your development will continue. This is self-help spiritual style and it reaches to every little part of your life on earth and will do forever more. And that, my friend, is the beauty of it.

The Essentials

Now to help you on this journey of spiritual sanity I refer you to the following tips and pointers on how to help defy the mental and return yourself to your wonderful state of spiritual grace. All of these are handy hints that I have learned on my spiritual journey; these are the best, the most useful and my absolute favorites. These are the ones that help transform your life by changing the way you see the world. I would whole-heartedly advise you to try these suggestions immediately. Perhaps try one at a time, embracing each for a day at a time, until you feel comfortable to bring them into your life full time!

Go Easy

It is not possible to become a super hippy guru overnight. It just does not happen, well not to mere mortals. You do not suddenly possess a halo and universal knowledge. Spirituality is a wild and crazy trip, and no matter how close you feel you are to getting your angel wings, you are still highly likely to trip over your two very human feet.

You need to know this, because I do not want the perfectionists among you to give up at the first hurdle, or for you to ever think you are failing. In fact, in spirituality, the more you fail, the more chances you have to learn!

My self-discovery is nowhere near complete. Some days I am far more enlightened than others. I can still be unreasonable and get lost in the shallows, but these days I recognize when this happens and I swim myself out to deeper waters. Getting to know my mind in a spiritual framework, means that I know myself and I cannot kid myself that I am right, when my higher self knows better. I believe that simply admitting to ourselves that we are not perfect is a vital step forward.

Some spiritual people give off a vibe of total perfection. I find this quite unbelievable. It is a little too self-important and I am sure that it stems from the ego. It is ego that tells you that you are perfect and that you deserve to be worshipped by everyone you know! If you start to think you are perfectly in control of your ego, then watch out, that may well be your ego speaking, a double bluff so to speak!

Being imperfect is the way we all are. Being imperfect is the point of life. It is our job to get closer to perfection, not to become it overnight. Go easy on yourself. Getting your spiritual sanity is a lifelong task. Do not be ashamed or upset should you fall at a few hurdles!

Mind Yourself

The Buddhist concept of mindfulness is absolutely key to defeating your ego. Don't worry, mindfulness is not about constantly thinking about what you are thinking about. That would be over-thinking craziness! Mindfulness is about being aware of your own thoughts and not allowing errant ones to crop into your mind and cause damage to your healthy thoughts.

Mindfulness can be cultivated by thinking more wisely and with more purpose. It can also be assisted by the avoidance of thinking, which meditation can assist.

Mindfulness stops all the inner talkies and it alerts you to the ego becoming mischievous. It is about living consciously with your mind and not allowing your brain to get lost on tangents of self-pity, worry, stress, nastiness or cruel thoughts.

It is about thinking before you speak or act. It is about not allowing your mind to cause you pain. It is about stopping the negative junk that you may occasionally allow your brain to wallow in.

Mindfulness is about mutiny; it is about taking back your brain from captain ego and steering the ship yourself.

Mindfulness, put simply, is being aware. You are often careful with the feelings of other people, but I expect you rarely extend that same courtesy to yourself. Now is your time to try this. This is entirely down to you. Nobody can really help you, and nobody can check up on you. So you must be sincere and committed to your spiritual self-development.

So how can you practice mindfulness? Watch yourself carefully for a week or two. Think very carefully and deeply about why you do the things you do. Are you being friendly to the new girl because she looked lonely, or because you want her to like you? Are you placing your happiness on new possessions or status? Are you being negative and allowing your mind to run off on unhappy tangents? Catch your mind in these behaviors and stop it. Try to actively change your way of thinking.

Ask your higher self, guides and angels to help you to be mindful. How they choose to do this is down to them, but hopefully they will help raise your vibration so that you are more alert of potential ego attacks, or over thinking.

Find a quiet space and a few minutes were you can be alone and concentrate. In this time sit calmly, light a candle and think or say aloud the following,

'Higher self, angels, guide and loving spirits, please help me to be mindful, allow me to understand my mind, and help me to control it for my best benefit. It is my goal to live spiritually and to develop myself as a person. I start with my mind and I trust that you will guide me, thank you.'

You may of course add extra requests according to your own mind, and where you feel you might be going wrong. For example you might request help with negativity, anxiety or BMW'ing tendencies. When you have made your request all you need to do is trust and allow the divine to guide you.

Keep a diary of your thoughts. This way you can easily remember your successes and your areas for improvement. Carry the diary with you and write in it whenever you catch yourself being 'mindless'. The thoughts that cause any negative emotional reaction are the ones best noted and avoided, particularly when the emotions are laden down with negativity about things that have not yet happened. Make efforts to write down how your thinking has improved and what positive affects this is having on your self-esteem and life in general. Being mindful in your own mind is hard work and you can easily fool yourself! The objectivity of putting it down on paper is powerful stuff.

Meditation

Meditation is an attempt to slow, soften and stem thoughts from rampaging through your mind. Whilst you may not always be able to fully turn off your thinking you can slow and focus it. In doing so you cut out a lot of the unhelpful clutter. By cutting out the messiness you can more easily access your genuine, helpful thoughts.

Meditation will help you differentiate between the thoughts that arise naturally from your genuine self, and those that are ego-based negativity that make you feel unhappy. Meditation will help you to understand what is going on in your own mind. It will give you some peace away from your ego and your over thinking to help you come to understand who you truly are.

If you are new to meditation then do start small. Ten-minute sessions three times a week will be sufficient to get you started. Get used to sitting, breathing and making efforts to clear your mind. You may find clearing your mind very difficult. But a meditative mind is not necessarily an empty mind. It is a mind that is full of clarity, and bubbles with inspiration, insight and truth. I find that many of my best ideas come about during meditation. I take these as gifts and understand that had I not quieted my mind, I would not have heard them.

Meditation will help you with your practice of mindfulness, and together they can give you back the inner strength to overcome your mental messiness. Keep a notebook handy for meditation too, because if my experience is anything to go by, you could attain great understanding of yourself and the world, simply by sitting and breathing!

Meditation is one of my favorite things. If nothing else, it relieves stress and centers the mind. I talk more on it in the chapter Connect. I recommend you start a mini practice immediately. If you cannot do it alone, find a local class, purchase a guided CD or download, or do it with a friend. Meditation is a powerful, easy tool and once started you will soon learn to find your peace within it.

Creativity

Embracing your own personal version of creativity will assist in your mindfulness. Whether you enjoy art, music, dancing or taking country walks, all of these things will aide you in turning down the clutter of your mind. Your inner creativity is your gift from spirit. I believe that all too often the society we live in makes us focus on all things external; appearance, achievement and ambition. Either that or we place our attention on things, such as television, fashion or magazines. As a result we all feel we are 'lacking' something, both internally and externally. This of course feeds our minds with more and more negative material about ourselves. Stop this negative distraction by doing whatever it is you love to do.

I know that bills need to be paid and jobs need to be worked at, but are you finding time for your inner self and her desire to create? When you are busy creating you have no time for ego, doubt, self-criticism or to worry about the goings on of your friends, family and favorite celebrity. Find your space, find your hobby, and find your future through embracing your individual creativity.

You may not know what it is that you are good at, or what it is that you enjoy. To discover this you may need to think back to your childhood and your youth. What did you enjoy doing back then? Seize upon that and go full throttle. We all too often make up excuses to stop doing the things we love. Yet if we enjoy them and they make us happy we are not being true to ourselves unless we do them!

If we can make ourselves happy through embracing our creativity then we are inspiration personified. Think of the people you know who do the things they love. Whether they enjoy cycling, gardening, dancing, yoga or making candles, their hobby gives them a depth and intrigue that those of us without a hobby envy. So do not be envious, do it for you!

If you cannot think what to do, ask your divine friends, guides and angels, to help show you. Ask them for signs and then keep your eyes and ears open! Meditate in silence and see what comes to mind. If somebody offers you an opportunity to do something fun or unusual, take him or her up on the offer. It may be just 'your thing'. Live your life fully and then you will have no time or need to sit around wallowing, over thinking or BMWing! Let your creativity consume you and pour water on the fire of your ego!

Be Grateful

Be grateful for what you have. Without wishing to sound like your mother, it is true that there are many people far worse off than you. Yes you may be victim to some lousy things in life. However you are alive, you are breathing, you have potential, we all of us always have potential. Being grateful for what we have is a direct snub to a spiritually insane mind. How can you be unhappy and harbor a deep desire to attain more, if you are contented with what you already have?

Being ungrateful is a state of disgrace. As lovely fair maidens we long to live in a state of grace, but if we choose to believe we do not, and feel that the world is against us we are being spiritually disgraceful and distasteful.

We are also opening the doors to ego. As soon as we deem our lives and our situation to be not good enough for us, we allow our ego space to start trampling on all of our good spiritual work. Being ungrateful is poison for the soul and I sincerely recommend that you make significant efforts to render any ungratefulness in your mind null and void.

Being grateful for everything you have negates the ego. If you are content and pleased with your lot, then you will not yearn for more. If you do not yearn for more then your mind and heart are satisfied, satiated and tend to naturally dwell in the current moment. Your gratefulness is your protection against unhappiness of all kinds.

Some of you may feel that you have little to be grateful for. If that means you then I am sorry to hear that. We all have off days where we would swap our lives for somebody's who we deem more successful, talented or impressive.

I find, however that those days are draining. In our ungratefulness for what we do have we can exist only in our lack. By concentrating on what we think we lack, then we are bound never to be happy. We are allowing a hole in our psyche that can do us significant damage.

Even in the worst-case scenarios you must find something to be grateful for, whether that is a small kindness from a stranger, or because you have a roof over your head. Even at your most down and out, the only way is up.

Gratefulness is happiness, it is hope and it is joy. Yes we will all struggle with it from year to year and event to event but it is worth pursuing. Gratefulness is the sunshine of your life; do not hide all your life beneath an umbrella of gloom.

The last time I was being ungrateful I was gifted an important insight. The reason for my ungratefulness was the cancellation of a holiday. I was stuck in a place of limbo and I was feeling sorry for myself.

Then I walked past a little boy, probably aged about 12. He had a bald head, not a shaved head, but a bald head, the kind that cancer sufferers get. He was talking to some other youngsters in a supermarket, no doubt dragged there by his parents. But in spite of his horrendous bad luck he looked so hugely happy. He sparkled. I realized then that I was being ungrateful. If he can stare into the face of adversity, and possibly death, and come out of it smiling, then he is a far more spiritual soul than me and a great inspiration to us all.

Acceptance

Accept that what you have is what you have. Accept what has happened to you in your life and accept all that you have done. Forgive yourself for any past troubles and accept that this moment right now is a fresh start.

Accept that you do not wish to be ruled by ego any longer and ask your spiritual self and guides to step in and assist you to achieve this.

Accept you are not perfect and commit to change, but without criticizing yourself or anyone else.

As humans we require very little to survive. In our society we believe we need a huge amount more than we actually have or than we actually need. As a result we are dependent on a great many luxury items, not only to boost our egos, but to feel complete, to keep up with others, and to feel whole.

This is all wrong. It comes from a place of desire, and desire is the opposite of acceptance. Desire is delusion and even a delusion fulfilled will never make you as contented as acceptance.

Giving up your needs is a difficult task, yet it's a very important and worthy one. Giving up the desire to need, need, need is what will make you whole and complete within yourself, irrespective of anything you can purchase.

Let me give you a very simple example of how giving up your unnecessary needs can make wonderful things happen.

This little story is fairly superficial, but I hope will demonstrate how you can get something wonderful, just by giving up wanting it so much.

Recently I have been growing my hair long. Which is innocuous enough, but lately it started to get longer and the ends were drying out and splitting. I got it into my head that I needed to buy one of the worlds most expensive and reputedly best shampoos to help cure this problem. I had used this shampoo before and my hair had been longer, so in my mind the equation was simple. Expensive shampoo means lovely locks. This was a mathematical sum based entirely on vanity and the wonderful world of advertising working its magic upon me.

The thing is, I could not bring myself to buy the product. Something felt wrong about becoming dependent on an expensive external to help ratify my self-image. So having given it a fair bit of thought I went out and bought the cheapest thing the supermarket had, which was roughly 40 times cheaper than the expensive one that I had placed my hopes upon. And you know what, the cheapo shampoo did just fine. My hair was in good condition and I was glad that I had not allowed the need to get as far as my purse. I no longer felt the desire to have an unnecessary product.

I accepted that the need for the shampoo was a delusion. I accepted my lot and sat in it quite happy.

Not long after this hair related revelation I visited my mother, who had recently come back from Tokyo. She had brought back presents and the first one she presented to me was a pack of large sized, super expensive, ultra modern and world renowned Japanese based hair products! Which was just so lovely. It was a treat. It was almost like a little reward for my previous refusal to cash out and sign on to the corporate glossy haired dream.

Of course this could go one of two ways. I could now become hooked on even more expensive Japanese products and spend a fortune importing them. Or I could see the gift given to me by the universe and treat it as something to be used sparsely and to be appreciated. I am grateful for this little present and see it as my reward of a job well done, not a reason to splurge in future. I remain unaffected by this, and will continue to purchase regular priced shampoo. I will not let it change me!

Like I said, this was a very shallow example of what I am talking about. Consider it a fable which examples a point. You accept what you have and you are happier. You may be rewarded for this and if not you will without a doubt be more content. This works on so many levels. I am sure we all have a friend who searched for years and years for love. It was only when she or he really stopped caring about finding it, and embraced their own life fully and without any need or wants, that they finally, and unexpectedly found it.

The more need and want we have invested in something, the less likely we will get it, or the less likely we are to enjoy it. This is because we are not accepting of our lives as they are at this moment in time. The divine world has a plan for us, and it may never involve getting quite what we think we want.

I believe that to be a fully rounded spiritual human we have to give up our needs to a very real extent and instead sit in an acceptance of what we have. We have to be realistic about what we can live with and what we can live without. We need to accept ourselves and the people we know, warts and all. We must accept where we are in our lives, what we have achieved, what we look like and the path we are on. This is not to say that you cannot strive forward and make changes, of course you can, but you must always exist in this moment and be accepting of the tools you currently have.

I challenge you to give up your needs and wants for a short time. Instead accept what you have and make good use of it. Try a week, or for the brave, try a month. Try living as your genuine self, without any requirements beyond that. Doing this will help you get to the now and to be your genuine self, without all the accessories that surround you and gild the lily.

Start each day with the mantra, 'today I accept what I have'.

Add a dose of daily gratefulness to that and you will soon be flying spiritually high!

Judge Not

Commit to a life of non-judgment and total love. Do not judge yourself or others at all; learn to love all people all the time.

Not one of us in this human incarnation is perfected yet and we all have a host of lessons to learn, so why not just allow others to live their lessons in peace. Choose to have no problem with their shoes, their hair or their attitude. Know that their actions are not personal to you and that your life is not beholden to them in any way.

It's easy to cast judgment... be it with a click of your tongue, a sly look, a smirk or a whispered remark. Sometimes you may feel that somebody deserves your judgment because of what they have done to you, or because of how they make you feel.

However what you deserve is to rise above condemning them with your thoughts, action and words. The strongest and most spiritual thing you can do is to think of them with pure love and compassion.

I recommend that you ask your divine helpers for their help on this one. Keep a diary of the times you judge and the times you purposefully do not make your critical judgment. In the first instance you may try ceasing to open your mouth and say those mean things. Avoid bitchy conversations, and if you have nothing nice to say, say nothing.

From that position you can move to calming your mind and your heart of judgment. When you get used to living in a kind way, you will find judgments that you overhear to be disturbing and saddening. You will know that you no longer need to cast negative opinions to make yourself feel better.

Love everyone, feel compassion, and forgive people easily. Let love into your mind and your mind will grow strong and spiritual quickly!

React Not

Calm down! Keep calm, first and foremost. In all situations that are getting a little bit inflamed, just take a deep breath and do nothing. Reaction is a flare up of the ego. As soon as you allow the reaction to take over you lose all your power and you give away your spiritual stance.

Getting angry never solved anything. Reacting to people in any way that is violent, argumentative, sarcastic or grouchy is harmful to you and is a form of selfish megalomania. Yes I know your colleague grinds your gears and that the person in the blue car really should not have cut across into your lane. But accept that they did. Who really cares, why does it really matter? Life goes on, forget about it, drop the judgment. Be calm, do not react, and move on.

The only thing you can control is you, your own reactions. People will always give you the opportunity to 'lose it' and in 'losing it' you lose your self. Remaining calm, loving and self-aware during adversity is a powerful indication of your transition from foot stomping shallow-end diva to enlightened, strong, peaceful seeker of spiritual loveliness.

Sometimes you may fail at this. But try and try again. Most recently when a friend of mine was being mean, my initial reaction was to be mean right back. Well I never have been a menace, so instead I just started to ignore her and block her out of my spiritual space. But then I realized this was not helping things. In my ignoring of her, I was reacting. It is a different type of reaction than flinging a few pens at her head, but it's a reaction nonetheless.

See how easy it is to lose your true self, without even realizing! As soon as I realized what I was doing, I shifted my perspective. I was not making myself feel any better by ignoring her, and I was allowing the drama of the situation into my life. My reaction may not have been dramatic, but it was part and parcel of my ego that was kicking up a fuss. Beyond that, ignoring her was a form of violence, and something that I am now ashamed of. I should know better, but that is life, and life is a spiritual path for you!

In answer to this I revisited my higher self and figured out that the best plan was to be loving, friendly and happy towards the person. Guess what... it worked! She was lovely to me in return and things are now on an even keel. We will never be best buddies, but in respecting her soul I was respecting my own. It turns out, of course that her behavior had nothing to do with me.

When you feel tempted to react always know that most times, it is not about you. Even if the person says that it is about you, be assured that it is more likely to be about them.

Reactions are nearly always about hurt feelings and misunderstandings. If we go around with love in our heart and good intentions then reactions become unnecessary and we can all live happily ever after.

Great times to test your reactions and ensure that they are soundly asleep are in the following situations: When you are being made to wait, when you are running late, or when someone else is running late and keeping you waiting, and in traffic jams. Never get mad at a traffic jam. Do not get mad at inanimate objects. If you miss the bus, train, plane, do not fume vent and kick things. What is the point? I know people who get angry. They spew out their anger into the environment and it always feels like an attack on the people around them. I hate it. Your reaction, if it is negative, is bad for anyone and everyone around, including yourself. Plus your reaction changes nothing. Kick the sofa all you like, but it will not change a thing.

You have got to let things wash right over you. Take the situation in and learn from it. See it as an opportunity. Reaction is hell on earth; so just try and avoid it at all costs.

Know instead that everything happens for a reason and that your reaction changes nothing except the state of your happiness.

The Final Word

It was because of my own problematic and troubled mind that I realized with huge clarity that spiritual interest does not a spiritual person make. The fact is you have got to keep striving and learning forever. The trip toward enlightenment is a constant battle. Or at least, it's a constant journey.

Spirituality is not a destination; it is an ever changing, ever complex, and always challenging journey. Accept. Trust. Surrender.

The ego does not disappear just because you want it to. The ego will never fully leave you, not ever, it is constantly on the edges of your mind, and only you have the power to stop it in its naughty little tracks. You cannot take a break from spirituality, because if you do there is a good likelihood that missus ego and missus anxiety, stress, strain and over thinking, will be there to greet you at the airport. If you hear the little voice that's telling you to feel sorry for yourself because someone has said something that upset you, or something has occurred, then alarm bells must ring. This is sometimes easier said than done, but an unbalanced, unspiritual mind is a tricky mistress and we must all end the affair. Accept. Trust. Surrender.

A friend of mine was doing me the kindness of reading through the first draft of this manuscript. When she had completed this section she found herself in a tricky state of mind, struggling to find her happiness whilst reconciling it with her spiritual intent. She decided to take the lesson literally, and driving to work one day she got stuck in a traffic jam, she chose to take herself out of her negative mindset and instead to breathe and look around and be grateful for the sun shining and the pleasant things in life. She slowly started to feel happier, then as she looked at the road a pick up truck emblazoned with the surname of her ex-husband zoomed past her. For a second she went back to the dark place that had accompanied the end of their relationship and the negativity started to flood in. But then she realized that this was significant, that she was allowing her peace and tranquility to be broken, when in fact he had zoomed out of her life many moons ago. She realized it was a sign!

She decided to accept, trust and to surrender to that, and to read the appearance of his name as a sign that she truly could be over that situation with the power of her own mind.

When she arrived at work that day this was compounded by realizing that this date would have been their wedding anniversary, which she had otherwise forgotten.

In choosing to accept, trust and surrender she realized that a simple change of focus, and release of toxic mental ways, can be powerful indeed.

She realized that her horrid mindset was homemade and that she could control this by choosing to be happy about the present, rather than focusing on those things from the past.

The signs were with her, and she empowered herself to free her mind from the ex-husband and the tyranny of emotions she felt toward him. She was able to let go. Accept. Trust. Surrender.

Following the guidance I have set out will help you find a

genuine starting point to let spirit into your life every day. When you are not worrying about keeping up appearances then you can begin to think about what is really important.

Essentially all of this helps you to become a better person and to begin a real relationship with the genuine you. As you become a better version of you then your world changes a tiny little bit.

You cannot ask for much more than that. Together we can transform our reality. Let's do this thing! Accept. Trust. Surrender.

Lesson 5 - Life is Hard

"I am so tired. Two car crashes etc etc! I feel lonely, empty, and sleepy and I have a headache. I miss James. I want my mum. Where has my normal self gone? I really need a hug." Alice's Diary 3 April 2010

Life can be significantly hard, of course it can, and when it is, there is a real likelihood that we will lose our faith. In this small offering I aim to give you a source of spiritual empowerment, and to open your eyes to how all parts of your life are connected and all parts of life relate back to your spirituality.

I hope that you will see the sense and order behind the chaos. I hope you will gain a little trust that everything happens for a reason.

I intend this next lesson to take you a little deeper into your own life. Once you have freed your mind, you will come across dozens of stumbling blocks. If they are handled badly, these blocks could easily incarcerate your mind once again. We do not want that to happen, and to preempt this we must accept that blocks will happen, and we must find the spiritual truth that lies at the heart of them all. We must learn to be champion spiritual hurdlers of all that life throws at us.

This lesson is about starting to understand the spiritual meaning of life. Of course I cannot lay claim to knowing the whole meaning of life, for that would be too grandiose a thing to say. However, I feel like I am starting to 'get it'. I believe that slowly, slowly you can 'get it' too. Day by day, trauma followed by hilarity, week-by-week, small pieces of the puzzle will start to slot into place.

I know that this sounds like a whole lot to take in. The meaning of life is no small feat to come to terms with for anybody. What I really want you to start understanding more than anything is the meaning of your life.

Over time you will start to understand why you personally are here, and what you are supposed to accomplish. In the first instance I aim to help enlighten you on a way to look deeper at the events that befall you.

In this section we are going to focus on situations and events in your life that might cause your spirituality to waiver, or that are standing ahead of you as blocks to you connecting with your divine self.

It is my self appointed mission to help you to see these things through spiritualized eyes rather than the murkiness of human emotion or societal pressure. Spirituality is everyday and it is every thing and every event. If we can understand this then we need not ever feel afraid or confused again.

In my life spirituality has never happened by accident. Divine happy accidents and traumas of a wide variety have pushed and shoved me forward on my spiritual path. Yes I have had human teachers and guides who have helped me access my own spirituality, but more than anything I feel I am self-taught. My most powerful spiritual education has occurred through the events that have happened in my life and the way I have handled them, in particular the difficult events and the difficult people. In fact, the harder the situation has been on my emotions, the bigger and better the lesson I will eventually learn.

The hardest push you will get into spirituality will be through emotional, mental and even physical trauma. The obvious example being people who have had near death experiences and claim to return to their bodies empowered with visions of heaven, divine love and the knowing that they had briefly returned home. Often they say that they've come back with a sense of their purpose and mission in life.

On a lesser scale, abuse, sadness and life difficulties can help achieve the same glimpses into infinity and provide countless opportunities for your soul expansion.

There is much to be said for going on retreat, having some imposed silence, set meditation sessions and yoga classes. I would dearly love to have a regular little guru guy or gal who ushers me into their spiritual sanctum and whispers the secrets of the world to me, but it has not happened yet. That is why I believe we can all become spiritual without countless trips to gurus, spiritual spas, or expensive weekends of meditation and self-imposed self-denial.

We have the tools we need in our every day lives, but first we must learn to recognize this and to know how to incorporate human strife into spiritual salvation.

An Adventure in Karma and Gurus

There are hundreds of gurus willing to separate you from your cash to help show you their version of heavenly love, angels, self-help and divine guidance. This is fantastic news for any spiritual seeker, and these people can truly help some people. Indeed seminars, workshops and talks are a fabulous way in to spirituality.

However, I'd say it is cheaper to start in your own back yard, in your own heart and with a true examination of why your life has occurred as it has. Sometimes though, third parties will catalyze this soul searching for you. Though not perhaps in the way you might expect... as I recently found out.

I have recently come into contact with two very different spiritual guru types. From this experience I have learned a great deal about myself.

Karma has been played out and incredible lessons have been learned. I am letting you in on this situation, purely because it shows how even in spiritual circles things can become woolly and confused.

Spirituality is never as simple as one, two, three, Alakazam! You don't rub a bottle and get a genie. It is complex and weird at times. This recent situation of mine shows how much stress, upset and effort can be put in before a very intriguing lesson is learned.

This event sums up how chaos, darkness and mistakes can total up to one big epiphany. I place it at the start of this lesson, so that you might bear it in mind as an example of life getting crazy, but also to show that learning can disseminate from that craziness. In this instance my learning was facilitated not only by the chaos maker, but also by my loving husband, and by an entirely unrelated third party. At the time this situation was painful, but in retrospect I see how far it has taken me. Buckle up and watch as chaos turns educational!

The last 'guru/teacher' I subscribed to made an exalted effort to try to come between James and I. I allowed his air of spirituality to blind me to the fact that he was basically grooming me. I had some negative intuition about him. But in all my wisdom, I chose to ignore that intuition, because I guess I thought the guy might be able to help me become more spiritual and more psychic.

I knew something was wrong when guru guy never once asked about me. He talked constantly about himself and he really did not know me. He said that spending time with me made him feel happier, it was his respite in a busy week of misery. Yet when I left his home I always felt exhausted, drained and dark. I visited him on four occasions, the fourth being the last time ever. Having had a rough few weeks in my life, the guru guy actually asked me how I was feeling. In my naivety, and I can be so naïve, I confessed that I was worried about James because he hated his job and I wanted him to be happy.

He offered to do a 'reading' for James, and being exhausted so I didn't quite have my wits about me, I agreed. My gut instinct probably should have known better at this point. The guru had spent the majority of the night drinking wine, smoking weed and trying to encourage me to drink more wine despite the fact I was driving. Sometimes though, the head over rules the heart and I guess my head was thinking, 'what harm can it do?'

The result of the reading was pure negative bile, in the guise of being caring and 'helpful'. He point blank dissected my marriage down to nothingness, basically saying James would never get a new job, he would be miserable, and he would sponge off me forever more. Following the reading he continued to pick fault with James, even declaring that if I had been single he would have married me and he would have made me happy, because I was so special and that was what I deserved. I deserved someone who 'really' loved me.

Looking back this was totally inappropriate, but at the time I was so drained. I attempted to defend my relationship, but he basically hushed me up, saying I did not need to defend it to him. I left not long after this feeling utterly miserable. To make things worse, I am pretty sure that when he gave me a hug goodbye he put his hand on my right butt cheek.

I arrived home and before I said a word, James, being hugely intuitive in his own right, picked up on the mood and immediately announced that said 'guru' was trying to come between us. He knew this without even listening to the tape of the reading, and without me telling him any of the detail of the conversation. Bless his little heart, he knew it. We argued over this and to my shame I tried to defend the guru. At this point I still thought that he was being genuine and helpful. A dark cloud was cast and a wedge was being driven.

A few days later, following a visit to a Sweatlodge (a very cleansing ceremony like a spiritualized sauna) that brought much needed clarity, I realized that James was totally right. Not only was the guy trying to drive a wedge between James and me, he was also trying to have some kind of inappropriate student / teacher relationship with me. I felt used, abused and deeply saddened. My guru had turned out to be all too human. He took his opportunity to pick at one area of my life and blow it out of all proportion, whilst offering himself as a possible solution. His ego was out of control.

This whole situation was a painful healing process, and one that eventually brought clarity and answers to me. Happily James got a new job within two weeks and even if he had not he would be welcome to 'sponge' off of me for the rest of his life, because, my lovelies when you love someone, cash, careers and dodgy predictions do not change a damn thing. For richer, for poorer and all that!

Since this event I have been forced to think a lot about karma. My understanding of karma as a subject has expanded as a result of this life conundrum. I explained karma in *The High Heeled Guide to Enlightenment* and to summarize what I said then, I basically concluded that all actions, thoughts, and words are subject to the law of karma. Indeed past actions from past lives may also be something we are accounting for. Basically what goes around comes around, you get what you give. Karma makes us pay back for what we have done, but in my mind it does this so that we might become better people.

If I am honest then in the past I did not really like the concept of karma – who does! But the more I have lived out my spiritual path, the less I can be in denial of it. I believe that most of us are a little bit frightened of the law of karma, and so we choose to believe that our karma is good. There is something terrifying about the theory that an unseen force is out to get its revenge on you. However, as I have learned, karma is not such a harsh taskmaster. Nor is it always pleasant. But karma does work both ways and so if you are good, then you get good back, and if you are bad then get ready for an interesting ride.

As it happens, I fell accidentally into communication with another spiritual advisor, a Ms Cher Chevalier, author of *The Hidden Secrets of a Modern Seer* (O-Books). She suggested we swap books, and I am awfully glad we did because it seems all spiritual seekers have similar tests, albeit in a variety of ways. That woman has been through the mill spiritually and so I hold her opinion in the highest regard.

I was moaning to Cher via email about my past 'bad experiences' with psychics. I was hoping she would give me a reading to counteract some of the negative readings I have had previously, in particular the horrid reading from the aforementioned guru type. Instead, Cher in all her wisdom pointed something out to me that I really did not want to hear. She told me that in her humble opinion we are often told what we deserve to hear. Ouch.

I took that one on the chin and went away to think about it. Having considered this deeply I could not agree with her more. In many respects I had brought it on myself, along with at least one other negative past reading I have had.

So how did I 'deserve it' or bring it on myself? I think I brought it on myself in a multitude of ways. I am generally of a sunny disposition these days, but prior to my spiritual path, I was seriously beholden to misery, BMW'ing, and thinking badly about my life. A lot of that was placed on my relationship; it is always easiest to blame the people you are closest to.

This situation, whilst it was horrible to live out, has actually forced me to readdress my own mindset and challenge it. I see the laws of karma playing out within this. I got what I had given. Whilst there may have been a time delay on my karmic sentence, it was still relevant, it was still the boot up the bottom that I needed.

Indeed I was forced to examine my own trusting nature. Since my first book came out I have been inundated with people who want to work with me, or to meet up with me. Two of those I now know to be official con artists! I have been forced to see that all people, no matter how spiritual or psychic they claim to be, are not necessarily to be trusted.

As per my conclusions in *The High Heeled Guide to Enlightenment* I still believe that unconditional love is key, and I do my best to offer that to all people, even those who have hurt me. But trust is an altogether different animal. Unconditional love does not mean naivety, and it does not mean ignoring your intuition. I embraced my naivety and ignored my intuition because my head told me I might learn something from my newfound guru. Well I guess I did. Just not what I expected to learn nor was it in the way that I wanted to learn!

Cher acted here as a fabulous intermediary between my own higher self and my every day worrying self. People like Cher can really give you a lift up the ladder of your spiritual understanding by just imparting a few simple words. They can open your eyes to the reality of your situation, rather than the ego fueled ramblings of hurt feelings. It is up to you however, to take those words and decipher them into your own existence. I could easily have ignored her; I could have taken offence and missed the value of the message. But there was a spark of recognition within me and deep down I knew that she had a valuable point. In many ways I did 'deserve' that particular batch of learning, not as a punishment, but as an opportunity to learn something vitally important for me about what I had been 'giving out'.

Your life is going to be full of similar situations. Everything that happens to you happens because it is supposed to. That sounds harsh, I know, but there is a great deal of wisdom within that.

The next lessons on chaos, darkness and death will elaborate a little more. I understand that when it comes to these topics we have a natural stop button. I know that when we hear something bad about ourselves, or about life, we want to press eject and go play at an amusement park instead. However your spiritual understanding hangs very much on your acceptance that bad things do happen. Once you understand that, then rather than feeling worse, you will actually feel better. Your life is how it is meant to be – there is comfort in that, there truly is.

Chaos

> "Faith in chaos, PI... I was warned about this ensuing
> chaos by my phone.... it's got worse" Alice's Diary 2010...

Another topic of life I want to talk about is everyday drama. We
humans are a theatrical bunch and as William Shakespeare so
aptly put it, all the world is a stage. And in my words we are all
a bunch of whining drama queens upon the stage!

Stress, turmoil, arguments and other raucous happenings are
enough to shake you out of your spiritual Zen with the force of
an earthquake and place you back in a land of soap opera style
emotions, actions and thoughts.

I have found that the more dramatic and violent these shake
ups are in our lives, the more there is to learn from them. In fact
the worse things become, the bigger the spiritual life changes we
can expect. Whilst life may feel on occasion like Satan has risen
from his fiery underworld and picked you specifically to
admonish his hell fire upon, there is likely to be a very good
reason for this choice.

We learn through our mistakes, but we also learn through the
chaos that we are caught up in. Oftentimes such chaos acts as a
hurricane sweeping in, causing ructions and leaving us with a
clean slate, all the negativity blown away. Chaos is sent to test us,
and sometimes it is sent to clear the blocks and rubble from our
paths. Whilst we're in the eye of the storm it is often impossible
to see how things could get better, but I assure you that they will.
Some people can never see past their own hardship and so their
spiritual learnings in life will be minimal. But as a person with
spiritual inclinations, I ask that you look to what good might
come out of your latest or next drama and crises. Because believe
me, good will come from it, indeed healing growth and spiritual
transformation will come from it.

Life can be a battleground and what starts as a fabulous day can end in tears, recriminations and heartache. How you handle such ups and downs can directly affect your spiritual well being, and perhaps in the long term your physical, mental and emotional health. Sadness, suffering and drama are opportunities to grow. Here is what I have learned that I feel you need to know about the dramatic art that is your life...

To release the pain and struggle of life is a hard thing to do. Maybe it is impossible to achieve with any permanence. But we can reign in the drama simply by changing the way we think about it, and understanding the spiritual nature of life, that all things occur for a purpose.

Again you must trust me on this. No, don't trust me, trust spirit, and trust your own spiritual knowing. Trust that everything happens for a reason and that one day this will make sense. Trust your process, even when that process seems to have placed you, wobbling, on an emotional tightrope, alone, terrified and liable to fall. Trust that you are there for a reason, that this situation will strengthen you, that bad will be swept away and that when the skies clear somewhat you will be able to see a good, valid and spiritual way forward.

Recently James and I went through a series of chaotic mini crises. Sometimes everything just goes wrong does it not? First we had mini dramas about our chickens. Whatever we did for them then something else occurred, and then another thing, and another. This mini drama was becoming episodic and exhausting. Then I had the awkward situation with the aforementioned guru, and a dozen other little lifetime events conspired to stress us out, remove our stability and send us reeling.

For a time life was chaotic and it felt that there was no way out. As a result we argued more and generally felt quite sorry for ourselves.

Then one day I pulled my phone from my bag and on the screen were the letters Pi.

Pi is a significant mathematical equation that apparently

makes little sense, but upon which the universe is formed. I am not a mathematician, and so that will be my summary of that! However I decided there was a message there for me, so I turned to trusty old Google. When I Googled the word Pi the first thing that caught my attention was the words 'Faith in Chaos'. These words were repeated across the page several times. What they actually related to (a film) is irrelevant, to me those three words, faith in chaos, were profound. They calmed and soothed me. They forced me to stop rallying against the chaos that James and I were experiencing and instead to understand that this chaos, like all chaos, has a good reason.

I believe now that the chaos we were experiencing was part of the natural processes of life. Our lives were thrown into tumult so that bad habits and issues could be swept aside to make way for our future. We have talked about having children in the future. But before we do this we need to get ourselves mentally, emotionally and spiritually prepared. I believe that the chaos we were living in was part of a spiritual intervention sent from the divine and our higher selves to help us feather our nest so to speak. And if it is not that we are destined to have children, because who really knows, then I am sure that other intriguing events are being well prepared for by this large dose of chaos.

The idea of having faith in chaos moved me deeply. As creatures hell-bent on living smooth lives, the idea of chaos is unattractive, maybe even abhorrent, and yet it is utterly unavoidable.

I ask you to sit down and think about all the chaos that has occurred to you in your lifetime, and about how at the time you could not see a way through it, and how you were caught up in the stress and emotion.

Then have a think about what good has come from that chaos.

What was removed from your life in your personal chaos that was an obstacle to where you are today?

What personality traits did you develop or lose as a result of the chaos?

And how has that chaos led you towards the spiritual path you have now embarked upon? Take some notes, meditate on this, and give it some real deep thought.

You know what – embracing chaos is deeply empowering. Knowing that it is happening for some reason is reassuring; it takes the edge off the pain.

I feel that I am still steeped in my current moment of chaos, but since receiving the message of Pi, I know that in time all will become clear and calm again. Chaos whilst apparently random can be a blessing in disguise. Just you watch and see!

Personal and external chaos is a natural state of this earthly world. It is sent to try us, test us, train us and teach us. We are not here to live perfect lives; we are not here to experience paradise. We get glimpses of wonder, happiness and perfection every single day, but it is the crazier elements of life that really push us forward.

Please do not expect your quest for spirituality to make all the hardship go away. Life continues unabated no matter who you are. Chaos and emotional trauma will be visited upon you from time to time. But it is not all bad news. Everything happens for a reason and it is the spiritual person's job to absorb it, learn from it, come through it stronger, and intensify her enlightenment as a result. Chaos is a healing guide, so embrace it and trust the process.

Spiritual transformation will result, and then before you know it the next drama will occur. Life is a roller coaster my friend, get in, get your seatbelts on, live, love, learn and enjoy!

Perfection

We need to go a little bit easy on ourselves. After writing my first book I was on a one-track attempt to be perfect. Every time I fouled this up I got so angry and frustrated at myself. I would brood over my spiritual failings. Ninety percent of the time I was a model of spiritual wonderfulness, showing love, kindness and caring to my fellow humans. And then 10% of the time I was human, I made mistakes, I would react badly to things and I would break all my own rules at a moment's notice. It appeared that I had set the bar too high, and when I failed to reach the standards of Goddess behavior I had set myself, I would come down hard on myself.

In particular I was vexed about the situation with my alleged guru! I was annoyed that I had not seen it coming and that I had refused to heed my intuition about the guy. Indeed I had even listened to my intuition and ignored it anyway. I knew I had constantly felt nervy and guarded when I was with him, but I chose to delete that from my brain. Perhaps my ego, with its desire for status, thought that the act of having a teacher/guru was one that cemented my spiritual understanding. Either way it does not matter any more. I learned what I needed to learn. Though had I followed my intuition, perhaps I would have learned it in a less dramatic fashion!

Not one of us is perfect. Striving for perfection is not a one-way track to spiritual peace and understanding, not at all. Tip top spiritual etiquette would involve constant kindness (including kind thoughts), never judging, being loving to everyone, not reacting to anything, being calm, placid and giving, whilst simultaneously listening to your instinct, consulting with your guides in meditation, and never falling foul of life in general.

Some of this is easier to achieve than other parts. Most of it can be achieved quite easily on a daily basis, but trust me, you are human, it will at some point go wrong, especially in your early few years of spiritual beginnings. At this point in the book I am going to give you permission to be human.

We human beings are put on this earth to learn. We would

learn nothing from perfection because if we were all perfect then nothing would ever be learned and there would be no point living on this planet. If that were the case then we might as well return home to our spiritual world and suck on eggs. You and I are here because we are not yet perfect, and because we are trying to learn more about life.

I have struggled deeply to become perfect in a short space of time and I have failed. That in itself is a lesson learned. Perhaps you should try it.

Here is your homework, try two weeks of perfect spiritual behavior and then get back to me, I'm intrigued by your experience of that. Yes you will raise your spiritual level, there is no doubt about that, and hopefully you will be able to overcome some bad habits and behavior that were getting on your nerves, but what about the moment when you fall short of perfection? How will that make you feel? My answer is that if and when you fail at perfection, there will be a very important lesson for you within that. So do not beat yourself up about it, choose instead to learn from it and benefit from it.

The realization that perfection is not necessary has been a recent area of healing for me. I hope that in my inevitable failings on this count I will learn to accept my mistakes as areas of growth and learning. The key is not to get obsessed about the details of the failure itself, but to look inside and to realize why that failing happened and what it has taught you about your life.

Spirituality has a mythic status that goes hand in hand with godliness. I do not want you to pressure yourself that way as it may lead you to thinking you have failed at spirituality.

Be assured that you, my dear, can never fail at spirituality, you are spirituality, you are divine and inside your body lurks a vibrant spark of soul. It is through your mistakes that you access this soul and strengthen it. Maybe 10 or 20 years down the line, perfection will be a more realistic prospect, but I doubt it, as life and all its lessons usually goes on a bit longer than that.

For now I advise you to focus on knowing yourself, trusting your patterns and allowing transformation and healing to come about as a result of this.

Spirituality is not about maintaining such high paragons of virtuous behavior. To be spiritual is more about cultivating and practicing good behavior, to the best of your abilities, at any given moment in time, and that means both happy and sad times. Failure is inevitable on some days. Failure is essential because failure sees us grow as humans and as spirits. So if biting your tongue and saying nothing in an argument fails and you shout at someone, or snap at your boyfriend about the washing up, or you bitch about someone behind their back, then the spiritual thing to do would be to acknowledge it has happened, rectify it however you can (an apology usually works!) and aim with your heart and soul to do better next time. Say a little prayer for the person you hurt, and for yourself, and strive to live and learn.

Life is here to make us grow; the twists and tumbles only add a richer dimension to that. Spiritual perfection is for Buddha, Jesus, the Dalai Lama and possibly Deepak Chopra – let's see. Us mere mortals need only follow their example and so the best we can do is to continue to learn from our errors.

Darkness

Let us now turn to the dark side that I believe we all possess and often suffer under. You have a really dark side, don't you? You can on occasion get really down and depressed and feel all gritty on the inside.

As much as we pretend everything is sweetness and light, we humans all occasionally suffer from the darkness. As women we are supposed to be pretty, happy and smiley. We are allowed our emotional outbursts as long as they are related to our hormones, or sometimes because we are viewed as sensitive little souls.

Depression and gloom is not something people want to hear about women suffering from.

If you are a guy then your pressure is different. It is still the case that men are expected to be tough old fellows. Emotion from a man is still a bit of a shocker and so whilst guys can be deep and brooding, they are not supposed to get upset, stressed, emotionally vexed, or tearful.

Whatever our gender, we are forever keeping up the pretence that our exterior calm comes easily, and that on the inside as well as the outside, all is shiny, easy, cookies and cream.

It is not really like that though. As a tarot reader people tell me things, sometimes incredible things. I have to say that in my experience the human race is dark, naughty and a little bit depressed.

There is so much written in spiritual books about the 'light'; a common phrase thrown around by spiritual types is 'love and light'. Whilst I wholeheartedly agree with the concepts, I do not think we can ignore that dark side. The reason I bring it up now is not because I want to help you dismiss your dark side, but because I want you to acknowledge your dark side as an essential part of your being and of your growth as a spiritual entity. If we did not have a dark side, we would be too perfect, and remember what I said about that...

I want to let you now that is it ok to feel sad, bad and dangerous. Accept and acknowledge your feelings and then do something about them. None of us could grow and become empowered if we were not coming from a bad place in the first place. There would be no success stories if we were enlightened to start with.

Your inner darkness is not something to be afraid of. It is the result of your soul being discontented. I have just had a dark patch. Between dodgy psychic predictions about how useless James is, to being super stressed at work, overtired writing my book, trying to run a home, and the never-ending chicken saga, I admit, it all got a bit dark. At times like this it can be very difficult to have faith in anything. But I did have faith, and James did too (and he listened to his intuition and shared it with me), and a few weeks' later things were looking up.

We all get moments like that. The problem with the dark place is that it is all to easy to dwell there, feeling sorry for yourself. Yes, you may have a damn good reason to feel sorry for yourself. But you will not empower your spiritual higher self or your angels and guides to actually help you out until you show ready and willing.

Once you start to make the right moves and plans for yourself, then opportunities, friends or help will be sent your way. I guarantee it. But the first move is always, always yours. That is how life is. It is your job to learn and so if you show efforts to move away from your dark place then you will slowly start to be showered with light. But if you sit in it and only wish for an improvement, you may as well just twiddle your thumbs, because nothing will change. Ask for help, make positive moves, trust your guides and have faith.

Let us start with this, a little prayer or mantra to your helpers to assist you through the darker times in life.

"Higher self, angels and guides please help me to have faith and to have strength. I ask that you support me and help me to understand what gifts this moment of darkness brings. Help me to find the light in the dark and be motivated to find my way to a happier place. Thank you"

I pray often. Mainly I do it in my head when I have a moment to spare. Most recently I got down on my knees and put in a serious word with the divine. However you do it, be sure to do it. If nothing else, it focuses your mind on finding a solution to the problem. It shows your higher self that you are ready for change and it prepares you to accept the change when it comes your way.

Concepts such as positive thinking come in quite powerfully too. When you're in a dark place, positive thinking and taking steps in the right direction, as well as setting a positive intent for what you would like to happen in your life, can make a huge and dramatic turnaround.

James and I were in such a rut, we were feeling terribly sorry for ourselves. When out of the blue he came to me with an idea about moving home and how great it would be. We both got excited. We sat on our sofa and laughingly asked out loud that the angels sent us some money to help our dream become a reality. The very next day James was offered a new job with better pay. The new job happened to be in the same small town that I worked in. A town that was close to the countryside and that happened to have very reasonable house prices. To top it off the job he got was right after the guru had said he would never get a new job. I specially liked that bit! This totally goes to show that the power in your life is truly in your own hands.

Finally the universe gave us a break. I took that as confirmation that our plans for a new life were in fact the right plans for us. Had the plans been incorrect for us, or unrealistic then maybe the job would not have come through.

As you may have noticed, the universe did not give us a break until we came up with the new plan in the first place. The moral of the story being that you must be motivated to help yourself, and then miracles will start to happen.

I am certain that you know one or two people who are consistently in that dark place, perhaps they always have been. It is their way of life; they have become life's victims. When you look at their lives you can see how one thing after another has gone dreadfully wrong, if you can not see it, then they will be happy to tell you all about it.

A life like this is a tragedy. But you have to wonder what might have changed had they realized that their own negative mental attitude was blocking good things coming to them.

As you become more and more spiritually aware, the dark times will become less painful and briefer. Now I actually find the dark moments to be quite useful. They let me know that something is not quite right or that something has to change. They make for fantastic catalysts. When things get really chaotic and I lose control and I feel down about it, then I tend to know that a big change is coming so I can prepare myself.

Much like the darkness of winter holds the seeds of a colorful spring. We too may feel desolate and barren yet in this darkness we harbor great potential waiting to burst forth in an intense rainbow of color and sound.

The dark feelings and external chaos swoop in to cause madness so that when the madness lifts, all that is left are things that are useful to life. True chaos allows for progressive, exciting and creative change. Life falls to pieces, but then on the other side and with a little faith, things can come up rosy. I told you, everything happens for a reason – even chaos and darkness.

Mistakes

Today I was given a very loud and clear message from spirit. I was driving along thinking of all the things that could have been but never were. I thought briefly about something that had it happened I believed would have been an error of judgement on my part. Suddenly my thoughts were interrupted, no, they were overdubbed by an intrusion. The intrusion quite loudly and clearly stated:

There are no mistakes.

Wow. I have most definitely been told. Whilst I often chatter away to guides, spirit and angels, and my life is full of signs, intuitions and messages, I have never quite been shouted at in that manner. I guess somebody felt it was important that I heard that and took it on board!

I do love that philosophy. There are no mistakes.

Well that is a relief! This feeds wonderfully into the belief that everything happens for a reason and that all things good, bad and indifferent serve a purpose in our personal and spiritual growth.

The fact that there are no mistakes can be a hard one to fathom, particularly if you are in the midst of feeling regret, guilt or sorrowful for some past action. I am sure there have been times in your life where you have held your head in your hands and cursed your name for something that you have said or done.

In living by the mantra that nothing is a mistake, we do not vindicate ourselves from responsibility, but instead we can intelligently seek out the meaning behind our actions and their repercussions. No matter how misguided they may seem, or how much regret we feel, we may utilize our mistakes as a valuable opportunity. Mistakes are simply fresh chances for us to learn.

Do not misunderstand me. Regret is a real thing. Regret is a struggle and a torture that can summon up a lifetime of misery. If only...? What if...? Perhaps if I had...? Regret is real, because like so many other human thoughts, we attach ourselves to it, we make it a part of our persona and we exhaust ourselves mentally by almost becoming it. But whilst it is real, it is also not real. It is a perspective. Perspective can be shifted.

Living under a banner of 'enlightenment seeker' means we are duty bound to shift our perspective. We must take those regrets and alleged mistakes and change them into something else, something more positive. This is true for all negative emotions; fear, sadness, pain, anger, stress, despair, depression and delusion.

We must realize that these negative thoughts and their associated emotions result from our own minds. No matter what terrible choices we have made, or what horrible events have befallen us, we have the choice to grieve for these for the rest of our time here. Or, alternatively we must find a way to cope.

And in my mind, the best way to cope is to turn a tragedy into a full-scale personal revolution that leads us straight up to our personal heaven's door.

Regret can be a huge burden on your soul. I suggest you make efforts from this day forward to live differently with your regret and your mistakes. Try to see the value in them, try to see the learning that you can achieve and then release the emotion that makes you feel bad about yourself. But first this...

Take a piece of paper. Write on it everything you regret, everything you think you could have done better or differently.

Then write down your emotions about this, how it makes you feel about yourself and the other people involved. Take this piece of paper, find a fireproof pot, go outside and burn that piece of paper. In doing so speak the following words in your mind or aloud:

"Angels, Guides and higher self. I release the burden of my mistakes to you.

I ask that you support and guide me so that I may have the wisdom to learn from my errors. Please assist me in understanding why I have done the things I have done, and allow me to rest easy knowing I have the strength to do things differently next time. I release my guilt, my anguish and my fear to you. I am ready to start again. I am ready to truly understand that there are no mistakes. Thank you"

Maybe sit and meditate on this for a few minutes. Allow the relief and the joy to replace any old, worn, tired feelings of regret that you hold. You are now free.

You have a fresh slate, one that you can base your spirituality and your life upon. From now on look at your life through the eyes of a person determined to learn. Become a master of your existence and remember this always... There Are No Mistakes.

Death

"Had a terrible dream last night. Dreamt that James had gone out and I knew he was gone, dead. But then I was allowed to have a final day with him again. The catch was that I knew he would die that day, and that I could not tell him how, or prevent it from happening. We were in a bar and a man in the bar would shoot him. Of course it happened and I couldn't even try to stop it. It was heartbreaking. Then as is typical of dreams James was stood next to me. James telephoned our friend Neil to tell him that someone else had been killed. Then James passed me the phone to let me tell Neil that James had been killed. I knew that when he passed the phone to me I wouldn't see him again in this life. Ouch my heart. I also wondered how I was going to explain to Neil that his best friend who he had just spoken to was actually dead! Heartbreaking dream. But so vivid, so intense. I know it spoke to me; it told me life goes on. We must cherish our lovers and friends, because we can't stop death, it will happen, it is planned. We will see them again, because life goes on, and whilst they may contact us in some way, essentially we won't see them again in this flesh and blood. Good Goddess that dream made me love James." Alice's Diary 2010

This is getting serious now. Death is scary. Death is sad. Death is tragic and it will break your heart time and time again throughout your life. I will not take that pain away for you. What I will do is frame it. I will frame it bluntly.

Death is not the end. I believe we go on, I believe that life follows death, follows life and on and on.

I believe that everything happens for a reason and death is one of those things too. So why do we die? My spiritualized guess is that maybe we have served our time and learned what we came here to learn but only for the time being. Maybe, in part, our death is so that others might grow and learn. Maybe death happens so that as a human entity we can experience death and all the wrenching emotions that go along with it. Whatever the reason, it is undeniable that death happens. It seems meaningless, yet I do not believe that this is the case. Death to me is not the end, it is the start of something new, and it is always a new beginning for everyone involved.

Through death inevitably comes new life. The life of those left behind is irreparably scarred by the death of someone they love. And whilst this may feel like it is never for the better, I believe that it can be.

Death can bring you closer to your spirit, which brings you closer to your loved one's spirit, which in turn brings you closer to the divine notion that life is just a blip in a never ending and wonderful sea of existence. It brings you closer to the knowledge that after we die we will be reunited with our friends, family, and even loved ones who died before we got to know them.

When this happens I believe we are going back home. Death, when looked at spiritually, becomes a transition. Our return takes us back to our true source, our natural spiritual state of being.

Let me say it again, death, like all things, happens for a reason. And whilst we all know it will come to us in its many forms, we are never prepared for the death of a parent, a child, or a beloved pet. Whatever I say in this section, I do not expect you to be prepared. You are spiritual, yes, but you are human too.

Whilst I do believe that suffering plays its purpose, I also appreciate that it may take us many years to grasp what that purpose is. You will find the relevant purpose in good time. Nobody is expecting you to don a flamenco dress to your husband's funeral and declare happily that you always did want to live in Spain, before salsa dancing your way out with your new friend Pedro.

It seems to me that some spiritual realms of thought aim to take the human being above and beyond the need to feel such gut wrenching emotions. However I have to query that. We are put on earth for a reason. We are placed in these primal, organic, emotional bodies for a reason. I do not think that reason is so that we can overcome emotion; control it, yes, maybe. But totally overcome it, well, not in this lifetime!

We need to take a realistic approach to death. I doubt very much that many people reading this book are so very spiritual that they can look death in the face and not weep and howl for their departed loved ones. Nor do I think you should be that removed. Maybe some real serious Buddhist monks and nuns can achieve that kind of detachment and infinite faith. But we will always be caught out of left field on this particular subject.

And I believe that we need to experience those emotions. They are part of the package of an earthbound life. I believe that we chose this life, and in doing so we opted in for all the heartbreak. Maybe in a few more lifetimes, we too can evolve to a point where death is seen as a release, as a return to spirit and no tears are shed, but for now we must allow ourselves the grief.

The intense grief you will feel throughout your life as death visits your door will be crippling. But in time it will give you opportunities for growth and to overcome those emotions in a myriad different ways. Many of you may feel guilty at that thought. You may wonder why it is right that you grow at the expense of someone else's demise. Well, death is not an end, it is a beginning for us all. Your loved one, I believe, is returned to their true source. They are not gone forever. Their physical presence is lost to us. But their soul will linger. It may even pay us visits. Their soul will reunite with their own higher consciousness, and perhaps their higher consciousness will have a word with your higher consciousness from time to time.

So when that good advice enters your mind, just as your lovely grandmother would have given, then rest assured, I am sure you have been touched by your grandmother's spirit. Just as all the other little moments and miracles you experience are likely coming from her too. You have to believe it. You must believe it. Believing it gives it power. When you allow yourself to have the belief that death is not an end but a beginning for you both, you free yourself a little and you open yourself to greater spiritual progression and understanding.

Little miracles can happen following a death that should, if we were not so consumed by our raw pain, allow us to glimpse an afterlife, infinity and the promise that we will be reunited one day.

I am desperately lucky in that so far I have experienced very little death in my life. People around me have suffered tremendous losses and they have kindly agreed to share their stories here in the hope that they may be able to offer you some hope and guidance. I offer these stories of hope after loss with the intention that you can relate to them, or find some peace amongst the abyss of your own grief.

Dad's funeral message for his family

My dear friend Claire lost her father Melvyn three years ago. It was unexpected for her, and left her mother a widow. Her family has truly suffered, and Claire even now, several years on has had her moments of deep struggle with what has happened. Yet since her father's death she and her family have had a series of little 'oh what if' style moments. Little miracles have occurred that suggest her dear old dad Melvyn is sending love and messages to them.

When I became closer to Claire she shared some of them with me. These include searching for sheet music for her father's funeral, and looking under the bed for it. Having been unable to find it, they looked again in the same place and there it was on top of the pile.

The actual music for the funeral was arranged. They played it before the funeral, just for Claire, her sister and her mother. At the end of the chosen track was a spoken word section by the artist. The words were beautiful and stunned the grieving family, they seemed to be a message from Melvyn, telling them how much he had loved them, and how much he was grateful to them for being in his life. When that same music was played at the funeral, the spoken word section simply did not play. It was as though the message had been for his immediate family alone.

More recently, on the anniversary of Melvyn's birthday Claire's mum bought a lottery ticket. She was happy to see she had won. She went to cash the ticket in and discovered that the exact amount she had won was £61. Sixty-one was the age Melvyn was when he died. Claire has a whole glut of similar stories, all of which suggest that Melvyn is actively sending messages to his family to let them know he is still knocking about and keeping an eye on them.

Sending a message

Melanie is my lovely manager at work and Jordan is her son. Jordan was tragically killed in a car accident very recently. Understandably Melanie was left devastated, as though a precious part of her soul had been ripped away from her.

Jordan, however, has not slipped away into nothingness. True to his playful and loving character, he has stuck around sending messages to his grieving mother through dreams, bizarre happenings and once even through me!

On his death Jordan did not waste any time in trying to

contact his family. Even before Melanie knew he had been in an accident it seems he was trying to get in touch. Not long before the police came to depart their horrific news, Melanie's daughter had a series of bizarre phone calls on her mobile phone. The number was total gobbledegook and when she tried to answer it would not connect.

In the time following Jordan's death, as Melanie struggled deeply, he kept up his assault of little communications. Pictures flew off walls, mirrors smashed, he spoke through psychics to other people who Melanie knew and he asked to be remembered to her – not that she would ever forget! On one occasion there was a bizarre noise coming from Melanie's kitchen. On investigating it she discovered that Jordan's favourite kitchen implement, an electric salt grinder was on the kitchen side, turned on and a little pyramid of salt sat underneath it.

Melanie has dreamt vividly of Jordan in dreams that appeared more real than ever. Whatever communication he has made, he always chooses to comfort, to show he exists still and to offer up hope that they will meet again. These events are small things to a cynical onlooker but to a grieving mother they are deeply significant.

When Jordan used me as a conduit for his message I was honored. It started as a fairly normal occurrence. Melanie's phone started sending me blank messages. I thought nothing of it, but after about the tenth blank message, I felt I'd better give her a call and let her know that her phone must be going off in her bag. As I spoke to Melanie to tell her that her phone had gone crazy, I had one final message come through. What I saw chilled me to the bone, but in a nice way. This was no longer a blank message. It had a photo attached to it. I had seen this photo before. It was one of Melanie just before an important event. Melanie had shown us it, because whenever she had tried to take the photo it could not be taken without a massive orb of light surrounding her. We had all said how lovely this was, and we had previously agreed that we thought it was Jordan up to his tricks again. To find this image attached to the message was deeply moving. The messages stopped after this. Though Melanie told me later that when she had checked her phone she found that there were about 15 messages stacked up in her inbox all headed to me. I am not even the first name in her phone's address book. Nor is it easy to accidentally attach a photo to a message and send it. It is hard enough to do if you're trying! We all believe that this was definitely Jordan's doing! I have never met him in real life, but for all intents and purposes I feel now that I know his soul a little bit!

I am sure that in your life you may have experienced similar odd little things that cannot quite be explained away. I know that when my grandfather died, and other members of my family on that side, weird things have occurred with the electrics. Things like house alarms and alarm clocks going off in an unexplained manner, or without batteries in them.

The day my grandfather died I called my father, just to check on my grandfather's health, I had no idea how sick he actually was. My dad sounded panicked and said he could not speak; he needed to speak to my grandma as grandfather had been taken into hospital. My father then called me back within five minutes to tell me that my grandfather had died.

As tragic as this was, I was struck by the fact that I'd felt prompted to call my dad and that when I did so, it was the most meaningful of times. This exemplifies small coincidences and big connections and incredible wonderful weirdness. Many people still refuse to believe in life after death and yet this kind of mini-miracle happens every single day worldwide to people who have lost someone. Ask around. Many people you know will have experienced something after the death of a loved one.

I asked some of the members of my online network and the results were testament to sprits power of visitation! I was given stories of actual visitations; alarm calls, dreams, orbs, smells and all kinds of intriguing ways that our departed loved ones have gotten in contact.

Dreams are a common theme and I too had a bizarrely intense dream about my grandfather, where he and I were both young together, lying in a field, and he told me he missed me. I said I missed him too, and I meant it like crazy, even though in real life we had not been so close that we would have ever laid around in a field together!

Dreams are one way of connecting to the spirit of a person on a divine level. I believe that they are not simply figments of our imagination, but they can be real and valid ways of connecting with the souls of our loved ones.

Another way to connect to spirit is through a medium. I am not always a great fan of psychics and mediums. But I have seen a few who are incredible. When my friend Deborah Ion *(Inspiration School of Psychic and Spiritual Development)* who is a talented medium brought forward my grandfather, she could not have been more spot on. My grandfather was a very particular character, one that could not be guessed from looking at me. He came through strongly, and quite hilariously. Whilst I don't necessarily recommend seeking out a medium, I know that should a good one cross your path and give you the insight you need, it can help prepare you to see the world very differently. If we have some form of proof of life after death, no matter what anyone else thinks of that proof, we can start to understand that death is not the end.

Death is a powerful process for all involved. I can only hope this small section gives you hope and inspiration. Perhaps it will help you come to terms with any suffering you have or are now experiencing. The key to all spirituality, and all religion, is that life on this planet is not the end result.

Whether you believe in heaven, reincarnation or something else entirely, I believe you are correct to believe that life does go on. That does not always make the grief over the loss of a loved one any easier, but it makes you stronger. Your loved ones are with you, and you are with them. We all surpass death and come out stronger. Believe it.

Happiness

Happiness, you did not expect me to say that did you, after all the darkness, chaos and death! Happiness is wonderful, but we can lose ourselves a little within it. We can easily lose focus. I find that after a period of happiness things tend to get unstructured. On a physical level, happiness may make me eat more and eat unhealthily, mainly because I am happy and so I just do not care! Or I may become so distracted by living and everyday pursuits to the extent that I let my spirituality slip, a small inch at a time.

This means I become vulnerable to a reoccurrence of ego, darkness, or I might lack the spiritual ability to cope should life suddenly become chaotic. As it has a habit of doing! Happiness has its pitfalls, it most certainly does. Happiness can make us complacent.

I believe that life is about striking a balance, and that periods of excessive happiness can tip that balance too far one way. Whilst that may be much fun, there is a possibility it will end in tears. Gosh, that sounds like I am being a bit negative about happiness. But I promise you I am not.

Thinking back over my own life, it seems I have periods of happiness, followed by periods where things go wrong and I cannot seem to get a grip on life as I would like. I believe that the periods of happiness, whilst wonderful, are somewhat disabling. They can lead you into a false sense of security. So when things do go wrong, as they invariably will do, you may not cope as well.

It is at these crux points between happiness and disaster that we can easily lose our faith. We can slip into the victim mode of 'poor me' or 'why me' or 'why Goddess why?' We hate to have our comfort taken away from us, and when we do we kick our toys out of the pram.

I guess it all goes back to the saying my parents parroted at me throughout childhood, which no matter how annoying, is actually unfortunately true, 'life is not fair'. We all have the capacity to regress to age six and whine and moan about how things are just not fair. They seem especially unfair when we were having such a good time. It is distressing to have our fun and games ruined, of course it is. But it happens, and as all loving parents know, it just isn't fair.

All I can say about this is that next time your life swings wildly from happy to sad, bear this fact in mind. Everything happens for a reason. Be calm about it, be rational.

Instead of thinking things are unfair, ask yourself what you can learn from this sudden change of affairs. Go deeper even, have a think about what it was you were taking for granted, or what you were not paying sufficient attention to. Maybe in your happiness you were becoming shallower, more ego centered. Not to worry, it is easily done; I do it all the time! But when the swings and roundabouts happen I pull my spiritual socks up and have a serious word with myself.

Change is a horrible thing to so many people. When change occurs outside of our control we freak out. The freaking is of course packed full of all the things I advised you not to do previously, such as not reacting, just accepting, and being grateful.

Next time life switches the balance on you I advise you to remain centered. Think about how every event has a meaning and watch as life enacts whatever purpose it has for you. Trust me, a purpose lies behind everything, even the temporary loss of happiness. Life is a journey, and the highs, whilst pleasant and wonderful, are only a part of that path. It is most certainly the lows that help us to grow, and the highs are a buffeter that makes the darker times acceptable and easier to cope with.

Trust in that. Know that happiness is fleeting. It rarely lasts forever. But with the help of a spiritual perspective, the lows do not go quite so low. Spirituality gives you a ladder, and by embracing it you can climb yourself out of the ruts more easily. Spirituality puts you on a more balanced and even keel so that any falls from happiness are not so dramatic, not so desperate as before.

Above all else, when you are in your state of happiness, then know you are happy and healthy. Be grateful for every last second of it. Enjoy it in the knowledge that it might be fleeting, and could be disrupted at any moment. So live in that moment. Do not think of the past and the future. Do not worry about what may or may not happen in the future, or what happened last week. Do not let your pesky mind ruin the good times.

Good times are our gift, they are our relief. Enjoy them, relish and savor them. Do not plead for them to last longer, just know that whilst they do last they are there for your pleasure, and for your growth as you mix and mingle with the wonderful things in life, peace, harmony, friendship, family and other minor miracles that make it all worth while.

In your moments of happiness be sure to thank your divine helpers for this chance to revel in life. When you are grateful for your happiness then you cannot descend into ego, you cannot get too lost from your spiritual path. Happiness is your gift, not your birthright. Think of all those who lead miserable tortured existences, and smile, not at their suffering, but at your own goddamn good fortune.

Be grateful for the simple pleasures and trust, trust, trust, that when your current bout of happiness is interrupted, that you can cope, that you are spiritually strong, and that you are accepting of whatever comes your way. Hand your life over to the divine and know that come rain or shine, this is your journey and this is precisely and exactly where you are supposed to be.

Lesson 6 – Dumb Culture

This book is not about to get suddenly highbrow and discuss the benefits of Mozart over Tchaikovsky or contrast Picasso with Leonardo Da Vinci. Probably the very mention of those famous names together is a clue to those in the know, that I know nothing. Nor am not here to talk about film, charity or high society soirées. The culture I want to talk about is the pervading culture of dumbness and idiocy that I can see taking over.

I am quite afraid that we are so busy dumbing ourselves down that we are in danger of letting any glimmer of spirit and soul slip through our fingers. The culture we live in, in the west is selfish, introspective and all about consuming more and more. We no longer live a life, instead we buy one.

To support all of this buying we go along with the absurd notions that we will be happy when we look a certain way, we own a certain thing, or when the weekend comes and we can get blasted out of our minds on cheap cider and cocaine.

Maybe this applies to you, maybe it does not. I know that it has had a massive effect in my life, and had I continued to follow that particular cultural choice, I would not have set foot on the spiritual path that I am on today. To be a modern, western human, it seems, we must indulge all of our human needs and longings, at a costly price, and without ever peeking outside of the constructs of the society that we exist within.

I feel strongly that in spending all our time looking in minute detail at our faces, our bodies and our pleasures, we become a very nice obedient society. We slot in rather well to the big scheme of things and we keep our mouths shut and our opinions quiet. That is presuming that we do in fact have an opinion about anything other than X-Factor or American Idol. We are easily controlled, we are mute, we are wrapped up in ourselves and we are less likely to cause trouble.

The thing is, many of us do not question the culture we have been raised with. We see it as, 'that's just the way it is'. Then we get our purses out and buy some mascara. We work in our nine till five existences, and then we are tired so we deserve to numb our minds with the entertainment on the television in front of us. We eat our healthy food and we know we are good people because we provide this entertainment and this roof over our heads for our family. We may never raise our head above our own four walls and question whether this life, our life, is something that is real, or something that has been pre-packaged and sold to us.

Maybe the culture we live in is not the only option? Maybe we could live differently? But first we would have to free ourselves from the maze of society that we have become enmeshed within. We all have debt; we are all dependent on our jobs and on the opinions of experts and officials to tell us what to do and how to exist. We take it as read that this is just how it is. And the thing is, it is how it is. I am not suggesting that you pack it all in and move to the Alps where you will raise goats and home school your children. Then again, maybe that's not such a bad idea.

What I am suggesting is that some of the things that we are lost within, are surplus to requirements. Some of these constructs can be abolished. We do not need to be dependent on them for our own self worth. We are not simply pretty consumers who like a bottle of wine on a Friday.

We are powerful spiritual beings in our own rights. We are connected to every other thing on the planet by the sheer fact that we are all energy. We can listen to our intuition rather than what the advertisements recommend. We can remove ourselves from debt, from the hamster wheel of life, and we can live how we choose too. You can be an individual simply because you are, not because the market place gives you a choice of sizes and colors.

The topics I will address here, beauty, lifestyle, shopping and hedonism, are only the tip of this iceberg. But this is an iceberg that needs melting. It is an iceberg that is built up around your heart to stop you from actually getting to know yourself. It halts you in your personal power and forces you to rely on institutions. It obsesses you with the unimportant details of life so that you forget you are a grand spiritual, divine soul.

I do not want you to be lost in the mirror or in the aisles of your favorite department store for a moment longer. I want you to find your spiritual community through inner exploration, not through the revelry of a drinking session in your local wine bar. I want you to know that you have a spark, an intellect, and even psychic abilities. I want you to embrace your intuition and to know that the universe is talking to you every day.

Seriously, tear yourself away from that damn television and look at the sky. I do not know where society has gone wrong with this dumb culture. I think maybe it has been done on purpose. I think maybe some of the conspiracy stories have truth in them. I think that maybe somebody out there does not want you to realize that you are a spiritual being, as opposed to a working, eating, spending digit.

Keeping your spiritual truth from you by drugging you up on self-obsession and the desire for a new kitchen is a very effective form of mind control, if indeed that is what it is. Don't you agree?

Even if that is not the case, if it just so happens that society has dumbed down totally by accident, then hell, let's not stand for this any more. Yes it is nice and comfortable, it is easy too. It is so much easier to sit in on an evening and focus all your attention on your toenails and your supper. It is easy but it is so dumb.

Instead we should get up and cater to our own spiritual magnificence because nobody else is going to do it for us. They will sell you a low-fat bagel, but they will not show you your soul. You deserve to know your soul my dear.

Dumb culture is killing our brain cells and our spiritual

connection off with every moment it is allowed to exist. We cannot allow this. Move over Dumb Culture you are stepping on my soul.

Lifestyle

"Everything we think we need is catered for and buyable by our 'pocket money' wages or via the loan system. We are entertained at every twist and turn and our desires are based on the fantasies of that entertainment. Our lives are marketed and sold to us week-by-week, fad by fad, distraction by distraction. We are not living, we are purchasing." Alice's Diary December 2009

Out beyond the drama of our own lives and minds lies a battle-field. This battlefield consists of all the things that society wants you to concentrate on at the expense of your soul. You are a spiritual being, but the western world would be happy for you to be nothing more than a walking credit card. This is not real life. This is not the real you. Nothing you buy or accessorize your life with is real. You may not realize this yet, but you are in a jail cell, and you are happily buying yourself into it, literally.

This whole lesson concentrates on the various consumer driven myths that we are all living. I intend to show you that these myths are blocking your spiritual development and that through spiritual thinking such ways of existing will lose their glamor and appeal.

Life is never simple, yet we are lucky enough to have a vast army of advertising executives burrowing into our minds, usurping our need to think and helping us to make a better decision. Lucky... right? At least we are not living in poverty or famine, at least we have a roof over our heads, at least we have ten varieties of soft drink and a choice of color on our desired leather sofa? We have it soooo good, right?

Well no, actually, I believe we are not so lucky. I believe we have fallen foul of corporate hell and that the media circus of reality TV culture that we live in plays havoc with our ego. Advertising, marketing and numerous lifestyle choices are ripping our souls up and throwing them into the nearest landfill or municipal tip. Who needs soul when you have got a flat screen TV and killer heels? Right? Who needs to think deeply when your favorite soap starts in ten minutes and a bottle of wine is ready for drinking? Right? Who needs to worry about the state of the world, the wars raging around us, or the homegrown violence of our youth, when there is a bubble bath waiting for us? Right? Right, right, right… right? Wrong.

Goddess give me strength. Our lifestyle choices are ridiculous. In every way, shape and form that they are touted to us; I believe they are ridiculous. They exist in a world of hyperbole, metaphor, perfect images and white shiny teeth. No image is more ridiculous than the one aimed at the market that is you and me. Young girls to middle aged women, a vulnerable collection of individuals who apparently need to purchase their weight in products to be acceptable.

You are the consumers of this planet. You may not be the war makers or the drug runners or the people in power. But hell sister, you consume do you not? And you do so with gusto. For some of you, it is all you do.

What's wrong with this picture?

What's wrong with this is that we have been given the vote but we have surrendered our voices. We vote on 'reality TV shows' – but that is not reality. Our happiness is entirely dependent on our lusts for new material objects being met. The fall out from a failure to 'afford' what we want is catastrophic.

As a generation (or two or three) we have succumbed to the almighty power of money. We have bought into the idea that money buys us independence and power. And yes it does, to an extent, it buys us purchasing power.

In spite of this consumer 'power' (or because of it) are you not on occasion losing your mind in the search for the perfect cream heels? Are you sometimes flipping out as you crave the chocolate with coffee and cream that you so, so deserve? Will you be a whole bunch happier when you have the perfect matching sexy underwear and bright red lipstick? Not to mention how fabulous life will be when you purchase that perfect little black dress?

Ladies, ladies, LADIES! Modern, western society presents us with a thousand choices, not one of them possesses even an ounce of soulful worth.

For many of us starting out onto our spiritual journeys, the ability to discriminate between real life and advertised images is as difficult as it is to find the ego and conquer the mind. Indeed the ego is the marketing man's tool of choice and so he taps into it and he sells you more.

In our battle to maintain a sound, sane and spiritual mind, first you must locate the ego internally, and secondly you are going to have to try to be the pure and simple you, minus the accoutrements of a full wallet.

For some of you this may be easy. For me it was reasonable. I do not watch that much television and women's magazines turned me off years ago with their impossible images and full throttle advertising. Some of you may wish to stop reading now. Perhaps you define yourself through what you can afford, your style, your taste, your social class or social networks and the fact you are renowned to have expensive taste. If so then I believe that you are a victim to somebody else's far more heaving and overflowing wallet. Please, do not stop reading, hear me out.

Spirituality is not simply about becoming deep, meaningful and soulful. Nor is it about expecting life to suddenly become magical and mystical. However if advertisers were selling spirituality that is precisely how they would sell it to you – with some pink and sparkly fairy dust thrown in for good measure. Spirituality is hard work, just like life is. Advertising literally glosses over the hardships of life to numb you, and to make all the irksome and painful events diminish. So we become addicts to their seemingly helpful offerings that will make our life complete, or easier, or more convenient, or more glamorous.

They offer deodorant and household cleaners as though they were the Holy Grail. They make you think that in purchasing one tampon over another your life will be free, and idealized. The crazy thing is that there are people out there who will judge you because you use a cheaper sanitary towel, let alone because you drive a cheaper car. In this haze of color, and happy looking young folk it is easy to forget about the real world. It is too easy to become disillusioned with your own life and hey presto you are back in the shop looking for a new one.

Relationships suffer too under the marketed belief that we deserve better. I do not want to start preaching old-fashioned values, but I do think that if we slowed down a little and stopped looking for the next better thing we would find happiness in our friendships and lovers far more easily. I believe we bypass so many difficult lessons in life because instead of battling things out we live in a dump and divorce society. People have gained expiration dates just like a moldy muffin. We do not fix things in this day and age, we trade up, cash in like a cell phone upgrade, and constantly look forward. Hence we never learn anything and our spirituality will not progress.

We purchase beauty products like they are going out of fashion, which of course they are as a new season starts and our old pink lipstick must be slung and replaced with coral, or mink or precious pearly palomino. Some of us rip up our flesh in the vain attempt to get better flesh, younger flesh. We take the hair of poverty stricken girls in far flung countries and we stitch, glue and staple it to our scalps. We don't stop to think how such lustrous locks came into being, the life they have lived or the hardships they have had to endure to ensure our own mane looks fantastic? What about all the children stifling in sweatshops as our babies luxuriate in the cozy cottons that those sweatshop children sewed for them?

We try not to think about any of that because at the end of the week when all the money is earned, when all the shopping sprees are accomplished, there is a likelihood that we will spend a good deal of time out of our minds and having all the fun we think we deserve. Drink and drugs help us to cultivate a fun, fun, fun party image, whilst allowing the trauma of the hard week slip away.

Brave New World eat your heart out. Many of us shop and party and dance our lives away, in complete disinterest to planet earth, her magic, our natural spirituality and the very basic concept of humanity as a thoughtful, caring, intelligent species. If I am not talking to you then I am talking to your friend, your parent, your child or your lover. It is time to change.

We are spoilt and we are ignorant. We have become creatures of consumption and self-glorification. You are hypnotized and mesmerized and I for one cannot allow you to remain that way a moment longer.

Click.

Life is more than what you can buy or what you can achieve. Fact. You are an incredible and powerful soul living a human life. You are deeply missing something, which is why you are reading this book. What you are missing is something you cannot buy. You are missing your true self, your soul, your angels, your guides, and you are missing the part of you that knows that all that glitters is not gold. You are missing the part of you that will give your life meaning.

This section is designed to look deeply at the areas of your life that could do with some spiritualization. I am no angel myself and having grown up in the same society as you, I have been equally its victim, and on a pre-menstrual day even now, I can still fall for it.

But for the majority of the time we need to get away from our old choices and open to something more spiritual instead. This does not mean burning your bankcards, learning knitting and moving to a remote mountainside where you can rear sheep for wool and food. Oh no, but it does mean becoming aware of your choices and how they affect you, and how they affect this spiritual planet.

I believe the world is changing. As a woman (or man), as a consumer, as a spiritual being, I believe that you have a role and a serious responsibility to act, to make a positive change. This reaches to so many levels, be they internal, environmental, spiritual, societal, past and future.

Let me put it simply; I want the world to be a better place. You want the world to be a better place. Nobody wants to live in a dumb culture. Your spirituality, your enlightenment and all our futures depend on this very fact. Come join me...

Beauty

It is hard to be a woman. Not only do we have the natural rhythms of nature to contend with, but piled on top of that is a trainload of pressure from society. Depending on the season, and current fashion trends we are supposed to have long legs, big boobs, pert boobs, ribs showing, toned arms, flat bellies, hairless limbs, lustrous hair, great skin and smiley white teeth.

This is something we can so easily lose our minds to. I have struggled with body issues in the past. As an ex-model I have seen the dark side of all this, the pressure, the criticism, the objectification. As someone who has studied feminism and women's issues, I am further acutely aware of the damage this can do to you physically, spiritually, mentally and emotionally.

In spite of my glamor girl past and a degree in women's studies, it was only when I became spiritualized that I realized how important it is that women lose their dependence and obsession with beauty.

This lesson is going to be a hard one to assimilate, because vanity is epidemic in our society. This lesson is essential because it is within our obsessions with our own physicality that we become deaf to our spirituality. We must learn to love ourselves for what we are – spiritual beings – not because of how we look. Beauty is a curse upon us all because it shuts down our spiritual senses. It keeps us from looking beyond our own exterior. We become shallow and this, my dears, needs to end.

The desire to achieve society's version of beauty is one of the main distractions western women have on their way to enlightenment. Indeed it is such a huge problem that many women never ever get past it. Feminists, sociologists and women's issues writers have written much about the objectification of the female form. It was a topic I became all too familiar with when studying for my women's studies degree. Depressingly familiar with. I would often find myself mid-way through a text on rape or female servitude and realize that I had been sobbing for the past ten minutes. When you look at the facts really closely, not only is it depressing, but being a woman can also be frightening.

Even now with all my spiritual anchors firmly in place, I still, on occasion fall prey to the pressure to conform and to be beautiful. It was only very recently that I decided to dye my hair from its usual blonde to a darker shade of blonde, nearing on brown. Having been a blondie all my life, this freaked me out. I am ashamed to say that I called James up in tears, because, and this is pathetic, it looked different. I looked in the mirror and the usual me was no longer there.

Whilst my divine self whispered words of consolation, my ego was having a fit. Who was this person, what did this mean, what would other people think, would I still be attractive?

I hate my reaction to this. You will be pleased to know that I soon got over it, and actually decided I rather like my new semi-brunette look and I am thinking of keeping it. However my initial reaction was based in fear. It was a fear of no longer fitting the image I had made for myself. It was the fear of losing my looks. It was total vanity, and I succumbed for one or two hours of my day.

I soon had words with myself and my divine higher self won the battle. My husband reassured me that my hair color had nothing to do with his feelings for me, and I got a grip of myself. I realized that this, like all things, was an opportunity. This was a chance to live outside my own stereotype. It was a chance to be me without the crux of being blonde to boot. It was my chance to opt out a little of the purely physical and live in a world where I don't need to stand out as brassy bottle blonde and instead sink into my soul for comfort and for depth. My blonde helmet had for too long been my armor, my shield against the world, and it was now my chance to just be in the world, defenses down and inner confidence alight!

As my confession will show you it is all too easy to become obsessed with our own looks without even realizing it. Our society preaches that the exterior surface of ourselves is vitally important for how we are received by others. The freedom of women has come at a price. That price being that our importance is often reduced down to the size, breadth, beauty, weight and firmness of our bodily parts. It is hard to be a woman, but we are not making it any easier for ourselves by buying into the western world's beauty obsessions.

A hundred years ago women were covered up, we were supposed to be pious, shy and quiet. When we demanded rights and freedoms, the freedom that an all male establishment gave us was the freedom of our sexuality. How very convenient for them! Hence birth control, legal abortion, free love, safe sex and the influx of pornography, sex trafficking, sexualization of children, teenage pregnancy and grown up women dressing like bunnies and kinky cowgirls. Everything women are encouraged to do, is touched by sexuality. We have total freedom to wear low cut tops, mini-skirts and to post semi nude photos of ourselves on the Internet. I plead guilty to many of these your honor.

Yes, our freedoms have moved into other areas too, our careers and life choices have expanded significantly. Yet at every twist of the road there are billboards flashing women's butts and boobs and impossibly long and smooth legs. Women are defined by their age and their hair color, whilst men are just that...men. It is still hard for a woman to compete in male dominated offices, but if she wants to express her femininity sexually, then heck, that is the easiest thing in the world. Allow me to repeat myself... how very convenient.

The facts are there. Women have not achieved full equality because we are still objectified beyond belief. The rise of the Internet and the huge, gigantic market for pornography has left us more exposed than ever as the sex objects society likes us to be.

Sadly the result of this mass objectification is leading more and more women to forget those latter qualities. We honestly believe we are insignificant and unworthy unless we have the bodies of the foxy, flesh baring starlets. Take a look at your female friends' pictures on Facebook and see how many sultry pouts you can count. I am guilty as charged when it comes to that, I have the pout, head tilt and come to bed eyes perfected. But I cringe a little bit inside when I see those pictures. Yes I think I look good, yes I look glossy, tanned, blonde and smiley. I hate it, but I buy into it. It is too easy.

I know how this story goes only too well. I have done it. I have bared my breasts for a photographer in the belief it made me special. And whilst there is not a thing wrong with beauty, indeed for some lucky ladies beauty cannot be helped, there is something seriously wrong with valuing beauty above all other qualities.

I have been "complimented" in the past because apparently I looked like a porn star. I have been told I am pretty enough to work in a bar – which is just a weird compliment on so many levels. More shockingly I cannot count the times a man, and indeed a woman has confessed to me that they were surprised when they realized I had a personality, lord forbid that I may even have a brain tucked under my blonde head of hair.

It is amazing how impressed these people have been by me. Indeed I have shocked a few people by being friendly too. Apparently as a blonde I should have been icy. I should act like an extra from some American high school drama, I should be a stereotypical bitch that gossips and snipes and plots against all the other girls. Officially speaking it is only a matter of time until I steal your boyfriend. As far as the stereotype goes, I have nothing better to do with my time. We women cannot win. We are not people; we are characters from Playboy's literature section. Damn.

We live in a beauty obsessed and overwhelmed society. We cannot be brainy and beautiful and we can't be brainy and loveable. So we are all constantly at odds with what we are, what we should be and which part of ourselves we should expose to get favorable reactions from everybody else. It is not real; it is a sad state of affairs. It makes us all very self-centered.

Into this mêlée and search for physical perfection how do we fit a little bit of spiritual inclination? Many of us do not. There is no time for spirituality when our hair needs straightening, outfits need to be thought about and the fat on your belly is undergoing severe gym attacks. But there should be. We need to stop following the advertising billboards and start following our hearts. Until we look beyond the end of our nose or our breasts (depending on which sticks out further) we will continue on this slavish path to objectification.

I am a proud feminist, I am a spiritual feminist, and I am a hippy feminist. I just want to see the world become a better place, I want to hug a tree and a man and I do not want to have to burn my bra because a decent bra is my Goddess given right - for the sake of comfort, ladies! I want women not to be obsessed with how they look to the point that they are dumbing their minds and selling their own souls, when they could be exploring their own intelligence and personality.

A search for enlightenment is far more likely to make you happy than an ongoing obsession with your allegedly freaky big feet.

I want us to move beyond the body and wake up to the magnificent beauty of the planet and the essence of our lives. I want you to see the beauty in a sparrow, the power of a smile, the sheer magic of prayer, meditation, tarot cards, whatever takes your fancy.

I want you to look away from the mirror and live your life to its highest spiritual purpose. I want your partner to love you because you are quick, witty, smart and talented. I want you to know that you are perfect anyway, irrespective of the color of your lipstick, the size of your lips and the height of your heels. Are you with me? Do you really understand that beauty is not the be all and end all? Shall we start a revolution? Should we rile against our constant objectification and the fact that our women friends are anorexic, bulimic and catching cancer like a plague from solariums? Should we get a little bit angry that we are expected to spend thousands of dollars on carving perfect breasts, butt implants into our body, and buying false hair extensions made from from the real hair of some poor Indian girl who was forced to have her head shaved as a penance? Should we wake up a little bit to the damage the beauty industry is doing to us as human beings? That we are becoming shallow, vacuous and selfish as a race because all we care about is the hair on our own heads.

I think we should. It is high time we stopped exploring the

flesh and started beautifying our souls. We must spiritualize our attitude towards our own selves and know that beneath whatever exterior we have been given, something more powerful and more beautiful than we could even imagine exists. It is this that will take us far in this lifetime.

Extreme Beauty

The past few years has seen a terrifying new trend that plays directly into our deepest beauty fears. It seems that every time I open a women's 'interest magazine' I am advised where to get the cheapest facelift, that it essential to have my vagina spliced, or how to get breasts like Pamela Anderson. This makes me terrifically angry, it offends me, it worries me, it frightens me; no forget all that, it makes me depressed. What has become of womankind that we are so desperately insecure and eager to compel our bodies, at the hands of a knife, into a macabre version of our 19-year-old selves?

Part of me believes that this is just society's way of making us spend our money on something else. We have the make-up, the clothes, the new hair and our holiday is booked. We have bills up to our eyeballs and the mortgage company somehow never, ever mislays our details and forgets to collect its dues, which is such a darned pity. We have enough excess money to enjoy a social life with friends.

So how can the ever more adventurous world of consumerism goad us into parting with a little more cash? Well, basically it does it by telling us we have small breasts, that our lady parts are hanging far too low, and our creased brows are reminiscent of the Grand Canyon. The key to this being that if we continue on in our hopeless, ugly bodies, nobody will ever love us as much as we deserve.

Of course the only way to gain control over our wayward and despicably aging bodies is to save up our wages and invest in surgery, that might leave us scarred, pitiful and stretched in the vain hope that people will love us more.

It is sickening...right? What would you have done if you could afford it? That seems to be a commonplace question among groups of well-heeled women (and men). In fact, despairingly, that question is more likely to be; 'what have you had done?' It is now so very usual. People I know, who I thought had more sense, are currently saving up to freeze frame their facial features with poison. People I know have had surgery – for no good medical reason. I cannot even believe that this is real life. I am so sad about all this.

So what does surgery and super cosmetic vanity have to do with spirituality? Cosmetic surgery has nothing soulful or spiritual or magical about it. It's a cynical, nasty business that feeds off people's insecurities, fears and anxieties. As a lifestyle 'option' that is 'available to all' and that can be paid for in 'monthly installments'. It is atrocious.

I am not talking about reconstructive surgery. I'm not talking about essential, medical cosmetic surgery. I am talking about vanity surgery. I am talking about the fact that some people live on this planet with their sticky out ears, receding hairlines, fat bellies and big noses and they are happy. I am talking about the fact that we all need to get a grip and get over ourselves. Literally get over your self. If all you can think about is the way you look, to the point that you cannot see beyond it, then you need a psychotherapist not a surgeon. Believe me on this...you are a loved and beautiful soul. You must get on with your life and you must, must, must look beyond your bust.

Cosmetic surgery is the ultimate in vanity, and vanity is all about the self and the ego. The more we indulge that ego the less meaningful our lives become. The more we obsess over a flabby tummy or a crows foot laughter line, the less time we have to open our eyes to anything beyond our own physical existence.

As I will go on to talk about a little later, I have a problem with commercialism. I believe that it distracts us entirely from the reality of the world and the planet we live on. We live via our purchases and the money we earn. With cosmetic surgery and extreme vanity techniques such as botox and acid peels and who knows what else, commercialism tempts us to be utterly self-seeking. It leads us to believe that the world will be a different place for us if we focus our full attentions on fixing whatever little fault it is that we believe we have.

Not only is this self-obsession utterly ridiculous but also it is harmful to the planet, to our children, to our friendships, our relationships and to our souls.

We are not immortal. The sooner we accept that the better. To know that we are aging and we may die any day now is the first step toward spiritual living. When we are aware of our immortality we naturally become better people. We make the effort to make the most of our lives and to be happy. Death allows us to utterly value what we have and to express that gratitude through worthwhile exploration of the life we are currently in.

Cosmetic procedures defeat all this. Cosmetic surgery in particular spits in the face of death and proclaims it knows better. It allows us to believe we can buy back the years, bit by bit. We can cash in and believe we can lose ten years on our face, our neck and our chest. We can focus on that as an achievement and in the very short term we will feel happy, ecstatic and beautiful. That is until we notice the veins, wrinkles and age spots on our arms, hands, legs and feet. It is a pointless fight. Pay out all you like but honey you are going to age and you are going to die. You may as well get used to it.

Radical beauty treatments are a delusion, and delusions are the mother of all things bad and wrong with the world. Delusion is what makes you think your needs are more important than anything else. Delusions are foul and they are the very downfall of our human existence.

Cosmetic surgery is delusional thinking gone insane. Cosmetic surgery is pandering to the niggling mental health issues we have. Yeah it is great to look great, but it is better to be a good, kind, loving, funny, warm person...or is it? You tell me. Magazines suggest otherwise. Surgery has gone from the seedy back pages to front-page news. It is no longer shameful and because of that we are led to believe that we all want a piece of the action.

Cosmetic procedures gone wild is the new commercialism that is preventing us from living genuine lives and from seeking the inner light as opposed to the fraudulent light that comes from instant satisfaction.

Perhaps your fear of your slightly too large outer labia could be fixed by some other route as opposed to chucking money to some robber surgeon who laughs all the way to the bank after slicing off two millimeters of your womanhood, leaving you in agony and the false belief you are now somehow 'perfect'.

Spiritual thinking would clearly and always say that perfection comes from within. Boring though it might be, the most beautiful people I know exude that beauty from their character, their personality, warmth, wisdom and kindness. I do love to look at a beautiful person, male or female. But I adore speaking with someone who glows from the depths of some deep and knowing soul. Beauty is lovely on the eye, but to make a real difference you must go more than skin deep.

What happened to the idea that age was a badge of honor? That you wore your experience and ideals on a well-worn face? The striving for perfection that western society demands is a shallow and vacuous cause. We have no faith in anything but this life, and so we concentrate our efforts on it. We focus on youth and nothing more, because we have little religion or understanding beyond that.

I want to tell you that life goes on beyond the here and now, and really your wrinkles don't mean squat in the big scheme of things. This obsession with youth disables those over a certain age and proclaims that only the young and healthy are worthy of anything. This is a terrible way to be. If we disrespect age then we have to listen to youth… constantly. And whilst the youth have intriguing, beguiling and intelligent things to say, so do those elders of our society who have lived it, loved it and damn well bought the T-shirt.

Shamanistic societies worship their elders. Respect is given to the utmost degree and it is the wrinkly old prune of a shaman who is likely to impart pearls of spiritual wisdom before any young warrior type. We need that wisdom do we not? But we will never possess any wisdom spiritual or otherwise if we allow the quest for eternal beauty to constantly be at the forefront of our minds. We should accept what we have been given and start to enjoy living through it.

Our bodies are merely the gateway to our spiritual selves, within which resides access to the temples of our souls. How can we learn anything and progress in this life if we refuse to go beyond the gates?

I believe that we reincarnate here to learn lessons, to live out karma and to generally do the best we can with what we have been given. To spend a lifetime fearful that our physical bits need chopping and changing is not a life well lived. Imagine explaining that to your guides and friends after you die.

Seriously though, let's imagine it. You die, you follow the light, you have a nice meeting with your soul mates and then you are called to meet the big shots to talk about the life you lived. What on earth do you say… Maybe it will sound a little like this…

'Well I meant to be a really good teacher / charity worker / inspirational friend / good mother, but unfortunately my thighs were too fat so I had to get liposuction, but it took me a few years to save up for it so in the meantime I got a bit obsessed with my skin and spent a couple of years investing in chemical peels and botox. Then I unexpectedly died, which was unfortunate because I really did mean to do something more with my life, once I felt pretty enough, if only I'd just had slim thighs!'

Yeah, that would be really classy. Just think of all the learning you will have missed whilst staring at your legs – scary!

As for looking perfect to try to snare a lover, or to keep one...well good luck with that. I was recently told that someone I love dearly had surgery to fight back time as her partner was younger than her. However, the cosmetic surgery did not work, maybe she looked younger, but it did not keep them together, so it did not work.

Perhaps if she had cultivated her inner self, instead of cutting her outer self up, things might have worked out differently. This is proof if I have ever seen it that the outside really, seriously does not matter. In matters of love or death it is what is inside that ultimately counts. In her case I am guessing she was several thousand dollars and one meaningful relationship down. I sound like I am being blasé, I am not, the whole thing is heartbreaking.

Surgery solves nothing. Surgery will not snag you a soul mate. Soul mates, in my experience and in my opinion, are a bit of a pain anyway. It is often their job to wind you up and be imperfect. If they were perfect we would never get anywhere and we could all just die and go and live in heaven. We need our soul mates to be a bit imperfect for us to learn. So having said that, why should you spend your cash trying to be perfect for them? Hang onto your wrinkles and give them something to think about!

Maybe it is their path in life to live with your imperfections, and if they cannot handle it then move along lady to the next soul mate in the wings. Life is not supposed to be perfect and no sweet cheeks or perfect rack is going to solve world hunger, global meltdown or cure AIDs. Switch your focus, forget your imperfections, accept yourself, and get on with feeding your poor hungry soul.

Life is all about progressing, taking opportunities, experiencing the weird and the wonderful and generally hopping on an adventure and seeing where it takes you. To fall for any of the hype around beauty is likely to lead you away from worthwhile paths. Or perhaps it is your path in life to meet the love of your life whilst waiting for your consultation regarding your 'nipple reshaping'. I seriously hope not, but if you do, I hope the love of your life talks you out of it and loves your nipples just the way they are.

Spiritual Beauty

Beauty and body obsessions are a serious barrier to a more spiritual life. We are all so busy trying to derive pleasure out of our own and other people's bodies that we can see nothing else. Our bodies are the totality of our existence. We spend our time perfecting and enjoying our own physical state, and if we do not do this then we are punishing and hating our physical state. Either way our obsession with the physical body shuts out all other elements of life that can lead to any kind of spiritual revelation. It is hard to ponder the possibility of your own soul when your stomach is rumbling from your new diet and your nails need a new coat of color.

In *The High Heeled Guide to Enlightenment* I touched upon a rough period in my life. In that rough period I had fallen foul of a lot of things. One thing I was completely obsessed with was myself. My week was spent planning my wardrobe, my make up and hair for the weekend. I felt compelled to present the perfect version of myself to the people I was going to see. I could not have left it to the last minute. My gym sessions were not in a bid to get fit, or to run a half marathon, but to be as slim and as attractive as I could be. I was depressed. The me that I had become was a concoction of perfume, flirtation, false eyelashes and fake tan.

I did not like that me, I did not know her. There was nothing to know. She was fake tanned flesh covering cocktails, tantrums and misery. That Alice was obsessed by her physicality, that Alice actually believed what Cosmopolitan says about the perfect sex life, that Alice was making herself depressed. Life had no meaning, except for the meaning that was injected every Saturday night by a mighty dose of booze and other substances. That me was dead inside. That me is now dead, and long live the new me is what I say!

Knowing yourself inside is the key to spirituality. Knowing yourself on the outside is as simple as looking in a mirror; there is no challenge in that. Becoming a spiritual person involves much soul searching, no eyebrow waxing required.

I started several years ago, and I do not expect the soul searching to end, not ever. Soul searching is not like the application of make-up, it is not ever perfected. But it does make you a whole lot happier. It is this that is my main concern, how can society even begin to become more spiritual and to raise its vibration and reach a higher consciousness if we are all worshipping at the altar or our own appearance?

I have escaped that particular rat race and I am headed elsewhere, it is a pretty cool journey and I hope I may convince you to join me!

If you want to be more spiritual then one of our greatest challenges as women is to try to overcome our own little quirks and personal foibles about the way we look. We need to open our hearts to our own innate value as people with brains, hearts and souls. We need to share this self-loving with our self-loathing friends and daughters. We need to take back our natural feminine attributes of nurture, kindness, sisterhood and compassion. We must remind ourselves that beauty comes from the heart and not from a jar, not even a really expensive, limited edition jar. Beauty will not cure world hunger, but a dose of confidence that comes from a spiritually enabled human being can take us a step closer to some kind of happier society.

Spirituality in all its forms asks us to be gentle to ourselves, and to show love to the world. We must love everyone around us, no matter what our critical self may think of them. The version of the self-obsessed me, could not love others in any kind of decent way. I was in no position to love everybody and the planet when I could not even properly love myself.

Becoming spiritual means loving ourselves warts and all. This may be a hard slog for you. You may feel ugly, unlovable, fat, spotty or awkward. But you must dig deeper to see your soul. We must take our eye off our blotchy skin and turn our hearts towards our emerging spirit.

I do believe that all our souls stem from one magnificent source and we are all the same. We are all sparks of spirit, we are all tiny, energetic fragments of soul, we are all equal and we are all perfect. We are all here to help one another and to progress.

All that stands between us and loving others and ourselves is our own consciousness. Our consciousness is saturated by different and particular ideas of perfection. Our first world consciousness is literally drowning in images of slim thighs and perfect teeth. We struggle to keep up with these impossible images and our consciousness forgets the truth and the spiritual reality that we are divine, we are amazing, we are so much more than what our bodies seem to be. And so we hate ourselves, and we re-shape ourselves and we hate those who do a better job at beauty than we do.

Know that artificialized physical beauty, in all its forms, is nothing more than what it looks like. Beauty is not confidence, it is not happiness, and it is not divine. All of those things reside in the soul and to know that on a daily basis will help you to focus your life and yourself on something spiritual.

You cannot justify to me the excesses of the cosmetics and diet industry when women in far-flung countries are being raped and murdered and their children are starving to death, while you apply your cosmetics and worry about the size of your nose / thighs / boobs. It is not right. It is just so not right. Come on, we have to stop this and we have to start with ourselves. The beauty industry has us in a grip and until we break through then we are blinded to the reality of the beauty and cruelty of planet earth. To be spiritual we must acknowledge both. We must see through the fog of powder and blush that has come to represent our lives.

Beauty does not last, and whilst sadly it can be bought, it is purchased at the expense of education, learning and creative thought. We save our pennies for a tummy tuck instead of going to college and following our passion for art, science or philosophy. The world is not going to become a better place because you have a flat stomach. I learned that a long while ago and I am empowered by the fact that I do not give a damn any more. As long as I am spiritually healthy, physically fit, happy, surrounded by friends, continually thinking and ever learning then I know I am glowing. Beat that Revlon.

Consumerism

You know what I hate and detest more than anything I can currently think of? Shopping. I hate shopping. I hate that shopping has become an activity, or even an art form! I hate that shopping is a way to purge and cleanse our souls. I hate that we have all bought into this, and that we continue to do so. I hate advertising, I hate products, and I hate the changing nature of fashion and trends. I hate that we are all on some gigantic hamster wheel that puts us in a place where we must make money, to be able to spend it. And what do we spend this money on; accoutrements, decorations for our ego.

Shopping, advertising, marketing, possessions, those four are the tenets of hell. Oh and the fifth tenet that comes as a result of all of these, Debt. I hate that too. Not because I don't want to be in debt, but because debt basically means trapped, jailed, captured. These tenets represent a society that is self deluding and ignorant. I do not understand that people go out shopping, all the time, just for the sake of it, just to buy new things. I hate that we are consumers. I hate that products are targeted at us, at our children! This might not be what you expect to hear from a woman whose book has 'high heeled' in the title. But hear it loud and clear. I hate shopping and I detest all it stands for.

Shopping of course results in more stuff. It is ridiculous how much stuff we all have. We mistakenly believe that wealth and 'things' bring happiness. If we were to think about it, we already know that true happiness comes from an acceptance of life's hardship, finding gratitude and exploring love in the present moment. We know that depth of soul is found through exploring life beyond the realms of your next purchase. And yet even though we know this we will still take a chance on that new fruit based drink because the advert says it will make you smile!

Our society as a whole with its focus on 'buying' the perfect life, the power of the media and the habit of consumption has a lot to answer for. I believe we have far too much stuff. Quite dangerously our feelings are invested deeply within that stuff. As such we are liable to suffer more chaos and hardship. If your favorite plate is broken in the dishwasher, your whole day can be thrown out of sync. For those people who have no plates and no dishwasher, perhaps life is far happier?

We have invited chaos into our western lives via overcomplicating, by placing our personality into every object we own and by building our mini fortresses of possessions and precious junk. We are attached to stuff, and we are barely able to handle the real world as a result. We believe ourselves to be protected, and often we are in for a nasty shock. As the world becomes more spiritual we westerners with our shopping and our possessions are key contenders for an extra dose of chaos.

First up, a confession. I occasionally go shopping. I have to. I still agree with clothing and food. So whilst I still agree with clothing and food, I have to go shopping. I understand that business is business and that people love making items for us to buy. That is reasonable and it has a place. What I loathe is the tactics that make us shopping addicts. I see this as some kind of anti soul neuroses, whereby you need not think about what is going on in the world, because there are dresses to be bought. As long as our minds are focused on handbags and gladrags then we are well-behaved citizens and we mind our own business about what is going on in the world.

Shopping and consumerism in general is a virus of our generations. It is a very effective way of keeping us busy whilst the powers that be get on with running the show. Have you ever read 1984 by George Orwell? We are living in it. Yes we have a tad more apparent freedom, but many of our best people are lost to consumerism. Our most talented lay strewn across the floors of giant department stores, picking out new sofas, trying on a dozen different pink skirts for the wedding season, and splashing our cash on new hair, nails, and even fake toe nails!

The culture of shopping is wrong, and it is wrong because it makes us slaves. We are slaves to ourselves. We are slaves to our hair, our wardrobe, our new carpets, our pubic hair, and our self-image. We are slaves to big corporations who provide us with ever changing items at reasonable prices and manipulate us so that this constant buying seems normal. We choose big brands over little ones and so the locals, the independents, the little guys get pushed out of the marketplace. If this carries on we will live in a one-store world and we will all become shopping drones.

We are not content until everything in our handbag, home and adorning our bodies is an expression of what we believe ourselves to be. We are slaves to our self-image and the media and the overlords that advertise it all know this. However whilst they are raking in our cash, they are quite content to let us run around and around that perfect little moneymaking hamster wheel. They will happily continue to provide us with new fodder and new trends so that once we are satisfied with our 'look', we must continue to tweak and change it so that it remains 'bang on trend'. Heaven forbid we look outside of the shopping bag and see what is really going on.

I think I need to vomit.

How is a soul supposed to thrive when to survive in a critical fast paced society it must concentrate on the exterior to the deprecation of all other elements of the self and of life? How can we live genuinely when our focus is minute and selfish? Who needs spiritual depth when our car is so superbly fast and shiny?

Today I was talking to a very beautiful, very interesting young woman who confessed to me she had a spending issue. She gets dark depressions and to lighten her mood she buys things, clothes, cosmetics, and dinner with friends. The lovely young thing purchases all of those bits and bobs and bling that a girl is supposed to buy to make herself smile. She then randomly confessed that she hates her legs. On occasion she hates them so much that she cannot leave the house. The lady in questions is a model, her legs are on show constantly, she is also a dancer, and these 'horrific' legs are in fact toned and lovely. There is not one thing wrong with that woman's pins.

It struck me that whilst she appeared to be intelligent, vivacious and attractive, she could not see beyond the mythical stench of perfection that we are all fed on a daily basis. In this society you are not 'accepted' until your shit no longer stinks. But Honey, it does, it always did and it always will. You do have hair growing out of your legs and possibly a hair or two on your chin, and if you do not keep up with a stringent cleanliness routine the rest of you would stink too. We are human, we are physical, and not a single one of us is perfect.

But it is the marketing myth that we can be an image of Goddessliness. A million pieces of junk are available to pull and prod your life into a semblance of the most wonderful you that you can be. But all of these plastic fantastic creations are nothing but plasters, covering the gaping wound that is our fractured self-esteem. And why is it fractured, why do we desire to look like the impossibly beautiful model in the airbrushed perfume ad?

We want to look like her because the marketing men and women have placed her out of our grasp. She is so far removed from what a real human woman looks like that no matter how much money, natural beauty or vivacious charm we happen to possess, we will never ever be as stunning, alluring and outstanding as she. She is an alien. She is a figment of the mass media's imagination. If we allow ourselves to buy into this then our bank balances will suffer, our mental states will fixate on what is not perfect about us and society will grow more vacuous whilst in an ever failing search for interstellar, unachievable, never going to happen, perfection.

Whilst we are on our mission for model like youthful glows, then what about our inner glow? Well inevitably we will forget about that. We may feed our bodies an organic, free range and low fat diet, and our skin may retain a glimmer of its baby like sheen, but what lies beneath that skin, nothing but cells and an absence of spirit.

The advertising men give us a prescription for the ideal life and we take that to heart. We wear it daily like a mantra, continually espousing their views as our own. I will be thin, I will be glossy, I will have a three bed property by the age of 27, I will have two children, I will be the perfect Mommy, I will make the best cakes, I will be the best shag he ever had, and damn it I will drink diet soft drink brand 'A' and smile.

We treat this prescription like gold dust, like a secret we have been let in on. When we achieve a little bit of it we tell our friends and perhaps advise them how they too can have successes like our own. We mean well, but really we want them to be impressed, maybe to envy us, ever so slightly. We thrive on the competition.

We barely know how to exist as human beings without all the accessories and accompaniments. And if we cannot exist in our own skin, how will we ever get deeper and find something a little more tangible. How on hell's good earth are we ever going to find our inner Goddess? Or will we continue applying blusher in the misguided belief that it brings out our personality?

This applies to nearly every aspect of your life. We are all so driven, in our own ways that the soul has suffered a death. No more do we tune into institutionalized religion of a Sunday morning to give us some kind of faith injection. Our faith is dormant and replaced by faith in our purchases. Strip it all away and we would be flailing, naked, lost little egos wondering where our battlements and defenses have gone. It is time to change this. It is time to say no to the powerful overlords of industry, the magicians of marketing, and look a little closer to home for our self worth.

It is time to challenge our egos to a dual to the death. If we wish to live a spiritually richer and happier existence then a fight with societal pressures must be fought. We must come face to face with everything we have been taught and everything we have become over the voyage of our lives and have a showdown. For those who want to take their spirituality and enlightenment further then this is a necessary step. This is purging and detox spiritual style and it will rip a whole in your mass marketed world letting your spirit soar and your soul develop into that of a fully formed wonderful human. Yeah you may still hang onto your blusher, but your personality will never ever be dependent upon it again.

Hedonism

There is currently a real Dumb Culture in the western world of getting hugely drunk, vomiting, snogging someone whose name you do not remember and blacking out at around 1am. Are we all so bored that all we can do at weekends is get drunkenly wrecked? Well yes, it seems that is the case for a vast majority of our people. Alcohol and drugs have become a rite of passage in western society, one that goes on beyond a few mad youthful years.

This is a rite that consumes lives and prevents a person from becoming their true self. To me it is another example of dumb culture dosing us up and medicating us so that in our stupor we forget to remember who we really are. In spending our free time 'out of our minds', we are less likely to question, to look outside of our box or to even look inside of our box. Living life for the weekend, and for the next round of cocktails, whilst tremendous fun, can also, if taken to excess be mind numbing and soul destroying. Alcohol and drugs remove us from any kind of real life, they destroy our spiritual capacities and they blur our concern, our empathy and our soulfulness. Hedonism is a frightening culture of distraction and the western world is currently very, very distracted indeed.

Alcohol and drugs help us to drop our barriers in so many ways. But they do so in a way that is delusional, a way that is not real. How many times have you had an incredible conversation with someone under the influence, only to clam up and have nothing to say to that person when you meet him or her again sober? I know I have done this on several occasions.

Alcohol becomes a useful crutch; it lubricates a stiff room into a party full of hilarious, happy people. When we are under its influence we become a projection of our ideal self. In that sense we become dependent on that drink to let us be who we think we should be. With the bottle, the pill or the rolled up note in our hand, we become gods in our lifetime, we feel we as if have become untouchable.

Drugs in particular take you out of the mind you are accustomed to being in and show you what some people take to be a glimpse of the spiritual side of being. Many drugs do expand the mind, they make you think in intriguing ways, they can make everybody seem lovable, and perhaps they can even make you see things that are not normally visible to a sober eye. Drugs too have infamously assisted many a great artist and musician to go outside of themselves, to surpass their limitations and create something incredible.

I do personally understand the appeal of alcohol and drugs, because I have used both for the very reasons I just set out, for the fun, for the confidence, for the distraction. Indeed I believe that in some very tenuous respects alcohol and drugs get you closer to your soul and closer to the divine. It is for that reason that they can seem so incredible. It is for that reason that they are alluring and for that reason that they are addictive. They can give you a very small sliver of heaven... but if you are unlucky, have a bad trip or become horribly dependent, then a slice of hell may open up for you too.

In our modern world we live terribly unspiritual, consumer driven, and media calculated lives. But you can have a glass of wine and suddenly you feel all warm and fuzzy and as though you belong. Intoxicants can make a stranger your instant best friend, and turn mediocre conversations into the height of entertainment. It is a damn strong pull and I have fallen foul of it a thousand times. Don't get me wrong, I have had some brilliant times on the wrong side of several cocktails, but for now my intoxicated good times are used up and I am enjoying my life in my own predominantly sober and spiritual experience.

Admittedly I have struggled with alcohol in the past. All the things I have ever done that I regret, I have done under the influence of drink. Whilst I believe there are no mistakes, I also believe there are certain behaviors that I wish not to repeat. All of which have always occurred with a drink in my hand. Everything happens for a reason, and often that reason is that we can live and learn and make the changes that we need to make so as to enable our souls to thrive. Excessive intoxication did not make my soul thrive, it made it weep. Enough said, game over, bye bye booze! I had enough of medicating myself on 'good times' and so I decided to wise up to what I needed as an individual.

I embarked on three solid months of being an alcohol free zone. I admit I meant to give up alcohol entirely and permanently, but in the end I felt it was perhaps more challenging, and realistic, to simply moderate myself. My three-month drinking hiatus included being utterly sober at parties, gigs, barbeques, family dinners and waving goodbye to a glass or two with my take away pizza on a Friday. Living free from intoxicants for that short while was, however, a fabulous thing for me. I personally needed to stop drinking alcohol, albeit temporarily. I did this to get to know the true me, even more deeply, and it has been a most awesome trip! I needed to know that I could just stop as and when I chose to. I needed to test myself in all manner of social situations without the protection of booze. I had to make myself vulnerable and know that the right kind of spirit had my back!

I took this step because I had truly started to dislike myself whilst under the influence. I did not like what I became and I guess there is a degree of control freak in me that detests how all my spiritual learning can come undone after one glass of wine. Spirituality is at the core of my life and anything that dislodges that has to go. I decided that for the sake of everything I cared about it was time to stop drinking so much. So at first I stopped drinking entirely, then I reintroduced slowly, in a controlled manner and with much, much moderation in my heart.

Since putting my drinking on strict lockdown I feel better connected to something divine and my life is smoother by far. I have stopped doing things I regret and I finally know myself in a way that I could not wholly embrace before. In many respects I feel alcohol gave me up! It decided I was no longer a fun party friend and so instead made me grumpy and sick. I hate to be grumpy and sick when life is so fulfilling and there is so much to learn, and so I could not allow it any more. I could no longer be that hyper drunk girl who spent Sunday in bed feeling ill.

In a moment of clarity I realized that drinking to excess simply did not suit the new spiritualized me any more. In the months since giving up and cutting back, my spiritual under-standing and intuition has intensified. My spare time is now spent being me, rather than being the version of me that resides in the bottom of a bottle. As a result I feel more myself than ever before. I am more in touch with my divinity than I ever thought possible. The spiritual effects are profound.

I am experiencing frequent prophetic moments. I can see my life clearly and with open eyes. I can see what I need to do, what I need to change and I can focus on that without the ill effects of a weekend hangover blurring my sanity. I am calm and I am happy. I do recommend you try it!

I believe there is a higher path to be trodden. I believe that for those serious about a spiritual awakening, putting a limit on drink and drugs is essential at some point in their development. If you find yourself feeling this way, then that is brilliant news. It means you have reached a place where you are happy and content in your own skin. It means you are confident to be who you are without the shield of having a drink for courage. It means you are ready to look around at the miracles of this planet through fresh and sober eyes. It means you are ready to drop the blinkers that dumb culture constructs and to get to know and construct your own true reality.

Cutting out the excess was the right thing for me, but why are drugs and alcohol unhelpful to a spiritual path in general? I am not sure that I want to say that they are unhelpful per se. I can only say that in my experience they were bad for me and I have witnessed them being very bad to others too, particularly alcohol. The very common use and abuse of alcohol to fill spare time is, in my opinion nothing more than a delusion to keep a person from exploring their own inner space.

Just as shopping and beauty obsession are unhelpful to an expanding spiritual mind, I believe intoxicants, particularly when taken carelessly or to remove oneself from reality are dumb, bad and are the antithesis of the spirituality we are trying to achieve. Being intoxicated is akin to medicating against life. But life is not a virus, or a plague and in my humble opinion it is best lived with clarity and knowing.

Yet still I will admit that the shamanic use of psychotropic drugs intrigues me, and as I mentioned I have slowly reintroduced some drinking into my agenda but with a view to strict moderation followed by several cups of tea! Plus, realistically, and honestly, I am sure I will still suffer the occasional hangover but only ever when I have something very marvelous to celebrate! But the very sensible side of me, and the very spiritual side of me, both agree that alcohol and drugs are a quick fix if you are looking for spiritual living. They are intriguing trips into the other side, but they are not something I would recommend as being spiritual necessities, or even spiritually compatible. Not by a long shot.

I cannot expect you to follow my lead on this one. Alcohol is a social institution. However, I want to raise the topic and be honest with you about it, because maybe one day, a few years down the line, you too might feel the need to drink less or even to abstain from alcohol altogether. It may be a hard step to stop drinking alcohol, and some people will judge you. Since cutting down I have been asked if I'm pregnant a few times when I refused even one glass of wine. Friends will encourage you to have 'just one'. But I will say this again with conviction. Alcohol can be a major distraction to a spiritual life. It can be destructive and it can blur your heartfelt attempts at life spiritualization. You choose your path, and if it is a spiritual one then intoxicants may not suit it. My path has chosen my divinity over my toxicity, 98% of the time!

Beyond my own path I find the path people take in terms of their alcohol consumption to be worrying. We live in a faithless society. Alcohol (and drugs) provide release and relief from the drudgery of life. This however is a temporary relief. It may provide us with crazy times, but it lends nothing truly meaningful to our existence. A few glasses of wine may give us confidence, but a few more glasses can make us dumb. One moment a room full of people are like best friends reunited, the next they are throwing punches. Intoxicants bring your essence up, it makes you feel more yourself, but drink too much and you come crashing down the other side and your true self is lost in a blubber of tears, overreaction, nausea and next day regret. Intoxicants are fast track delusion, played out over a space of twenty-four hours or a weekend. To inject a dose of joy you reach for a bottle or a pill, you believe yourself to be happy, but it can all go badly wrong and what you thought was 'good for your soul' can leave you feeling very much the opposite.

I am glad I have experienced both, I am glad I have been totally out of my mind, and believe that in doing this I have (eventually) learned not to do it again! I have lived the dumb culture of intoxication and beyond truly limited memory and some crazy fun looking photos I didn't gain that much. Intoxication was a true education. Though I have now graduated from that school and am currently enjoying the trip that is spiritual and personal growth.

I am enjoying being aware and alert and refusing to medicate myself against the world. Hell, this is my life, and my planet and I wish to experience it for real and not to become a delusional drunken/drugged zombie who hides from it. I will not allow intoxicants (and the society who sells them to me) to take my voice, my individuality or my spirit from me a moment longer.

I now live from the heart and there is nothing that a bottle or a pill can fix in me that I cannot sort out with a dose of meditation, prayer or a good chat with a spiritually like-minded person. Spirituality can get you to a place where you love and like yourself, irrespective of how much social lubricant you have ingested. When that happens, no mind-altering intoxicant can beat it. My spiritual life gives me all the confidence and security I will ever need. I am warm and fuzzy in that knowledge. I no longer need a bottle of chardonnay to back that up or prove myself to anyone.

I wholeheartedly recommend it. Be who you are naturally. Live genuine. Find yourself in your soul, not in the bottom of a spritzer!

Final Word on Dumb Culture...

Dumb Culture is disabling us all. It is distracting us from everything that really matters, putting a price tag on our happiness and washing away our worries, not with wisdom, but with wine. Buying into dumb culture means you are denying living as your true self and embracing a life that is especially, spiritually, yours.

When you choose to look beyond the ordinary, the usual and the box you have slotted into, you will find a powerful new world waiting for you.

I know that you have read this far, I am sure that you are spiritually wise. But sometimes it is the ordinary acts of life like obsessing over a new kettle, or having one too many glasses of red wine that can send your spiritual radar all skewed and unhelpful.

Refusing dumb culture goes further than opting out of the world of marketing and consumerism. It is also about refusing to immerse yourself in the nonsense that it breeds. Do not get me wrong, trash television and gossip magazines make marvelous screensavers for the brain, but if you are doing nothing else, then your brain may as well just get switched off.

Once you are ready to step outside of that dumb culture you should be prepared for an awakening of epic proportions. I do not just mean a spiritual awakening, though that too may follow. What I'm referring to is the fact that as well as a spiritual world around you, there is also something else, there is also the real world. This is the world we choose not to speculate upon and instead raise our rose tinted sunglasses and sip on a chilled Pinot Grigio to make it all go away.

For those of you ready to step outside the realms of dumb culture I ask you to explore the world you live in. I ask you to make yourself aware of its pains and suffering and its injustices. You may start by simply looking at the Amnesty International website, this will certainly bring you down to earth with a bump. Alternatively you could look up Greenpeace or research local charities and find out who needs helping in your vicinity. Educate yourself on suffering and then think what you might do now to help relieve it.

Refuse dumb culture and look to real culture in all its horrific glory. If you really want to defy the hold of dumb culture, you could get out and about and actually sign up to things, volunteer, make others aware, and go to meetings. I truly recommend that you burst your commerce-laden bubble and realize that life of all kinds exists outside the false world of shiny-floored malls and high streets that smell provocatively like donuts. Until you educate yourself of the real, true, heartbreaking world, then you will forever be bubble gum flavored in your resolve and candy floss ignorant.

Wake up! You are not Barbie, you are a powerful spiritual soul, get real and get empowered. It is only in your empowerment that the world might start to look a little fluffier and how we would all prefer it to be. A spiritual world can start with your decision to do one thing today to empower and assist your fellow humans.

You are a spiritual being, you are spirit. Dumb culture may be fun, it may be addictive, but I can show you something better. Take off your blinkers and become the real you in your real world. Get ready for a fight, some fun and some world changing attitude adjustments. Come join me!

Lesson 7 – The Body

"Our bodies are not simply fairground attractions taking us from A to B. They are spiritual tools. It is through them that we are forced to exist and within them that we find our own divinity". Alice's Diary April 2010

The body is the one thing that we have available in this lifetime to experience our spirituality through. It is a gift to us. But more often than not we only think about it in terms of its basic needs (food, water, sleep, breathe), or of vanity (muscle tone, weight loss, shiny skin).

Lesson 7 aims to look at the body, not as a funhouse of pleasure but as a tool of spiritual life. Rather than going into the issues of bodily matters and the pressures of society to be slim, size zero or to be tanned, toned and taut, I want to talk to you about the body from a spiritual perspective. You had enough of the lectures on societal pressure in the section on beauty, so let's instead focus on the body as a valuable spiritual instrument.

I have met spiritual people who believe that through defeating the body, pummeling, starving it, testing it and generally treating it like dirt, they can attain a greater degree of spirituality. Indeed a great many spirits have done this, and come out wiser, Buddha and Jesus being the first two that spring to mind. However I do not adhere to that way of thought. I believe us women have our fair share of bodily trouble throughout a lifetime and so if we wish to gain the most from our rhythms and nature, then treating ourselves with due respect is a top priority. If Jesus had periods all his life, then he too may not have felt the need to fast for forty days and forty nights! Imagine what that would do to your menstrual cycle, ladies!

In my humble opinion spiritual deprivation is simply deprivation by any other description. Life is hard enough without adding hunger, pain and physical isolation to the list of traumas we must undergo. I have failed miserably at any attempt of rigid self-control, for example the detoxification. Detox diets are generally hard work and in my opinion the wooziness that comes from that is not to be mistaken for spiritual awakening. I do not care how light you feel after a week-long juice diet, that lightness is what comes before fainting and is a symptom of starvation, not of spiritual ascension.

Whilst I am not one for starving myself I do see the benefit in spiritualizing my diet. Eating the right thing is of far more spiritual value to me than eating nothing! This is not to say that I do not wish to be adventurous with my body. I do believe that there are benefits in treating the body well, and even on occasion pushing it to the limits. I deeply admire those of us who can complete marathons, undergo intensive training or who live super sporty lives. One of my favorite tests of physical endurance is found in the spiritual undertaking of a Sweatlodge.

A Sweatlodge is a Native American and South American tradition, which involves sitting in a circle with others in a tent-like construction for several hours, with hot stones in the center of the lodge. The effect is like a super intense sauna – that goes on for a prolonged period of time. It puts you through a range of emotions and mental states, and in essence it cleanses your soul. I love it, and for me that is quite extreme enough!

I guess I am a moderation kind of girl and I recommend that you follow that same route in the beginnings of your spiritual path. If one day you feel an urge to throw yourself with abandon into some intensive spiritual physical activity, then go for it! But for now I want to tell you about the day-to-day benefits of embracing the body as a spiritual piece of equipment.

I have found that my spiritual path has led to several quite astonishing things...

My Body...

As a result of recent spiritual awakenings and changes in my life I eat far more healthily. It has taken me a long while to get there. But in the last few months I have found myself in a place where I crave fruit, vegetables and I cannot drink enough water. It is weird. This is not who I was. Who I was loved pizza, I do not even miss pizza, and when I do eat pizza I feel lousy for days. My life has changed and my body is having it is wondrous way with me. Its wondrous way is now addicted to bananas!

I really and truly did not see this coming. This all started when I decided to undertake a week of purely healthy eating. This involved eating lots and lots of colorful stuff, mainly fruits and vegetables.

It is old news that eating fruit and vegetables is good for us, but on what level was it good for my spiritual enlightenment? This was the real question that drove me. So for a whole week I deflected all offers of caffeine, chocolate, meat, dairy and processed rubbish and went all natural.

For years I have struggled with what to eat, how to treat my body and whether or not to eat meat. I have been an on / off vegetarian for many years now. The meat eater within me was disgusted with herself and the vegetarian wanted a huge shove to the forefront of my mind. These two characters were battling it out and whilst the veggie knew that one day she would win, I needed to ensure that her succession to the throne would be permanent. You cannot claim to love and respect the souls of animals, and eat them still. Something had to give.

Prior to undertaking this task I spoke with my higher self and my spiritual guides, I asked them for help and guidance. I wanted a lifestyle change, but didn't know how to do it. I wanted this lifestyle change not to be about weight loss, or even fitness, but about inducing a deeper spirituality within my very bones. I asked that I was spiritually assisted in finding a truly spiritual way to consume food and to be true to myself.

I needed to curb my love of junk and feast instead on the delights of Mother Earth. Above all I wanted to get some control, I needed to see food as sustenance rather than as a boredom subsidizer. I wanted a healthy relationship with what I ate and I wanted it to reflect the spiritual me. It seemed a lot to ask... but if you do not ask you do not get!

My heart was really in this task and because of this, almost immediately a switch was flicked deep inside me. I believe that this happened at the right time, and perhaps my guides had already prompted me in that direction, knowing better than me, that it was what I needed. Perhaps the very fact that I wanted to be healthier was because I was already being guided in that direction. Maybe my prayer for assistance was an affirmation of the fact that I had listened to my higher self, and not the other way around. I will never know the true source of this need to spiritualize my diet, but I know it felt right!

Soon after my request for help with my eating, I was inundated with many signs in the form of information on veganism, on healthy eating and on the benefits of both for a spiritual path. It felt as if I was being presented with an intellectual choice. I could continue eating unhealthily, indulging in alcohol and consuming meat against my better judgment. Or I could embrace my spirituality within my physical body and grow further as a spiritual person. This almost felt like a matter of honor, and a rite of passage. "You are either committed to this spiritual lark, or you are not," said the little voice in my head. There was no judgment either way, but there was the matter of my life, and my own truth to contend with.

I asked for help, and one way or another I received it. I stuck to eating fruit and vegetables for a whole seven days and now I simply cannot eat meat. I still eat my fair share of (high–cocoa and dark) chocolate, but beyond that I'm pretty impressive on the healthy food front. I eat when I'm triggered by hunger, no longer by boredom. The best thing about this is that this has all just happened. I opened my mind and my heart to it, and the universe, my higher self and my angels have allowed it to be.

I seem to have chosen the path of spiritual loveliness, without even really thinking about it. I feel that I was lovingly manipulated by the spirits in the correct direction and my prayer was effectively answered. Though it was my mind in the end that needed making up. So I did, and it is great, and on a spiritual level it really, truly works! I made a decision and now every fiber in my body has backed it up.

A healthy diet keeps me balanced and as a result my spirituality has space to thrive in my more ordered, calm and vegetable filled world! I feel so free. I am no longer blocked by my bodily senses. My delusions around food, and the false thought that food makes you happy, have been dropped from my mind as an option. I am less clogged up by harmful chemicals from meat and processed food. No doubt my hormones are calmer as a result of this. Most recently I have quit drinking tap water, and go for bottled spring water instead. Now when I drink tap water all I can taste is chlorine, so I avoid it like the plague. Of course I always remember to recycle all those plastic bottles too!

I am so much happier as a result of all these changes. Indeed I have noticed my intuition has sharpened in a way that is quite dramatic. I love that fact. Intuition is key to contacting your higher self and understanding your own needs, wants and true feelings about things. Since reducing booze and barring meat and rubbish from my body, my psychic and spiritual affinities have gone into supernova. It is massively interesting and I love this new development so much!

Beyond what I put into my body there is also the issue of exercise. Exercise was always a love / hate of mine. Now I love it. I do it because I want to. It helps me focus my mind and it makes me feel fresh, healthy and at home in my skin. When I feel at home in my body I find my spiritual life comes easier. I sleep better, and therefore my spiritual dreams are more easily reached. Exercise helps to make me calmer, and when I am calm I am prone to moments of profound thought. I find that following a workout or a walk in nature I can better access spiritual messages in my brain, amongst all the other clutter.

I no longer stress about how and when I will go to the gym. I make the effort because I know it is worthwhile. I know that giving my body a work out helps my soul to feel better at home in a physical self that is suitably used. I am treating my body like gold dust and it is all coming so easily. I believe I am being spiritually supported in this, and I hope it continues into the future. I recommend it highly.

These areas of my life were always aspects I previously struggled with, and to be fair, they were aspects I enjoyed. I am a big food lover and if you have read *The High Heeled Guide to Enlightenment*, you will know I was partial to a glass of wine, pizza and the occasional cocktail or two (or three or four...) But all of a sudden I have changed. I have not forced this change on myself. It has just happened. My higher self has intervened to help raise my divinity and my consciousness. Now I cannot consciously fill my body with anything that poisons it. I practice self-love through the foods I choose to eat and by showing my bones the love they deserve! I wanted this to happen, despite my love of pizza, and I think that the fact I wanted it, is the key to my success.

All of a sudden all those issues around gym, exercise, food and drink have dropped out of my life. The best thing about it is, I do not give a damn about my weight or my appearance, not really. I am living true to myself, and because of that I accept myself, my fluctuations, my changes bodily and mentally. I am aware of myself as a spiritual being, and I treat my body with love accordingly. I will not be harsh in judgment or in punishment to myself. I will simply be me, and my body and spirit will let me know what it needs moment-by-moment.

This is hugely empowering. Not only spiritually, but also as a woman in our critical, image orientated society. I suddenly feel free. I do not have those demons on my shoulder monitoring my various intakes, or judging me for how much or how little I have chosen to move my lazy bones! I am energetic, happy and healthy, and it has all just happened as a result of my spiritual progression. It has been a long time coming, but now it is here, I embrace it wholeheartedly.

As for my physical appearance, I would be lying if I said it had not altered. My skin is glowing and I have lost some weight, though I do not know how much weight as I refuse to weigh myself nowadays. I know that I fit nicely into my clothes and I feel free and comfortable in my body. That is all that I care about. I do not advocate this as a diet, or as a ploy to lose a few pounds. To do it genuinely you must want to spiritualize your body, not spiritualize your weight loss. There is a huge difference. In all honesty I do not believe I have lost a great deal of weight, as I still eat a lot, and manage to tuck some chips and chocolate away on occasion. I am not yet a raw food cabbage snorting diva! The biggest benefit for me was to be true to my soul and to find a way to exist where my body is happy and I am not worried about the state of her.

I can now get on with spiritual living unhindered by worries of the physical or feeling trapped in an unhappy, unhealthy frame. Spiritualizing your body sets you free on so many levels. If you feel ready then do it today!

Say a prayer to your guides and request their help, stock up on wholesome foods and commit to being the best you. Do what feels correct for your very special and unique life. Embrace your inner spirit, feed her well, take her to the park for a run and all the rest will follow!

Eat Well

If you want to take my lead then here are some tips how. Start off by aiming to complete a spiritual eating week. Keep a diary and be sure to speak to your loving higher self and guides, ask for their support and then get stuck in. Find a quiet space and some time out to meditate afterwards, then speak to your higher self and guides with something along the lines of the following...

"Guides, higher self and my angels. I choose to live a healthy and spiritual life. I ask for your support in helping me to make healthy, soul supporting choices when it comes to what I eat, what I drink and what I do with my body. I wish to do this so that I may grow closer to my divine self, and so that I might support my physical self in the best way possible. Thank you."

For the seven day period focus on cleansing your body and filling right up on good, wholesome, healthy foods. Do eat lots of fruit, vegetables and whole grains. Be sure to cook things yourself if you can manage it, then you know for sure what you are feeding your spirit. If you can afford to then go organic, this helps you to avoid the consumption of nasty chemicals.

Do not eat processed foods. Processed foods are the foods that have been messed around with and have had most of the goodness taken out as a result. Do not eat saturated fats because they are manmade nastiness that is just plain bad for you. Do not drink alcohol and do not eat meat. Finally do not eat dairy products. I recommend that you purchase a good vegan recipe book. You will find that the recipes offer optimal healthiness, using all vegetable ingredients, and are hugely healthy without you having to alter them in any way.

It is most important that you remember that this is not a weight loss diet. It is a soul cleansing situation and so do go crazy on nuts, berries, and fruit. Find good replacements for your usual staples of meat and dairy. Trust me there are some incredible vegan ice creams out there, you will not know the difference. Yummy. Eat, eat and eat. If you starve yourself this week then you will end the week by running back to the arms of your favorite naughty comfort foods. This week is about feeding off the abundance of nature. The aim is to show you the spiritual, emotional and physical benefits of eating foods that are full of natural love and spiritual power.

After the week try to incorporate many of the good foods into your life. If you choose to drop out and eat the occasional pizza, takeaway or giant tub of ice cream, then forgive yourself. I still enjoy junk food from time to time; just yesterday I indulged a chocolate craving quite publicly (all over Facebook)! In the main I stick to the good stuff. I do so because my spiritual path is aided and abetted by it, and if you can get a glimpse of this in your week of eating well, then you may find that following my lead comes quite naturally.

The Body and Health

I wrote previously about the myth of beauty and perfection as one of the greater ills of the female condition. But many of you reading this will be sick for different reasons. Some may be depressed, some may be tucked up in bed with flu, and others might be suffering from something altogether more serious.

My spiritual explorations have led me to believe that our health physical, mental and emotional is intimately entwined with our spirituality and self-knowing. I will explain why now...

Modern medicine and healthcare, as wonderful as they are, concentrate almost solely on the treatment of already existing sickness and symptoms. This methodology and practice is played out within the use of pills, surgery, chemicals and other external treatments that aim to remove or purge sickness from within us. More often than not, the treatments offered up by science tend to leave us sick in other ways. Medicine is an attack on the body and whilst it may save your life, it leaves you with further recovery to be made.

I believe that the body is an energetic organ that is vitally connected to our soul and spirit. I believe that whatever pain or suffering we go through in our lives, may eventually be visited upon our bodies, perhaps in the form of a compulsive sore throat, or maybe, if you are unlucky, in the form of something more destructive.

I believe that a holistic approach to illness, taking into account our previous life events, and the way we think about our lives could bring about a healthier planet. Many of us barely think about our health or illness until we become sick and so we do not realize that we could possibly prevent that illness by living a balanced, spiritual and happier life.

I guess what I am saying here is that I believe that we may very well be responsible for our own ailments. Just as smokers know they are dicing with cancer, maybe we are all dicing with disease through the way we live, think and feel. This is a big leap for many people to take, but I wanted to introduce you to this possibility. Read on and then take this idea away and do with it what you will.

We live in a society that only treats an illness once it has already arrived and is in full swing. It is not contemplated that we have any power to prevent illness, or that illness might stem from our own thoughts and actions. As such illness is rife. Not only does negativity cause us problems but also our lack of connection to our divine selves leaves us floating around the planet acting, reacting, storing up negativity and eventually succumbing to it in the guise of disease, accidents and potentially even early death.

I believe that all of our negativity, bitterness, fear, cynicism and anger have the potential to make us very ill. We are energy and our thoughts reach out and affect the world around us. It follows perfectly that our thoughts and feelings will significantly affect our flesh. If these thoughts are sad and bad ones then our bodies will echo this over time. When our body is sad it becomes sick. Therefore sadness of the soul becomes sickness of the body. Medicine does not fully recognize this link yet, but you can.

I believe that the sadness that we suffer, and the way we react to it is key to preventing our future illnesses. How long have you been carrying that heartbreak in your gut for? Surely to feel such immense pain for so long could lead to further unhappiness, and then in turn to physical, mental and emotional difficulties.

The sickness of your emotions overflows into a sickness of your body, so then surely it can flow into others and into the state of the planet itself. Why is this, you might ask? Well let me refresh your memory.

I believe we are all energy; we are linked and connected at a deep spiritual, divine level. Our spiritual conscious resides here on earth, but also elsewhere, in the place and dimension of our spiritual origin. Every single thing that happens to us on this planet happens to all of us. Emotion is not just a feeling, it is a real thing, it has energy, and that energy has an affect. Sometimes that affect will be illness.

Ancient health systems devised by Shamanic traditions tend to believe that a person visits their bad health on themselves by storing up a plethora of unresolved personal issues. These issues sit within that person and eventually cause an outpouring of bad health. Have you noticed how stress brings on a cold you thought you had avoided? Well think of that but on a bigger scale.

Imagine a year's worth of anxiety traveling around your body, with no or little chance of escape, and then imagine a part of the body ceasing to function efficiently as a result. This happens often. Lack of food brings malnutrition, oral thrush and weakness, possibly even depression and mental health concerns. Lack of soul food leads to stress, migraines, stomach ulcers and so on. It is not a huge leap to make, and to me it gives us more reason to start to look after our souls.

I am not saying that people deserve their illness. But, for example, a lifetime of stress is liable to lead to a stress related illness. We easily accept that the food we eat, or the exercise we do, can cause or prevent illness, so to me it naturally follows that the way we think, and the feelings we harbor may also contribute. This is not a judgment on people, but it just makes sense... don't you think?

I believe sincerely in modalities of energetic healing such as reiki, spiritual healing or shamanic healing. I believe that within them we have a key to help solve the sicknesses that stem from our emotional and psychic wounds. However before you turn to a healer to diagnose and cure you, you must realize that your health is always, in the first instance, in your hands. You can treat yourself before an illness even occurs. Through the power of your mind and a faith in your energetic vibration being a real thing, you can enact prevention so that a cure will not even be necessary.

As individual beings we are in charge of our own little bodies, our thoughts and our minds. Modern medicine has allowed us to believe that it is the doctors and nurses who are in charge of our healthcare. We do not realize that we too are responsible for our well-being. This responsibility lies deeply rooted in every thought you think, every thing you do and every emotion you allow yourself to feel. For every single resentment or anger you harbor, I believe that you could be storing yourself up some future problems. It is only you that can stop those thoughts becoming a physical reality.

To help prevent illness you can see as many healers as you like, you can consult doctors, shamans, white witches and crystal healers. They may be able to help, they may steer you in the right direction and they may even minimize your pain and suffering. But if you choose to stay in the same mindset, the same old ruts, the same negative emotions and hard feelings, then no healer, doctor, nurse or medic will be able to save you from yourself.

It is akin to the smoker who uses patches, sees hypnotists and reads all the right anti-smoking books; as long as they choose to keep smoking, there is a possibility it will make them ill. This is not a judgment, it is a fact. The same applies to everything we put into our bodies, be that crystal meth, red meat, fried foods, or anxious feelings. Everything has a knock on effect. This does not make you, or your sick relatives, bad people, it just means that we need to start taking care of our spirit in the same way that we take care of our physical bodies.

Next time you get ill it is important to remember that sickness, as well as being painful, exhausting and frustrating, can serve a very real purpose. Conventional medicine sees illness as a real evil that must be purged and destroyed. However sickness is also an indicator to us that something is not right in our life or in our way of living. Sickness is a sign, it is a divine and blessed sign.

Do not view illness as some kind of karmic retribution, rather take it as an opportunity to examine your life and to see what is missing or what can be improved. Action taken now, whilst recovering from a bout of flu, may very well prevent you coming down with something more serious in the future.

I believe that this counts for accidents as much as it does for illness. Anything that affects our bodies can be taken as a sign from on high that all is not well. As I have written about previously I recently had two car accidents. The first one occurred at a time of great chaos in my life, and at the exact moment it happened I had been thinking quite negatively. This was the shunt I needed to change that fact and that thought pattern. It could not have been better timed. The second accident was more elusive in its reasons. I choose to believe that my higher self and the spiritual universe conspired to give me a double whammy so as to really set me on the spiritual straight and narrow!

The double whammy worked. It was since my accidents that the majority of this book has been written. I have changed my lifestyle immensely and my outlook on life has completely altered. Whilst on the surface my life is not much different to how it was six months ago, my inner attitudes have transformed.

So when illness or accident befalls you, take it as a gift. Use the time and space given to you to examine your life. What negative behaviors are you indulging in? Do you need to forgive and forget something that is causing you heartache? Perhaps your lifestyle or your work is slowly rotting away at your heart, and this sickness is a call for you to do something else entirely with your life? Maybe the illness is simply telling you to slow down, take a bath, and have a little time for you.

I believe in the power of spiritual universal energy. I believe all our bodies are made up of energy and that this energy is free, copious and magical! It is currently an unseen component of our existence and of our health. If our energy gets out of kilter, which throughout life it often does, then it can eventually have the knock on effect of making us ill. Embracing spirituality and all the good loving advice it gives to you is one way to create a shift in your self and in your development that is more preventative than any number of vitamin supplements!

I believe that becoming more spiritual can act as a preventative method of healthcare. To be spiritual you must purify your thoughts, your emotions your body and your mind. In doing this all your negativity is released and your energy is cleansed and positively charged. Continuing to live with spirituality in your heart is, for me, a recipe for a healthier life. It will not prevent death; we all still have to depart this place one day! Of course, as a spiritual person you will soon see that death is not the end anyway!

I hope that with new areas of research into health, energy and quantum physics there will be a shift in how we as a world population see illness. But we should not wait for the scientists to tell us before we start living better. There is a great deal of money resting on our requirement for medicines, so this may be a secret the pharamceutical companies want to keep.

We really can't rely on anyone else, especially not corporations to help us on this one. We must start to view ourselves as mistresses of our own physical destiny. We must want to heal and help ourselves. We must accept that we have that power; we have the control over what we think, feel and do. In essence, we create our own lives and this includes the creation of illness, anxiety, stress disorders, mental health issues and even accidents.

We are all divine; we all have the power of divinity and spirit residing in our souls. If we learned to utilize it and empower it then we will no longer have to weigh the balance of our lives completely in the hands of doctors. Instead we can take some responsibility for our health and embrace a healthier, happier, spiritual future.

This does not mean the total avoidance of medication, not yet anyway. But you can address the sadness and fear inside and make efforts to think yourself healthy! Life is always going to be a little hard but our spiritual mission only asks that we aim to be better people. It does not take much but I believe that happy thoughts could save your life!

Your body is so much more than a pretty ornament upon which to hang lovely summer frocks. It is your singular way into a more spiritual life. Your body and your spirituality are intimately connected at this stage of your existence. We cannot afford to see them as separate from one another. You are in your body for a spiritual reason known to your divine self. So no matter what you think of the façade that houses you, you must love it, treat it with respect, and above all give it what it needs.

Our bodies are sometimes wiser than our minds. If it wants

feeding, feed it, if it wants a day lying about, then spend a day lying about. It needs it, and doing this may stave off some breakdown of energy and vitality. Beyond the daily functionality of your body the bigger spiritual lessons will help your health too, I am sure. Continue along on your spiritual journey. Find a way to forgive and forget past hurts, whilst transgressing any fears and worries you currently embrace. Place love in your heart and kindness in your mouth. Make efforts to conquer any anger, sadness or distress that sits in your gut and make sincere efforts to heal yourself whole.

Know that this little house of yours is a one-off opportunity. How you act, think and feel will have profound effects on the structure.

Living spiritually is about knowing that all aspects of your life are spiritual. That very much includes every inch of your flesh, hair, mind, organs and your teeniest tiny toenail. Be good to your body. Love your body. Offer your body the opportunity to take your soul on a crazy human journey and give it the thanks and respect it deserves. Your body is part of the journey, love it up and live it up! Your body is your temple, Amen.

Lesson 8 – Love

"Enlightenment is found in love, it is deeply set within every love you have ever felt for a child, a pet, a spectacular view, a book, a lover, a parent, a friend. These things will not die. In spirituality there is no abandonment, no forever suffering and no true helplessness. If love never ends then our essence continues, our ashes are long blown away but our heart, our soul and our love will be infinite." *The High Heeled Guide to Enlightenment* by Alice Grist

I named Lesson 8 Love, but in many respects it is about people. Because whilst love can be felt for anything or any living being, it is most likely and most obviously found in your feelings for the people you know; your family, partners, friends and fleeting acquaintances who bring sunshine in their smile. Whilst many people get on your nerves and test you beyond endurance, it is love that we must embrace if we wish to do well on this planet in this spiritual incarnation.

Love, and how you express it, should not be limited to a close handful of intimate buddies. Love is universal and it is entirely possible to love a stranger in a platonic but heartfelt way. I believe that we are all connected, everyone you meet is your divine relative, so love can be expressed in every action, reaction and meeting you will ever have. It is through the understanding and acknowledgement of this that we can start to make a better, more spiritual world.

Beyond people it is also fabulous to spread your love to trees, animals, scenic landscapes and great food. Love does not require flesh and bones to be enacted. You may love a memory, a photograph, a small pebble you picked up on a well-remembered beach. Love is the key to spirituality. It is the key to happiness. I shall not continue on these lines, because I will start to gush. I have said it before and I will no doubt continue to say it, but if you can get the love thing right, then you, my dear, are well on your way to high heeled spiritual living.

This lesson on love covers heartbreaks through to family matters. Love is a big deal in the world of spiritual living and so I hope to give you the lowdown on living through the ups and downs of a loving life.

Perfect Love...

Love is perfect. Human beings are not. You are human so immediately we have problems! No matter how spiritual you may become this lifetime, you are utterly prone to humanity's weaknesses. I find that in this day and age the mass media markets love as an ideal, just as it does everything else. So like all other areas of life there is a very real danger that we will compare all our relationships with the ones we see on television and on advertisements, and we are often left wanting.

The media is keen to promote the disastrous nature of relationships too. If a couple is not hugely happy, then we see them fighting, falling out of bars and having affairs. All the perfectly loved up and contented celebrities appear to be in hiding, and so we have very few examples of happy relationships to help light our way. As far as society is concerned relationships fall into one of two categories, the sublime (desert island, sand, beautiful people) and the crazy (drunk, staggering, fights, drug addiction).

We are very confused. We have no real say in what constitutes a perfect relationship for us, because we are focused on what makes a perfect relationship for that writhing couple on the billboard we pass twice a day. As a result, many of us chop and change partners, desperately seeking the right person for us, whilst not really recognizing that we are not yet the right person ourselves.

The search for love and partnership is such an unconscious, primal, example-led task these days. The view of love we are sold is very much a sexual one. Just as our diet drinks are sexy, and our cars are sexy, everything has to be bloody sexy. It is ridiculous. If things are not sexy we reject them. The same goes for love.

Gosh I'm going to sound old fashioned, but whatever happened to friendship, partnership and companionship? Yes sex is important too. Of course it is. But it is not the only thing we should be looking at. The sexual revolution was a great thing, but in so many respects it has knocked our love-o-meters right off track. We are all thinking with our genitalia, and so our chances of finding a 'true' love are diminished considerably.

Plus I believe that love should be a little bit difficult. It should not always be roses, romance and complete unquestioning adoration. That way a stalking obsession lies! Think back to the section on chaos and life being hard. That applies here too. I do not think anything in life is supposed to be perfect, seamless and fault free. That is simply not the way of this human world. Relationships and love are supposed to get our blood pumping in more ways than just the one!

As little sparks of soul we are here to learn from each other, and give to each other. Not always through our perfections, but also through our faults. Relationships of all sorts are building blocks upon which to cement our understanding of the world. Our spiritual know-how of the world is empowered by our inter-actions with others. So please, let's put down the stereotypes of how a perfect relationship looks, and instead focus on how to feel a perfect love.

A perfect love is one without conditions. It is a love that is powerful, strong and true. No. Matter. What. That might seem beyond you. But it is not. You can love someone in spite of cruelties they inflict on you, even if that means leaving them. You can love someone and forgive them and walk away at the same time, if need be. You might also love someone and take on board his or her faults, and between you slowly, over time, sort them out. Love is a complicated thing but only if we allow it to be. Nothing on the planet is more simple than just allowing love to reside within you and turning that same love out onto the world at large.

It can be done. I have done it. My life used to be more compli-cated. I had the media's view of love firmly implanted in my mind. I expressed my love for my other half through sex. In my opinion we were not having enough sex or we were not having the right kind of sex. That sounds hilarious now. But I was a product of a highly sexualized environment that we call the United Kingdom. As a female I felt valued for my extremities and my sexual abilities, or lack of them. It seemed strangely vital that I buy into this.

Beyond this, my love was reserved for a handful of other people, friends and family. Oh and animals, I have always loved all animals. But in my desire to be a perfect and well-loved girlfriend, I forgot about the animals, other people and the planet, for the longest while. My life revolved around the pursuit and maintenance of love, as portrayed by the popular media.

It was my mission to be easy on the eye and to ensure that the guy in my life stayed put. I was following a well-worn path trodden by women determined to get their man and keep him keen. My view of love was shallow, arbitrary and entirely unspir-itual. My attitude towards love was one based on fear of losing it by not doing as society suggested. I was lost in my own mind and had forgotten who I was beneath the veneer I had applied.

When I started my spiritual journey, I began to realize that this perspective of love was not normal, right or natural. I soon figured out that I could be loved beyond my lady lumps, and that I could love people right back irrespective of anything at all.

That was my first big dose of sexual freedom and free love! It was my own personal and mini sexual revolution right there. When you are no longer focused on keeping up with the Samantha Joneses, then you have a lot more true love to go around.

Heartbreak

"There she lies with her bloodshot eyes, no feeling surrounds her, she whispers goodbye. Still holding on to what's already gone, it's too late, it's over the damage is done" James Mabbett (husband) Lyrics from Eden Lake

Relationships, flings and anything to do with sex, love, crushes and rejection can be enormously informative on a spiritual path. They can also give us fantastic experience, offering up unconditional love, to the very person who we probably believe least deserves it!

To achieve anything meaningful from heartbreak you have to want to stop drooling over the possibilities of a failed love affair and identify instead the possibilities you have received as a result of it ending. You must stop living in the past, drowning in sorrow and decide to discover what that heartbreak has taught you about life, love and yourself. What has come into your life to fill that gap and where could this take you into the future?

Women are brought up to be concerned for other people and to be nurturing, and we can fall into that pattern at the most inappropriate of times. We care what that lover who dumped us really thinks. We care how our ex might be feeling, we care and wonder and spend evenings with our friends discussing the pros and cons of a telephone call from a guy we met in a bar. But do we sufficiently examine our own hearts and heads? I think that maybe we do not. We become a victim to our own crazy mental states and inevitably we fall foul of false, fantasized love, as opposed to searching out a love that is key to our own personal success.

When one door closes another door always opens. This may not always be obvious, and it does not mean that heartbreak will lead to a more perfect partner. Nor does it mean that suddenly opportunities will flood your way. In this life we make our own opportunities, and before the floodgates open, you may have some soul searching to do.

Relationships are a minefield of potential open and closed doors. Yet within this minefield there is massive room for learning. Heartache goes hand in hand with the evolution of you as a spiritually enlightened being. So whilst rejection or love-life confusion may sting like hell, in the long term it can be spiritually very good for you.

I feel your pain ladies, honestly I do. How can rejection by the love of your life ever, ever be meaningful? How can that passing fling have been so 'passing' instead of the permanent love nest you hoped it would transform into? Why did that gorgeous fellow sweet talk you into bed with magnificent promises only to go cold and factual the following week? Whilst I cannot answer on behalf of these errant ex-partners I can say that the answer does not lie with them.

Before I met my husband I have been known to rant and rave into the ear of a willing girlfriend, for months, or years, about some poor chap who had the gall to reject me, not return a phone call or blatantly dump me. In true female form I would of course blame myself, then him, then myself again. He would be a bastard and I was the innocent love fool. It is hilarious really. What I did not recognize was that the guy does not hold the answers. Not the answers I really needed anyway.

Spiritual lessons come through people, all people, even the really nasty ones. Especially the really nasty ones. Just because a love affair was 'not meant to be' does not mean it was not meant to be whilst it lasted. We attract people to us to help us to grow and learn. So if a relationship did not work out how you expected it to, then instead of wondering what the other person is thinking, try to see what it means for you. Think of yourself and what you can garner from the remnants of that love. Consider what you have learned about your self, about your behavior, about ways of being that you might want to avoid in the future. Indeed consider the good and the bad and be sure to take this on-board for your future love growth.

I believe that some of our more dramatic relationship disasters were planned before coming into this life. They are fantastic ways to promote your growth as a soul. You may have asked a fellow friendly soul to be born as a guy or gal you were going to hook up with, and you may have planned that he or she dumps you out of the blue, or kisses your best friend. The reasons for this may be multiple.

Perhaps you rejected that soul in a previous life and to amend your karma you are asked for the situation to be reversed. Maybe you just needed to feel real heartbreak. Or perhaps you just wanted to fall deeply in love briefly, and then move on to something more significant, perhaps your purpose in this life is to do something else entirely. Maybe that soul will inspire you to great things. Maybe your ex is simply a stepping-stone on your way to a more suited lover in your future. Heartbreak at any age does not mean a lifetime of singledom. It might mean a wiser choice at an older age and a better understanding of who and what you can tolerate in a relationship scenario.

I believe that the more we feel during a lifetime, and the better we react to our own emotions the more progressed as souls we become. So whilst the broken heart may make little sense right now, it is likely that you are stronger as a human as a result and in turn will be a tougher, more knowledgeable soul. The possibilities are huge, and exciting, and every horrid little incident has something to be gleaned from it.

Relationships of all kinds mess you up – on one level. On

another level they are an opening into a better understanding of yourself and other people. It depends how you take your medicine. I believe that the world would be a better place if we stopped dwelling on what we did or did not do wrong and instead took our learning like good girls and got on with the show.

Taking a positive attitude toward relationship disasters enables us to move on and learn the spiritual lessons that all relationships have for us. All human beings are messengers, whatever clothing and guise they come to us in, be it saint or sinner. All people, without exception, carry important life lessons for us. Yes it is difficult to comprehend those life lessons when all you can think about is how much you miss snuggling into a certain person's neck, or how cute the little wrinkles around their eyes were when they smiled. Facts are facts, if a door has closed, do not stand staring at it for the rest of your life; think about why it closed, what have you learned about yourself and about relationships? What about this situation can make you a better human being and a more successful and well-rounded soul?

If you can, then I recommend that you project unconditional love to the person who hurt you and then walk away, physically, emotionally and mentally. A break up should not mean the end of loving their soul, even if you never want to see them again, so do them and yourself a favor and send a little loving sugar over the energy vibrations to them. It will do no harm. After that you may want to project a little sugar onto yourself. Work at getting happy again and finding a way to assimilate this loss into your lifelong spiritual learning.

Human life was never supposed to be easy, we are here to learn. We continue to reincarnate here until we have learned sufficient amounts about pain, emotion, kindness, and love. One huge and fast way to learn about pain and emotion is through our relationship heartaches. Love is a rip-roaring, soul wrenching occurrence that when handled correctly can fast track and deepen your spiritual wisdom.

Soulmates

Soulmate, what a lovely term, what an amazing concept! Don't we ladies all just want the perfect soulmate to sweep us off our feet, understand our every need and to be that ultra perfect fit?

The thing with soulmates, spiritually speaking, is that they do not really exist. Well they do, but not in the fairy tale, prince charming manner to which we have become accustomed. Now before you bury your head in the sand or turn the page swiftly, let me assure you I am not setting out to vandalize your personal vision of 'happy ever after', although I may be about to inject some spiritual reality that you may not like. Brace yourself.

There is no such thing as the perfect relationship. We are conditioned from birth to expect a knight in shining armor to whisk us away to safety, pay for all our expensive tastes and give us the best, most mind blowing sex of our lives. In reality relationships are hard work, they can be wonderful hard work and they can be painful hard work. No human being is perfect and once the initial misty love sensations have worn off you may begin to see some small faults in your beloved. Life is very much about learning to live with these or moving on and finding someone preferable.

It concerns me that there is a genuine danger of people self-sabotaging their own relationship whilst in a vain search for something that does not truly exist. We go into relationships with blinkers on and can be disappointed too easily. If we wish to attract a perfect love, then we must first accept that perfect love is a myth and be prepared to see perfection in something slightly different.

Now on my personal spiritual journey I have been intrigued by the concept of soulmates. I know we all want one and secretly a lot of us believe we have one, often we just feel we have not met them yet. So to save your carbon footprint searching the globe for Mr or Mrs Right. I can let you know you probably have met your soulmate already. The problem with your soulmate is, well the problem is that your soulmate is human.

In all my spiritual researching and living I have come to conclude that soulmates are basically extremely good friends of ours who are with us for the human ride. Occasionally they may trip you up, challenge you or just downright get on your nerves. That does not mean they are not your soulmate. The fact is that as much as they may annoy you, you are likely doing the same thing right back to them.

It worries me that people are seeking a perfection that does not exist. Yes we all like to aspire high, but certain heights cannot be reached. We should see perfection in potential, and in the feelings that lie within us. We should not expect constant perfection in terms of actions or deeds, because we will get let down. That ladies, is the problem with soulmates, it is not black and white, they are not perfect, and we are not perfect. Moments can be perfect, gestures can be perfect, intentions can be perfect, but humans, I am sad to say are currently far from it.

The thing about soulmates is that I believe they are here to challenge us. Life is not, in my opinion, supposed to be easy. We are supposed to face hardships and difficulties and even deep loneliness that could be the result of our soulmate leaving us, hurting us or abandoning us. The quickest way to learn is by being burnt and if life is a playground for learning and improving then we are going to leave this planet pretty scarred up. The best and worst way to get scarred is through pain inflicted by those we care about most.

Now this of course is dangerous ground and I am by no means advocating abusive or violent relationships. But then again if you find yourself in that situation, maybe it is your job to learn how to get out and how to be your own best soulmate. And yes honey, you may very well have to leave your soulmate in the process.

But I do believe that some way down the line you have other soulmates laying in wait that will, with any luck and a dose of self-love and understanding, treat you as you deserve.

So how can we cope with this new and devastating news that perhaps a perfect soul is not laying in wait to whisk us off our feet and show us Mexico, the Bahamas and the depths of our soul. Well, for a start we can love ourselves a little more. We can look to our own selves for affirmations, respect, interest and love. We can get to know ourselves, so that when a good match comes along we are ready for them. If we already have a good match then we can learn to love them despite their flaws.

I have found a soulmate and I have married him. Whilst some days he is the light of my life, on occasion he is also the bane of it. Whilst I adore him to the ends of the earth, on occasion I swear I could bury him in it. And whilst there is no other man on the planet who can measure up, on occasion Keanu Reeves looks tempting.

I do believe my James is a soul mate. I have been regressed hypnotically and that was revealed. But to be fair I should have known it anyway. Even in my darkest hour when my mind filled with doubts, I could not walk away from that man. Before I lived my spiritual path, and everything was everyone else's fault, I did consider just packing a bag and leaving. I was hugely confused, mixed up and a little bit depressed. The most logical (or illogical) thing I could think of to do was start life all over again, on my own.

James knew I was on the edge and he told me that if I wanted to go, I should just go, because he could not take it any more. I sat and I looked at his beautiful face and I realized that no matter what was not perfect about this love, it was indeed perfect because it was my home. No matter what else was going on in my life, there was still something utterly transfixing, perfect and familiar about him.

When I committed to my spiritual studying, I began to realize that the shape I had in my head of a perfect 'lover' was so unrealistic and so unfair to James that I let it go. I decided to love him for precisely what he is, not resent him for what he could never be. I also realized that I too have a mass of imperfections and annoying habits, and yet he still loves me. A lot of soul searching was involved, but thank sweet heaven that it was, and guess what, we are both happier for it.

A soulmate meeting is an opportunity for growth by both parties. If the growth goes well you may find that small slice of paradise. That is the thing with soulmates, when you love them despite their human flaws, and they love you right back despite your glaring flaws, that is truly heaven on earth. If you put in the hard work, then and only then can you find your personal glimmer of bliss. So, you see, I am not such a cynic after all!

Family and Friends

What I have said about love relationships applies equally to relationships of the family kind. The spiritual basis of all our relationships is of learning. Yes, your interfering mother-in-law might drive you barmy and to the brink of divorce, and your sister's choices in men may leave much to be desired.

In some instances, family may incur your venom and wrath for the cruelties and abhorrence they have committed against you, and for that I am sorry. However as hard as this pill is to swallow, each of their minor and major irritants has occurred to teach you something about love, about life and about yourself.

We are teachers to others and all the people we meet are our teachers in return. This includes your family and your children. No matter what differences lie between you, be they age, status, authority or opinion we are here to learn from one another. Just because you changed your son's nappies a thousand times and protected him from harm, does not mean he cannot teach you a thing or two.

I totally believe that when we are not incarnated on earth we hang around with a gang of soul friends elsewhere. I believe that we probably know thousands, if not millions of souls, and we all agree to influence each others lives when we return to the earth in physical bodies. We are acting a role so to speak, but that role is improvisational rather than scripted!

We might be born into circumstances that affect our personality and the way we are, and so throughout our lives we are attempting to resolve these and return to a closer version of our spiritual selves. Other people surrounding us can make this difficult or easy for us, depending on their level of spiritual progression.

We may have a past life history of love or conflict with these people, and whilst our minds may not remember that directly, our souls are aware. We may have all kinds of contracts and agreements with the people in our life. No matter what problems your loved ones pose, I believe it is your role in this lifetime to try and resolve them.

Love will always play a big part in your relationships with family and friends. I suggest that you make a promise in your mind to love them all, no matter what. Love them for their faults, their failures and for their glorious aspects too. Love them for what they have made you suffer, and love them for the times they make you smile. Know that these people are your team and your support and that no matter what they do or say to you, it is all for a reason and can facilitate much learning and growth. Make the conscious choice to love them, and make the conscious choice to learn.

Parenting

I am not a parent, and so I cannot comment from experience, perhaps that will be the next book! But there are a few general spiritual thoughts that occur to me that I think will aid the rearing of your youngsters, and your sanity as you do so.

Your child is always going to be your little baby, and I can imagine on occasion that there is an overwhelming sense of love, duty, burden and protection all rolled into one. As such your attitude towards your brood is going to be one that is somewhat extreme, quite naturally so, of course. However in terms of the idea of protecting your child, or cosseting them and comforting them, it is important to remember that that child is a soul unto itself. Whilst it is only right that you keep your children from harm, on occasion influences may occur in their lives that you do not appreciate. It may be an interfering grandparent who 'knows better'; it could be a neighbor who insists on giving them sweeties and sending them home buzzing and hyperactive. It might be an overzealous teacher, or maybe as a teen they become friendly with the wrong crowd.

In such circumstances I imagine most parents would wish to place their child under house arrest. But think back into your own life, think of the good and bad influences other people have had upon you, and what these people have taught you. Would your parents have approved? Would you change anything if you could? Or would you keep it the same because hard, fun and bizarre experiences have made you who you are?

Perhaps the overzealous grandparent will form a lasting bond that child will remember for life, not because they were overbearing with you, but because they encouraged the child, or the way that person told them fairytales or sang to them when they were alone. The bad influence teens may cause a blip in that child's development in your eyes, but perhaps to the child much formative learning will be had, and harsh lessons will be enacted that will see them stronger into adulthood. The sweet giving neighbor will become a little piece of history, someone kind and generous that will pepper his or her memories.

I know as a parent it is your absolute duty and responsibility to protect your youngster. But at the same time you must value their individuality as a soul. You must remember that your children are here to learn, just as much as you are. The fact that you are older does not always make you wiser. Yes, you have a slight advantage in that you are more experienced of this earth, but they have the advantage of fresh, clean eyes. They can see things that you dare not. Just as you can see things that your own parents dare not.

The most loving thing you can do for the soul of your child is to love them dearly and then let them make their own mistakes. Remember though…there are no mistakes, only learning, and so take your role as teacher seriously. Be there to pick them up and dust them off. Show them unconditional love no matter what partner they bring home, or what direction they choose in life.

You can introduce spiritual concepts and ways of thinking to them from a young age, just as you introduce manners and routines. Give them rules as necessary but allow them freedom to grow.

Be vitally aware of your life as a living example. Show them through your own example of how to live a wise and spiritual life. What you do, is the greatest teaching you can offer them. Show them forgiveness by forgiving, show them justice by being fair, show them calmness and clarity by refusing anger. Show your child the example you wish you had had, even if on some days you struggle. Be the best that you can be and they will soon follow.

Whilst raising children is undoubtedly an emotional roller coaster, try to always keep your cool. Non-reaction is a key factor here and I believe that when dealing with children you must remove the excess emotion so that you can speak to them through your highest self, rather than through your hurt feelings. Know that whatever faults you portray, your children will learn and emulate. If you are delusional about the grass being greener, then they will be too. If you are ungrateful, then they will be too. If you BMW, this will be normal to them and they will BMW too. Remember what you want to be and be it now. Be your spiritual self personified.

Speak to your child in terms of spiritual concepts, explain why delusion is unhelpful, or reaction is bad for the heart and soul. Teach them to identify and trust their own instinct and intuition. Tell them frankly that they are a soulful spirit, that life is hard, but that you believe we are here to learn and we never truly die. Treat them like an adult and respect that they too have incarnated before, that they are an old soul, possibly an older soul than you are. Respect their opinions and give them room to breathe, do not force them to think how you do, but give them the option.

I believe that the generations of children now and into the future are deeply spiritual beings. Such children are known as Indigo or Crystal children. They are being born here to help push humanity to a better more spiritual place. Remember this and give them their dues.

Encourage their psychic moments and their invisible friends, even if it does give you the creeps! Perhaps if their spirituality is encouraged we will have a generation of people able to link to their divinity quite easily. Just imagine that, a whole generation of young adults in touch with their intuition and their higher truth. The world would be destined for great things!

Counter negative desires with intelligence and loving distraction. Society would have your child bothering you for every new toy, food and sweetie. Counter this soon so as to avoid that child growing up to be dependent on money and possessions. Indigo and crystal children have a whole lot of energy; find ways to channel that and to keep them interested in life. Make efforts to inspire them.

Turn off the TV, interact, and be in nature. Instill in your child a love of their home planet and teach them respect for animals, plants and the environment. Children naturally find miracles in nature. Follow them and ask them questions as much as they ask you! Let them know that their answers are valid and intriguing.

Childhood memories will be warm and fuzzy when they are older. Do not allow their memories to be warm and fuzzy ones of a box in the corner. Take them out, show them the world, and teach them spirituality through living your life well. Show them unconditional love and expect nothing back. Encourage them at every opportunity and above all allow them to show you a thing or two!

I also think it is worthy for any parent to take some time out to think about their own parents. In my first book I talk a lot about what I have taken from my parents. My father was a vicar who became a Wiccan high priest, and my mother was a gay feminist anti-bomb protesting type!

For a long while, in my late teens and early twenties, I was resisting being any part of either of those things. I was keen to buy into the prescription of young womanhood that society wanted to sell me. It wasn't until I returned to my spiritual, egalitarian, feminist roots that I found who I was again.

I think it is so fascinating the effect that parents can have on their children. In my case for the good, but for others, it is for the bad too. Either way, there are always plenty of lessons there for a person to learn. Any parent should consider deeply the profound affect their parent or lack of that parent has had on them. We must forgive parents their trespasses and embrace those lessons they gave us. Whatever your parents did is what has structured your world and is what has made you uniquely you.

Inevitably our children will one day think like that about us too. They will wonder and consider all the things we did to them, some that they appreciate, and some that they do not. They will see our faults as clear as day, and they will feel them deep inside. I believe that by understanding the spiritual nature of the debt we owe to our own parents through their achievements and their mistakes, we can start to be better parents ourselves.

Admit your mistakes and know that whatever mistakes you

make, intentionally or otherwise, will all go towards forming the character, guts, determination and perhaps the very saving of our offspring. Because, as ever, there are no mistakes.

We can teach our children the value of imperfection and how all the things in life that gives us joy or sadness can be tools for growth. Give them a happily positive upbringing but remove the rose tinted glasses of advertising and perfect people. If you instill that into a child's mind then they will be ready to accept a spiritual path as and when it calls to them. Above all love them, accept them and choose that love and acceptance to be entirely without condition.

Love is easy...

Love is actually easy, it is people that are the problem, are they not? Well, maybe and then maybe not. We control our own world through our thoughts and it is our choice to love or not to love people. We are guilty of clogging our own love spout up and preventing our heart from giving as much as we potentially could. Often we place strict rules on who we love, and then implement stringent expectations to those loved people so that we may continue to love them. None of this is necessary. You could just choose to love them.

One of our biggest spiritual challenges is to find the love within ourselves and to turn it around onto others, unconditionally. This includes not just the people you know and like, but also everyone you meet, be they the plumber, a bus driver or your boss. Anybody who features on your radar, even if you only see them on the television or in a magazine, is worthy of your love.

I do not believe that this is optional. Whilst it is down to you to interpret your spirituality, I guarantee you that finding love for people will fast track you towards a greater understanding of your own compassionate spiritual humanity.

I do appreciate that the love of humanity can be a tough one.

But because it is difficult it is worth doing. So how can we become a beacon of love and how can we get past our own natural defenses that seem to limit and block the flow of emotions in our hearts. It goes back to the very simple point I have repeatedly stated. You are spiritual because you are spirit. We are all spirit, we are all energy, and all of the energy is linked intimately. It is only in these human guises that we see ourselves as separate and individual. Deep down we are all the same, we are tiny parts of a bigger more amazing whole. We do really love each other. We just have to try so hard to remember that fact.

In recognizing the divine spark within others, we light our own way too. By seeing that divine light, acknowledging it and acting with love towards even those people who are very difficult to love, we help light their way too. It is a never-ending circle of joy and lovingness, but to embrace it we first have to give our love out with the faith and certainty that all living souls deserve it.

I can tell you all day long that you will get it back. But it is not always guaranteed. Some people are impossibly rotted in their stance of coldness and non-intimacy. Let them get on with it, is what I say. Hopefully in their own time they will come round to a little bit of loving. It is not our path to forcibly love a scarecrow in the hopes that it might return the feeling. But we can love and respect that scarecrow from afar, so that when it is ready, it too can find its heart. Love is not about give and take. It is about giving. Receiving back is lovely, but it is not a prerequisite. We do not receive love back to be able to give it. Nor should this be a reason why we do or do not choose to give our love.

Love is easy... all that stands in your way are your own social mores and your fear of looking silly. Well do not worry, loving people is not all about throwing yourself at their feet or espousing their virtues through poetry. All you need do is feel the love. Feel it baby and then act in whatever way that love guides you. Love may make you polite to a stressed receptionist, it may make you smile from the eyes, it may make you hug a helpful stranger, and it may simply make you a peaceful presence instead of a whirlwind of argh!

We are so used to expressing love in categories and degrees of depth that we may need a little bit of practice at unconditional love. So here goes...

Think of the pure love you have for a pet, a child, a memory or a sibling. Now apply this to everything and everyone. You do not have to wander the streets in some loved up haze attempting to cuddle people, but you can hold a space of love in your core. You can then bring that love into your smile, your attitude, your kindnesses and your actions.

Try if for a day or two. Check out the reactions you get, and if you find it acceptable, which I believe you will, then keep the love there for eternity. Hold it close and spread it wide. Perhaps sit and say this little prayer to your helpers for support.

"Guides, angels and higher self. I am willing and able to tap into my unconditional love. Please support me in this task. I intend to find love inside myself and to feel it and offer it to all living beings. Thank you"

After this you may wish to take on a more challenging love exercise. Think of someone you do not get on with at all... Whoever this person is you have just thought of them for a reason and I believe that it is now time for you to find a way of making some kind of peace with them. If you can manage this, both your lives will improve and you can learn to relate at a soul level as opposed to a level of human disagreements.

I want you to make it your mission to be loving and kind towards them. If you have an argumentative relationship, then simply drop your side of the argument. This might be an intensely hard thing to do. Perhaps you will be concerned that they will think that they have won and you have lost. Maybe they will think that. But as a spiritual soul you must rise above this and offer them love in whatever way is appropriate. Give them a hug, tell them you don't want to argue any more, change the subject, buy them a drink, and tell them you love them. Whatever it is that is keeping you two from relating in a friendly and loving way, just drop it. If they try to pick it back up, do not join in.

If you do not succeed at the first hurdle then ask your guides and angels for support. Maybe have a word with that person's guides and angels, ask them to support you in improving your relationship. Find a moment to sit still and send messages of love and caring psychically to the person. Forgive them whatever they have done to you, and really, really mean it. Then all you can do is be patient. Be patient with yourself and with your emotions and be patient with that person. It might take them a little while to fall into your all-new way of relating. But keep love and peace in your heart and make this world a better place, one awkward relationship at a time!

Love Yourself

My final word on love and I will keep this brief. Love yourself. It is so easy to focus your love on a partner, a place, or an indulged pet. But turning that love inside can be very difficult. Once you learn to love yourself for everything that you are, then your spirituality is going to feel much more at home. When you know what you want out of life, you are less likely to follow the wrong path and trip up over a dozen inappropriate love interests. Love, when applied to you, unconditionally, can transform your life and provide a great little starting platform for your spiritual journey.

Spend some time alone. Enjoy your own company. Laugh at your own jokes. Spend time treating yourself to whatever you want to be treated to. When I started on my spiritual path I started by pleasing myself. It was probably selfish but it was what I needed and it worked. I had been so busy pleasing everybody else for such a long time that I had quite forgotten who I was and what I wanted out of life. It is vastly important to put yourself first fairly often. You are a special little soul machine and it is important that you keep yourself happy so that you can complete whatever your soul's mission is.

An unhappy soul in a tired neglected body is unlikely to be of any use to anyone. Remember that and then take yourself to the spa, meditate, eat out, watch your favorite film, have a long bath. It is all very good offering your unconditional love to all and sundry, but you must remember that you are worthy of it too. Lap up your own attention, get to know yourself, fall in love with your special self. Go on, put this book down, wrap yourself up in your own arms and have a great big one-person hug. Kiss your hands and smile. You are very, very much worth it.

Lesson 9 – The Natural World

Lesson 9 is close to my heart. I am a crazy, passionate nature and animal lover. I hope that animal and nature loves me right back. I sincerely believe that they do. I see spirit in every creature that I meet and the thought that animals have no soul is entirely laughable to me. I believe that animals are here as our equals and that should we choose to see this, they might be able to teach us a great deal. Indeed they might become our friends as well as our pets and our entertainment.

Lesson 9 is about understanding that we humans are not the only beings with a little spark of divinity in us. It is about realizing that the planet we live on is as precious, valid and spiritual as we are.

Nature is a force to be reckoned with. She is a great educator and if need be she will bring us to our knees to teach us all about her power, although the lesson may not be pleasant. We are all made of the same vibrating energy as the wind, the rain and the earthquakes. We are all linked and so it is not unreasonable to state that nature and the planet is a living being, it has a consciousness. Maybe this consciousness is not one that we can currently understand, but it has one nonetheless.

I believe that there are greater forces than human intelligence afoot, until we realize this, we will bluster on by in our raping and pillaging of our earth. One day she may well get exasperated and kiss us goodbye in a great ice age, disease, pestilence or a flood. This may sound impossible, or extreme, but quite frankly I believe she could do this, and you know what else... I wouldn't blame her!

It is unfortunate that humans pit themselves against animals and nature and declare that we are the more intelligent, the more worthy. I believe we see our intellectualism as superior to the animals' alleged more basic instincts. We see our creativity as far above the creativity of nature that we believe to be accidental or unconscious. However if instinct and accident means living in perfect intelligent harmony with the environment, then I choose those qualities every time. I also question what is so dumb and thoughtless about peace, harmony and natural flow? Nature at least has some forethought, she sticks to her rhythms and she feels little need to pollute herself or commit heinous sins against her inhabitants. We act like a virus and, if the cap fits, perhaps we ought to wear it.

The problem here is that mankind is more adept at using its mind to create, to solve problems, oh and to apparently tip gallons of oil in the sea, bomb cities, destroy rainforests and render many wonderful creatures extinct. This is alongside a hundred and one other planetary abuses we commit, never mind the violence and abuses we commit upon one another.

This to me is not intelligence. It is greed. It is egocentric madness. It is cruel, thoughtless, selfish and despicable. It is all done out of delusion, out of the insane belief that by oppression, subjugation, control, power and hoarding money, someone, somewhere will be happy. I do not believe humanity has ever given peace and love a proper chance.

We may well be intelligent, but the intelligence has had no heart, compassion or nurturing behind it. Perhaps this is because the female energies of the western world were until recently rendered silent. Women were to be seen and not heard, and so half of humanity had no or little say on our progress as a culture. Whilst we might make efforts to raise caring and sensitive children, all sensitivity can be wiped out by the need to compete with one another and to make more dollars in the boardroom.

Our own animal nature as a species has been looked down upon. Women in particular have been looked down upon because of our closeness to nature. We have been viewed as more primal due to our menstrual cycle and the fact that we must lie like animals and push a child from our vaginas. Never mind the fact it was a man's primal juices that helped place the baby in our bellies! A woman's more evident nature has helped add to her subjugation. Women have been deigned nurturers and carers, but those roles have been undervalued in the extreme. We have been allowed to sit in our place of nature, allowed to commune with the animals, allowed to have our softer side. This was all quite fine, as long as we did not bring it into the arena of the 'real' world. However it is my hope that the real world is subsiding, because the real world is of man's making and is not, in my opinion real at all. It is a construct.

It is my deepest hope that the true natural world is taking back her place in the scheme of human dealings. I believe that women, and female friendly individuals will be spearheading that return to our more natural, instinctive, harmonious ways.

Animals as Guides

Ancient shamanic faiths have always turned to nature and animals as messengers and guides from the Great Spirit. The Great Spirit to me really represents the conglomeration of all intelligent, conscious existence. It is the knowledge of billions of souls, and out beyond that it is the wise, awareness of the universe. Not the universe as we know it, but the universe as a living, energetic mass of life beyond our current comprehension.

Just as you can connect to your own higher self through intuition and signs, I believe that the natural world is equally as connected to you. She has messages for you on a global scale and indeed on a more personal level.

Think back in your life to a time when your pet, or an animal has helped you in some way. I hope you have an example, for if you do not then I hope this lesson can empower you to start receiving some animal help. My life has been littered with tales of animal guidance. Whilst a Lassie dog has not saved my life, I have had many warm moments with my animals, and as I will go on to detail, I have had my eyes opened to life and death by my sweet little pet chicken.

I believe that my first love was a kitten. She was not mine. She was a kitten of a neighbor, back when my father was still a vicar and I lived in the vicarage. I remember this kitten well. She would wander up the road to find me, and I would take her to my room. My mother remembers apologetically returning the little cat to her owners on several occasions after she found me and the kitten hiding underneath my bed sheets doing whatever it is a five year old and her cat friend do.

I have been in love with cats ever since. They have brought me love, comfort and happiness throughout my life. Any cat or dog lover will understand that their animal has soul, that they love you unconditionally and not just at feeding time. They seek love from you and they return it also.

At the present time my dear cat Molly has been acting as though she has seen a spook. For the whole week whilst editing this book she has been darting around jumpy and afraid. She refused to leave the bedroom and when she once ventured down stairs she was terrified and soon ran back to her safe haven. It broke my heart. But as a sensitive animal soul, I wondered if she was feeling all the extra energy flooding in to help me write this book and it was freaking her out? She is not an energy lover. Whereas my cat Jimi, when recently injured, went outside of all his usual habits and routines to come to me for some reiki healing. Animals know things. We must give them credit, because they are often wiser than us in our staid, proforma type world of routine, commitment and technology.

Indeed just a few moments ago I lit a candle to the Goddess to help me on this the last day of editing this book. Molly then decided to venture down from her upstairs haven. I told her not to be afraid of the energy and that the Goddess was with us taking care of things. As I said that she immediately looked at the candle I had lit, then back to me. That girl knows stuff. She just does.

As a happy ending to this tale, know this. In the very moment when I had finished all the hard work of editing Molly suddenly became Miss Normality. She trotted downstairs, unafraid and her usual perky self. Whatever was assisting me certainly gave her a fright. But as soon as the book was edited, my little cat was back to her usual self. Animals are so very aware.

When I split up with my first serious boyfriend, my wonderful ginger tomcat Mr Thor came and slept with me all night. He never did this again, well not until a time many years later. The second time he did it was one of the last times I saw him before he died. After this he was too old and weary to get up the stairs, but that last time was sweet. So in all his lifetime, he saved that precious intimate moment for a time when I needed him as comfort, and a time when he knew it was a goodbye snuggle.

Just before Mr Thor died we had a little family reunion for my mother's 60th birthday. My brothers Michael and Joseph attended and we were all together for the first time in years. Mr Thor was clearly on his last legs, and yet he looked so happy and contented to be with his human boys and his whole family. It was heartbreaking but I knew in my soul that he had stuck around simply for this one last get together. He stopped eating entirely and died shortly after.

Mr Thor's brother, Icarus is still alive, but very much an old man cat. Michael lives in Japan, though we hoped he would come home to England to see us later in the year. My mother, who is no big animal lover was sitting with Mr Icarus one day and she quite casually informed Mr Icarus that Michael was coming home and could he please stick around on earth long enough to see him home safely. She declares what happened next to be an, 'Alice moment'. Apparently Mr Icarus looked at her straight in the eye and very solemnly nodded his head. Try as she might she has not been able to get him to repeat this one off affirmation. But she doesn't need to, because whether she admits it or not, I know she believes that Mr Icarus knew exactly what she said, and in that moment he chose to respond. Bless his little tailless self.

Animals know things that we have no conception of. They are in tune with life in ways that we rarely are. They sense weather conditions; earthquakes; and scientific experiments have proven that your dog is very much aware of your imminent return home, even when you are not working to your usual schedule. Animals are sensitive and I believe it is because they are deeply in touch with the energy of this life.

Ancient faiths see animals and the environment as a way to access the Great Spirit. They view the Great Spirit at work through the behavior of animals, the cycle of a blooming forest or the dance of a mating bird.

We modern humans are not as attuned to the rhythms of the Great Spirit, and so we cannot discern her messages as easily. I do believe though that we can start to reclaim our natural intuition, instinct and connection to Great Spirit. I see this in the glut of new environmentally friendly products and the many thousands of people committed to saving the planet and the animals. We are getting there slowly but surely.

Following the guidance of the animals and nature is a respectable starting place. They will help us to understand our true nature, and that our nature is intimately wrapped up with the nature of all else living here. Nature is an intelligent force, she is our intelligent force, and we are hers. She has allowed us to play around with her, and have our fun. Now it is time to realize that her pain is our own. She will guide us through this disorder and help us to find our own souls. All we have to do is let her...

Beverley Chicken and Lessons in Life and Death

Until recently Beverley was my chicken. She and her sister

Barbara lived happily at the bottom of my garden for two years. They laid fabulous eggs and enjoyed having the run of the place. The chicken sisters' destructive tendencies, in eating all my favorite plants, were made up for by their quirky characters and the way they wobble when they run!

I came home from work on a Wednesday and joked to James that because he had not checked the chickens one of them could be out there lying half dead. I couldn't have been more right. I went out to discover that Beverley chicken was horribly sick. She had gone lame, was coughing and her wing was paralyzed. I knew then and there that she was dying. I helped her up to bed, and I separated Barbara, in case it was contagious, and I set about trying desperately to fix her.

I Googled every chicken disease under the sun. There are so many. The information highway was fabulous and useless at the same time. All chicken diseases seem to have the same symptoms. All websites give different opinions on the likely survival of your beloved chook. I was ranging from 10% to 100% likelihood of death. I knew in my heart that it was 100%.

I expected Beverley to die that night. She was straining to breathe and my intuition told me that this was the end. I had seen this moment in my mind's eye many a time. I had always 'known' that Beverley chicken would die early, and that it would be an ugly death. I guess my intuition or natural psychic ability had foreseen it. I have noted this with my other animals too. I always tend to worry about an animal prior to something happening. Most recently I felt strangely concerned about Jimi, and it was a week later that he came in with an injured tail asking me for some spiritual healing love. I had distressing thoughts about my Molly only last week, and as I have mentioned, she has been acting like a real stressed out and scared pussycat.

Perhaps our connections to animals are strong because we do not have the usual issues with them that we do with humans that block us from getting too close. Whatever it is I have found that

I am quite well attuned to my four legged and feathered friends.

Of course I did not dwell on my little prophecy about Beverley, and had put it down to a chicken's mother's anxiety. That night I put a little spiritual healing magic into Beverley's head and immediately I saw her face and body calm. She seemed to fall asleep under my hand. I said my goodbyes and went into the house for a night of dreams, nightmares and fears of what I would find the next day. I cried for my girl's little chicken soul.

The next day I awoke and James valiantly offered to go and check on our poorly babe. She was still living but only just. She did not raise her head for him and just lay there her breathing even more laborious. As James headed off to work I went to say my goodbyes. When I did she suddenly perked up. She lifted her head and looked right at me with sparkling eyes. She even made a little noise of greeting. For a few minutes I hoped she might be making a recovery.

Soon after she placed her little head back down, and try as I may I could not get her to open her eyes or raise her head again. Her breath grew heavier and her body made tiny little jerking movements. I knew she was on her way out. I told her that she was free to leave, that we loved her, that she should not be afraid. I gave her a little more healing over her suffering body, and with a heavy heart I left for work. I begged all the angels, Goddesses, and animal spirits to take her out of her suffering.

Work that day was horrendous. I pondered over whether I should have disturbed her suffering to take her to the vets. Although I feared if I did the shock and strangeness of it all was liable to finish her off anyway. James and I spoke many times by phone. We felt there was only one option left to us should we arrive home to find her still alive. The option was to put her out of her misery, either by the vet, or by our own hands. My chicken adoring husband decided that he would do it. He did not want anyone else to do the deed, and it seemed ridiculous to go to the vet and pay for her to die at stranger's hand, in a brightly lit room and far, far away from her home and her sister Barbara.

But I truly did not want James to have to do that. I knew it would likely be traumatic, even though it would have been done out of love and mercy. I admired him beyond belief for making such a hard choice, but at the same time I sent desperate, pleading thoughts to the universe asking that when we returned home from work we would find little Beverley already gone. I wanted Beverley to slip away in peace and of her own accord. I prayed like a desperate woman for this outcome. It felt it was an appropriate time and situation to ask the angels what would become of this situation and what advice they may have to offer me. I got my angel cards out and the card the angels chose for me that day was 'answered prayer'.

Indeed my prayer was answered. When we returned home Beverley had passed. I took it calmly because I had spent a good deal of time at work sobbing for her, wishing her out of her pain. To see her no longer struggling was a relief, I was happy for her. I was happy that James had not had to do it for her. It was an awful situation, but in that moment of seeing her death, all I could do was feel happiness for her and, in all honesty, for us.

Life is Hard

Beverley's life was not the easiest. When we first brought her home she was bullied terribly by her sister Barbara chicken. Little did I know when we decided to keep chickens, that chickens can be cruel creatures when the mood takes them. They are known to cannibalize each other, particularly the sick or weak members of their flocks.

Her first few days with us were spent with James and I defending her against the vicious Barbara. If you have never seen 'the pecking order' in action, then you are lucky. The pecking order I had thought was just a catch phrase. Previous to my adventures in chicken keeping it had no real meaning to me. But to see it being established between two birds that you have brought home as pets, is distressing, no… it is mortifying.

We would stand there helpless as Barbara attempted to peck the living daylights out of her new sister Beverley. We would attempt to defend her, and she knew it. She would hide behind our legs and run to us. She was an extremely timid girl, she was a little afraid of humans. But she knew that in this instance we were her only saviors and she would dash to our side to be rescued. This was the closest Beverley and I became. Because once she and Barbara had sorted out their differences, Beverley went back to being extremely shy of humans – unless of course they were humans bearing sweetcorn or spaghetti!

Forgiveness and Unconditional Love

Beverley loved her sister Barbara. I am not sure Barbara felt quite the same way, but she tolerated Beverley. Once the pecking order was established and the actual pecking attacks died out, it was clear that Barbara was the boss, and Beverley was her lady in waiting. They both seemed to know their place and they got on rather well.

In spite of the previous assaults upon her person Beverley was lost if she did not have Barbara by her side. If Barbara wandered off to tug at a worm, and Beverley lost sight of her, you would see her become panicked and start looking around for her big sister. Once she spotted her she would run over to be by her side. Her wobbling, waddling little run was something that was endlessly cute and amusing!

It seems that all had been forgiven regarding their initial first impressions. Beverley did not resent her sister, nor did she seem scared of her. Indeed she appeared to worship the ground she walked on. I am glad it was Beverley who died first, because I am not sure that she would have coped if she was left alive and Barbara had died. Beverley certainly knew how to forgive, and how to go straight from forgiveness to friendship, companionship and love. Little Beverley could teach us all a thing or two.

Little Beverley Chicken was a shining example of a spiritual life well lived. She had it hard, but she got over it. She loved, she lived, and she enjoyed herself by destroying my beautiful garden – bless her little chick heart! Then she died, really, really quickly. She has left us all with a chicken sized gap in our lives, but I am sure that her life was a blessing and a lesson to us all.

The Dying

Beverley's actual death was not something I witnessed thankfully. But the way she died was echoed in the dream that I had the night before she died. I dreamt quite vividly that she had died and she was in a position which meant she would have fallen or jumped out of her roosting box. It was as though she had done a kamikaze suicide bid. When we found Beverley in real life, her death was very similar. The day of her death I left her almost totally unconscious in her roosting box. When we came home later that day her body was on the floor of her chicken coop. I do not know, nor do I want to know how she got from the box to the floor in her weak and unconscious state. But what I do know is that this was identical to what I had dreamt would happen.

The night that I had that dream, I also had another dream. I dreamt that I went to see Beverley to check on whether she had died or not, and she was alive and happy and normal. This dream came after the dream of her kamikaze style death. The only thing I can take from this dream was that Beverley had died, but that she was still alive, that her soul was free, happy and healthy again.

Shamanistic people rely heavily on dreams; and they feel that dreams about animals are particularly potent and meaningful. It seems that our communication difficulties with our pets and four legged friends are easily solved by the instant satellite link up power of the dream. If you dream of an animal, or your animal, do not discount it. It is sure to hold a potent message for you. It is another method used by Mother Nature to show you that she cares and that you are her child.

Beverley was a brave little chicken, and I am forever blessed by the fact that she raised her head and looked at me not long before she seemed to go totally unconscious. I am honored that she said goodbye, although it must have taken all her strength to do so. I feel happy that she met her demise alone and that she saved James from having to take her life for her. My mother's partner Karen said that perhaps this was her final gift to us. I believe that to be true.

Beverley's death has brought about an acute awareness in me of death, and what that means. I am so ridiculously lucky that I am 32 years old with a near whole set of grandparents. I have been to two funerals that I remember, and only one of them is somebody who I actually knew, my Grandfather. I am drastically lucky. I know that unless I keel over dead in the next five minutes, I am likely to see much death and heartbreak in my life. I know it will never be easy.

As an abstract concept I can cope with death, but then a chicken dies and I go to pieces. This kind of thing puts everything in perspective. Earlier in the week James and I had been bickering, but given Beverley's death I have no idea what our problem was. Suddenly the small things drop away and what is important is remembered. Life and love and death are all intimately related. A heart can be broken, mended and broken again, if we allow it, with every heart break we can strengthen something else within us, our spirit, our soul, our belief that life goes on. What we learn and what we take from this spiritually is what keeps us going.

You know all nature hangs on a spider's web of life. This death of Beverley, whilst relatively minor, compared to others I will undoubtedly suffer, is significant. It has taught me to see spirit in all things. To take notice of nature's patterns, and to appreciate that animals are in contact with something far greater and far more generous than we currently realize. These days we squeal at death, we may see it as a punishment on our souls. Perhaps if we open our hearts to the signs and symbols of this mystical, magical world, then death will become a journey. Our understanding will grow and we will accept the inevitability, if not the excitement that is encapsulated in returning to whence we came.

Whilst some people may squirm and wonder why I am putting so much meaning on the life and death of one tiny chicken, I ask them in return, why wouldn't I? Her death has shone a brilliant light on her spiritual place in nature, and her importance as a teacher to me. I have no problem with my most recent teacher being poultry.

In her leaving this planet, she leaves those mourning her with a whole new set of experiences. She has given James and I some real food for thought and the events around her death have renewed my spiritual beliefs ten fold. Beverley's death brought my heart into concert with nature. I saw her life and her death in all things, and a series of meetings with birds confirmed to me that I am related to nature intimately. I opened my eyes and I saw nature sing to me... read on to see more of her song...

The Birds

Prior to Beverley's death I had no idea she was sick, not until she was really, really sick. The disease was rapid and the symptoms all came at once. So for about a day I was in blissful ignorance. But one thing I did note, and that I mentioned to many people, was that in the week or two leading up to her death I was surrounded by birds.

Everywhere I went there were birds. They took to flying out

in front of my car crossing it or leading the way to wherever I was going. I gleaned great spiritual strength and messages from these non-coincidental happenings. Indeed I felt the animal kingdom and Mother Nature herself reach up and pat me on my head. Be still little one she whispered, for we are all one, and you and Beverley and we, will all meet again.

The messages from my feathered friends started in the form of ravens and crows. Now most people relate such big black birds to death, but I see them more as a magical bird bringing messages. Maybe in this instance it was a little bit of both. I saw them everywhere. At first I just thought there were an awful lot of crows and ravens about and thought no more of it. I presumed that everyone else was noticing them; maybe it was simply the time of year. I mentioned to my car share friend Shireece who was with me on many of the occasions that I had seen them. She however did not know what I was talking about. She had not noticed any. Either I was seeing things, or the birds, on this occasion were there for me to notice and not for her.

The most striking crow experience occurred when I was coming out of the supermarket one day. I was strolling through the urban car park, full of cars and people, and suddenly to my left was a crow. This sweet little creature proceeded to eyeball me and hop along beside me, watching my every move. If I had bent down I could have touched it. It was one brave crow! It was after this event that I started to wonder what all these crows were trying to tell me.

The day of Beverley's sickness, I noticed two sparrow hawks hovering near the car on my usual drive home. I have not seen one of these creatures for some time, never mind two in one day. In particular I noticed how they simply hovered, they did not actually attempt to take their prey. They hung in the air, in their limbo like state. Perhaps an omen that something was afoot, that death was ready to strike, but not quite yet.

On the morning of Beverley's death I could not help but notice that all bird activity ceased. I saw the birds, but instead of swooping down in front of me, they simply watched me pass. I felt as though I were at a funeral procession. The skies were quiet and I felt strongly that my worst fears were being confirmed.

Alongside the sparrow hawks, crows and ravens, herons have also visited me. I have seen about five or six flying herons within as many days, probably one a day. Every time I have left the house I have seen one crossing my path in the sky. I might normally see one heron every few years, and not often in flight. Indeed just ten minutes ago as I sat down to write this about Beverley, I looked out my window to see a heron circling the sky near my house with two crows accompanying it. I knew then for certain that these birds were acting as messengers to me.

An interesting non-coincidence came to me as I was writing this section. I decided to look in my photo archives and take a look at the pictures taken the day the chickens came to live with us. Besides lots of images of curious cats and perky headed young feathered friends, I was taken aback to see a photograph of the sky.

Smack bang in the middle of that sky was a flying heron. Whilst this was brilliant in itself, it caused me to remember the strange phenomena that had taken place the day we brought the chicken's home. On that day our garden was visited by dozens of birds. This was noticeable because we have cats and it is very rare to see a bird in our space. So to have many come flying in was most noticeable. There is something afoot in the bird world me thinks…

All these magnificent birds are my messengers of death, and my messengers also of life. A crow is a magical underworld style birdie and a heron is a smaller version of a stork, which of course is traditionally represented as the bringer of babies. To me their presence signals that Beverley has gone to a better place, she has flown home, her life was important and that the messengers of spirit want me to know that I'm not wrong in thinking that.

These creatures of the air seem so well in touch with the world and the energy around them. I hesitate to think that their messages were solely for me, but more for all of us, for themselves, for the connection that we all share. Whilst us humans are often oblivious to that connection we can access it if we simply choose to observe.

The presence of these winged messengers has given the entire trauma and upset such great significance. It raises Beverley's death above the ordinary. The birds seem to be guiding me through my loss and showing me that they are with me. We all feel the loss, but we all make great gains from it. I hope you too will make great gains from this story of little Beverley's life and death.

Attention to detail is vital in interpreting such signals and signs from Mother Nature. The ability to believe in what you are seeing is another key ingredient, but it is something I hope you will soon be able to access. The animal kingdom will speak to us often; it is our choice to observe and to listen. But trust me, the messages are there; they are there for you, as they are for your sister, your brother, your mother and your flat mate. We are not separate entities in the way our society believes we are. We are part of a community of spirit living earthly life, and that community, that Great Spirit wants you to know it.

Interestingly enough, as I write this about storks and herons in flight, my very good friend Natalie is in labor with her second child. That imminent birth is helping me through the death I have encountered with poor Beverley. The circle of life is going crazy all around me and as the heron and crows mingle together in the sky, I see that the cycle of life and death are hand in hand.

The Deer

Continuing on with the theme of messages from nature I will now tell you about my most recent animal lesson that was brief but intense. At the time I believed it related to something else, but with hindsight I can see more clearly what it was telling me. This sign came to me prior to a huge awakening in my life. I had recently been involved in the previously mentioned car crashes. I had been off work, in pain, and was feeling utterly fed up with my lot. I was reverting to human ways of moaning and whining, and I stood in a place of confusion, disorientated and unsure of my next step.

To alleviate some of the stress, James and I went for a country walk. At this place we experienced two encounters with animals, both fascinating and intriguing. Indeed both carried different messages for us as a couple and for me as an individual. Some people will see these as mere chance encounters.

From a spiritual perspective, nothing is ever just a chance encounter. We gain meaning in our lives from every soul we meet, and everything we observe. Here are my stories...

We parked our bottoms down next to a herd of wild deer. They kindly allowed us to sit in their space and we sat chatting. There was nothing hugely special in this, until we realized that the deer were having frequent visitors, in the form of jackdaws. The jackdaws were landing on the deer, pulling their fur out and returning presumably to feather their nests. This was a relentless pursuit, and the birds carried on their comings and goings without rest or relaxation. Occasionally a huge raven would swoop down and for no reason at all attack the jackdaws. They would flee in terror, but would soon return to the task at hand.

This event coincided with my James starting a new job and us talking about the possibility of moving homes. These birds and deer were helping to show us the power of cooperation, persistent hard work and bravery in the face of marauding ravens. They demonstrated how nothing happens overnight, and that life can sometimes swoop down and cause you a little bit of fear. In spite of this fear they stayed true to trust, to their mission and to the pursuit of their lives. This was valuable information to a young couple, recovering from a time of difficulty and looking for a way forward.

Having observed the birds and deer, we went for a little wander and came across a lone one-antlered deer wandering on the other side of a river. She approached and stood opposite us for the longest time. She was begging for bread and looked scraggly and stressed. Jay and I fell in love with her, despite the fact that she looked vexed, and like she might have a few mental health problems. As we left she crossed the river to our side. All of a sudden she looked really odd and as though she was going to have a fit. We were getting quite concerned for her welfare when she decisively struck her head on the concrete path making her one remaining antler fall off. She then ran off like a baby bambi, happy and free into the woods.

This got me thinking...I believe she was a sign for me. She had spent all winter growing her antlers. She only had one left now. The antlers were a part of her, part of what she has achieved and done with her life. But it was bothering her. It was stressing her. It did not feel right any more. So she wandered into unknown (human) territory and very purposefully bashed her antler right off. After that she immediately regained her personal power and ran up a hill into the woods. It was all very symbolic. Not once did she look back for her lost antler. I feel it was a vivid sign for me.

I had allowed myself to become similarly stressed and straggly with the events of my life. I was hanging on to outworn behaviors and elements of my character, that were no longer serving a good purpose in my life. Like the deer I needed to free myself, to shatter my crowning glory, take my life by the antlers and start afresh. So I did. I changed a great deal of things in my life and started to live wholly by my spirituality. This coincided with my trip to Glastonbury that in turn also helped heal me and set me free.

Since then I have not looked back. I have embraced a new me

with gusto. That deer was my inspiration and my muse and I will be forever grateful to her for bringing her personal problems into my world and showing me how to tenaciously and swiftly solve them.

From the examples I have shared with you I hope you can start to see the relevance and power of animals and nature in your life. This world is far more than a human metropolis awaiting your credit card. It is a beautiful place whereby all things are equal and spirit is inherent in every grain, atom and ray of sunlight. Understand this and you seize upon a whole new world, right here, where you already live.

What is spiritual about eating animals?

Well that depends on your standpoint. For many cultures and religions the sacrifice of animals to be eaten is culturally, socially and spiritually significant. The society I have been raised in is one such society, a roast joint of meat on a Sunday, a Turkey at Christmas or Thanksgiving if you live in the USA, a prime steak as an extravagant Saturday night treat. For other people of other faiths, the idea of eating flesh of any kind is abhorrent.

As a vegetarian, I stand by the idea that eating meat is revolting, vile, cruel and unnecessary, and yet until recently, as an on/off, part-time vegetarian, I still did it.

My personal spiritual values err on the side of The Great Spirit, and whilst shamanic cultures do not practice abstention from meat, my natural values lead me in that direction. Yet until recently it would still happen that my head or my stomach ruled my heart and I would happily tuck into a bacon sandwich. Or the vilest curse of them all, a cheeseburger. I hate it, I love it, I hate it, Arrrghhh!

Let's be final about this. I hate it. I do not love meat; I prefer the vegetarian option every time. I believe all animals on the planet to be equally splendid souls; none should be viewed as lesser. I hold no water with the belief that any creature was put here for us to eat. Yes, it remains true that a deer may well be placed here for the lion to prey on. But I am no lion; I do have a choice, and a very clever consciousness – when I choose to engage it. I love those darned furry things, yet eating meat stood in direct opposition to this so-called love of animals. I was a hypocrite with blood on my hands.

So if I believe that eating animals is unpleasant and unspiritual, why did I continue to do so for so long? I will be honest here; sometimes it is easier to just not think about the consequences of our actions. The poor creature is already dead (once it is conveniently delivered from slaughterhouse to supermarket). I can afford it, and it smells great roasted.

In such instances I chose not to engage my consciousness or my higher wisdom. Which I am ashamed to say is just about as ignorant and arrogant as you can get.

However I cannot be unconscious any more. I want to love animals genuinely and that does not include the ingestion and digestion of their lifeless muscles. There are no options. For me it is vital that I never eat meat again.

The reason I feel so strongly about this is because I have now engaged my brain with my soul, and there is no turning back. My spiritual soulful conscious thought knows this. I think that all animals, and all living creatures are part of this world. I believe us all to be connected on a basic, fundamental level. I have preached my way through the pages of this book about how important it is to be good, forgiving, and compassionate to our fellow humans. Yet I truly believe that animals are made of the same psychic, spiritual, energetic matter as the rest of us. Animals have souls. Animals deserve to live the best life they possibly can. I shall have no part in causing their lives to be a misery.

Animal rights are a frontier that many traverse only partially. We may wail and mourn for the puppy that was cruelly tortured and abandoned, but we think nothing of the life of torture and deprivation of basic comfort inflicted upon chickens, the dairy cow or other animals whose lives are irreparably limited for the benefits of our hungry stomachs.

You would not condone the slavery of humans, so why condone it on our fellow living creatures? Is it because they cannot speak, because they submit to our will, because the Bible says that we can use all plants and animals as we choose to?

Our consciousnesses must be raised, and this topic is vitally important in that battle. We must start to look outside of our own minds at some point on our spiritual pathway. Yes the mind is a great place to start, followed by our hobbies and our habits, but soon we must turn to the state of the world. What we eat, how our food is produced and the effect this has on the well being of the planet, on so many different levels, must be addressed.

I was going to pussyfoot around this subject. That was only because I was pussyfooting around it in my own life. I cannot afford to do that any more if I want to like myself and live what I believe to be correct. I must commit myself to my spiritual cause. It is time to get fierce with my food. It is time to wake up and realize that what we eat can affect our spiritual sanity, our level of personal spiritual awakening and the lives of millions of animals and people worldwide.

Let me be blunt. I believe that eating animals can block your spiritual progression. If you are in denial about the harm that is caused every time you sit down to a meat-laden meal then you are not raising your consciousness to a spiritual level. I'm sorry if that sounds harsh, but I sincerely believe it to be true.

Animals are not happy when they are kept in confined spaces, they mourn and moan when their offspring are taken from them and they live in confinement, only to be killed. If all things are made up of energy, and our thoughts can become our lives, then surely animals' feelings go straight into the energetic remnants of their flesh. Which we then consume, and so we eat their misery and we eat their fear. This is not good.

When meat comes packaged in cellophane it is easy not to allow those thoughts in to your mind. It is easy to see a great deal on offer and put yourself and your family's finances first. But really you are not doing yourselves any favors because whilst you grabbed a bargain, you are living against your better knowing. Nor are you being kind, loving and generous to the world around you.

In buying meat you are purchasing a product that has caused great suffering to the creature that died to provide it. You cannot get away from that fact. Your consumer choice is promoting the suffering of that cow, duck, chicken, pig or turkey. You are saying yes to abominable cruelty and telling the people who make those products that you want more.

Of course there is the option of free-range meat. I questioned this for a while. I figured that if the animal has had a happy life, then maybe eating it was ok. This, however, is again just my mind overruling my heart. No matter how happy that animal's life, and how painless the death of it might be, it is not my place to choose if that animal lives or dies.

My natural reaction to the killing of so much as a fly in my presence is one of pure horror. I cannot tell you how bad I felt the time I squashed a fly on my desk at work. That creature was having a life, no matter what I think that life consisted of, that was what it was doing. How dare I come along and decide to cease that life. How dare I presume lordship over and above that creature's natural survival instinct? Or there was the time I thoughtlessly put slug pellets out on the garden because I was sick of the slimy things eating my new plants. I came down the next day to slug Armageddon. I could not stop my heartfelt weeping. Perhaps if I saw the lodgings and treatment of where my last burger came from I would weep some more…

My natural spiritual position is one of non-violence, peace, love and respect of the planet and all who abide upon her. Eating meat does not fit into that equation. When I eat meat it goes against my soul's knowing and the knock-on effect of this is that my spirituality stalls. So now, for all these reasons, I do not eat meat.

I believe that because of my choice to live consciously in all aspect of my life I am psychically raising the bar. I am more sensitive than ever to the world around me, and I have been having profound psychic moments. I have also been happy to embrace a whole host of happy non-coincidences that are destined to take my spirituality further. I am respecting my place on this earth as a spiritual being who is connected to all other things. I am certain that Mother Nature and the spirit that we are all made of is showing me some respect back.

Veganism

To truly road test the benefits of not eating meat or animal products I decided to go dairy and meat free for one month, in the hope that I would feel cleaner, less guilty and at the same time fill myself up on bundles of literature all about the harsh facts that comprise the making of our daily milk and cheese.

Our terribly innocuous pint of milk has a history, likely one that if it occurred to a human would be nothing less than a human rights abuse. Yet we pour milk on our cereal and stuff our rolls with sausages without giving it a thought.

Life is not a product, yet the meat and dairy industry market the life of others to us every single day. It is all wrapped up in nice packaging, at great prices with promises of so many health benefits. But however you look at it, it is another creature's life we choose to ingest.

I understand that not everyone has feelings regarding animal rights. Some people think that animals' emotions are fleeting, that they live day-to-day, moment-to-moment. Other people have assured me of their belief that animals volunteer for their role as meat/dairy stock before being incarnated into their animal bodies.

That theory worries me, because it essentially says that we all choose our suffering, and therefore deserve it. The same people do sometimes believe that is true for us too. That kind of explanation can make the believer frighteningly irresponsible and allows us to excuse any travesty that we stumble upon. Taken to an extreme we can justify murder, rape, genocide, because hey, the souls signed up for it! This way of thought would make us loathe doing anything to ever improve our lot in life.

No I do not adhere to that belief at all. I do agree that we may volunteer for certain things to happen to us in our lives, who knows, maybe cows volunteer to be slaughtered or to become dairy cows. However I do not believe that this happens so that we can eat them. I believe it happens so that we can practice some humanity, so that good can come from bad. If an animal does happen to sign up for cruelty in its life on earth, it is not so that the cruelty can happen without conscience, it is so that it can be noticed and so that somebody can stand up to it and stop it from happening.

To me this is the same as you volunteering to split up with the love of your life, so that you can practice getting stronger and getting over it. Animals sign up for hardship so that some brave soul will rescue them and cause some goodness to come out of the situation. Animals do not reincarnate as fodder for our lunch, though of course, their suffering may cause fodder for our souls.

I believe that horrific things occur on Planet Earth as an opportunity for us as sentient human souls to exert change. If something is happening that is no good for human or beast, then what stops us from stopping it, or altering it, other than our inertia? Or the financial implications? Oh, that's right, yeah… of course the financial implications are what stands in the way of progress. Somebody is making a lot of money from the provision of meat and dairy products worldwide. Forget the rainforest and the environment.

As a spiritual person I must take responsibility for myself, and I cannot blindly pick up a carton of milk knowing full well that a degree of misery has been caused to make it, no matter how cheerful the image on the wrapper is. A month of veganism was called for to help me sensibly assess the reality of life without animal products, and to discover for myself what I am willing to do in the long term to help the greater good of the planet, people and the soulful animals on it.

My month of veganism was fabulous, but it was hard work. It was difficult to get the right levels of vitamins and dietary requirements when working full time and reliant upon only the small town local supermarket for my fuel. The choice of dishes in restaurants was dismal. There was either none, or if I was lucky there would be one, usually labeled 'green salad'. I forgot to take supplements and to be honest I stopped the experiment after three weeks because I felt I was becoming run down.

You know what though, in spite of my failings on this count I have become a mad wannabee vegan. I am now slowly and gently heading down a semi vegan route. I avoid milk like the plague and eat cheese only very rarely. The majority of my meals are vegan, and I will continue to practice this into the future.

I have decided that I will still eat local free-range eggs, and honey too. The eggs I eat come from the marvelous free-range farm where Barbara chicken has gone to live, up the road from my home. As for honey, well I am entranced by humankind's relationship with the Bee and I truly do not believe that it is a hardship on a Bee to do what they do. I am certain that some fair relationships can exist with animals whereby we might share in their products in exchange for a warm shed/hive to live in and a nice life! Eggs and honey are ones I currently feel comfortable with.

The reason for my desire to be vegan is simple. I cannot ignore what I have read. I cannot ignore the suffering of animals being used to provide my food. Particularly not when there are really great alternatives available. I no longer wish to be party to the mass consumption of animal products. I no longer wish rainforests to be cleared to make way for fields for grazing cows, who then fart their way to a hole in the ozone layer. Not to mention the fact that the space they take up could be used to produce masses of soya, and that all this soya would feed far more people. And let's remember there are hungry people in the world. Not to mention the fact that a vegetarian diet is proven to be far healthier, whereas meat and dairy clog up the system leaving us open to high cholesterol levels, high blood pressure, heart disease and cancer.

The ethics of the meat and dairy industry are on the whole as heartless as the cruelty inflicted on the animals in their care. The world of food commerce is messed up beyond belief, and my spiritual self will not allow me to get mixed up in it for a moment longer. I absolve myself of this responsibility and I am bowing out. I hope one day to own my own little farm, with my own chickens and maybe a cow that, might, if she has any spare after feeding her calf, lend me some milk. But for now soya is my mixer, rice dream my crème de la crème, and my long term aim is for the only cheesy thing in my life to be a proud ownership of Take That's greatest hits.

Nature is our Friend

Mother Nature and all that dwell upon her are a spiritual seeker's best friend. Through nature we can disseminate the patterns and powers of our own lives. When we grasp our connection to the planet then we expand our minds exponentially. I hope that you experiment with this, try it out for size. Allow yourself to be nature and nature to be you. Find a way to express this in your life, however it makes sense to you: by purchasing environmentally friendly products, by spending more time with your pets, going for a walk in the woods, putting nuts on a bird table through winter, or joining a local wildlife group.

Forging your connection with the planet will see you well in the future. It will establish you as a creature of honor amongst billions of other little lives that share the earthly life. Connect to the messages from nature and you connect with the harmony of your own existence. If you can see what that seagull means to you, then you can appreciate that the seagull is an extension of your energy, and that you are part of the same pattern in which the seagull is present.

All is one. Our human energies are profoundly connected to the world around us, and the sooner we realize that the better. I want to show you three ways in which you can connect to your true nature and to the animals that are the representatives and cohorts of the Great Spirit.

First make an effort to be in nature and to bring nature into your life. Depending on your circumstances this might mean bringing a plant into your home, going for long country walks or a weekend away somewhere wild and wondrous. Get outside, be and exist outside. If buildings surround you look up at the sky, check out what the clouds are doing. Find even the smallest green space and sit in it. Meditate if you can. City dwellers watch a pigeon, or an ant, observe their nature and know that it is yours too. Allow yourself simply to be a part of the scenery. Observe the happenings of the beasts, birds and bugs around you. Walk barefoot on the grass; watch the wind in the trees and feel it in your hair.

One of my greatest messages from spirit came through a crazy gust of wind. I was sitting alone in a wooded area, it was a calm day, and I spoke gently in my mind to the Great Spirit, thanking her for the gifts in my life at that time. From nowhere, as if in response to my thanks the whole wood shook with a fierce wind that swung through, causing everything to vibrate and move as if alive. The woodland floor became a sea of brown as the autumn leaves blew towards me in unison. And then it stopped just as suddenly as it had started and the woods became business as usual. Beautiful. Message understood.

Secondly, look for a message from an animal. Have faith that one will be received. This may not come in the form of a physical animal; it may be the repetitive image of the same animal or an animal that comes to you in a dream.

For a period of my life I saw horses everywhere, on the side of lorries, on television, in real life, at the airport, everywhere! Animals will reach you no matter what. You can live in Texas and be visited by a Polar Bear; you just have to know where to look. That Polar Bear might visit you in a number of ways and it is down to you to think carefully about what that means to you.

Then again it may be that your pet, or an animal you pass in the street has something to say. Watch them wisely, offer them peace and love, see if they let you in on a secret!

Finally I suggest that you make your life a haven of environmental loveliness. This can be hard and is not always convenient, but it is a must. If you eat meat, then eat less of it. Perhaps swap your milk for soya or your battery produced eggs for free range. Plant a tree in your garden, or if you have no garden, give a tree as a gift. Experiment with vegan recipes and even try going vegan for a week or two if you dare. Grow your own vegetables; it is easy and hugely satisfying. Replace your chemical laden beauty products with organic natural ones. Mash up your own facemask with an avocado or a body scrub with sugar and olive oil. Walk or bike when you can and leave the car at home.

Live your life in concert with nature and ask the Great Spirit to guide you to better more natural choices. Believe that this will occur and watch as nature lends you a helping hand.

Nature really is the greatest teacher and the most wonderful friend. I adore her. Whenever I am in nature for long I come home buzzing. My whole body seems to vibrate and echo the sentiments of our living earth. She seeps up my negativity, she grounds me and she spurts forth with vegetables, fruit, flowers and a home for the insects. Enjoy her, respect her, and believe in her, feel her in your soul for she is you.

Lesson 10 - Connect

Becoming a spiritual being is all about connection. It is about seeing the power of every little event, the synchronicity of it, and tuning in your inner radar to help make sense of it all. The following lesson covers intuition, non-coincidence, your thoughts, love and spiritual space. The idea behind this lesson is to hasten and improve your spiritual understanding. Each subject will assist you to connect to all things divine. This lesson will be fresh in your mind for when you go forward emerging as the enlightened butterfly that you are.

Connect is all about embracing the spiritual faculties and incidents that are often and readily available to you. The following topics are essential accessories to your spiritual living and every single one I highly recommend to help cement you as a finely tuned spiritual being.

I have left this till toward the end of this book because I want you to understand the other elements of life before you start to rev up your connection. I believe that at this stage of the book you are becoming well tuned in to a new spiritual existence, and so it is high time that you started to actively bring a little something spiritual into your life.

The divine is waiting for you; it is your time to shine....

Non-coincidence

Coincidence does not exist. Although it is with a seeming 'coincidence' that your spiritual life might emerge or be kick started. I find coincidence to be a word that badly summarizes the fact that actually, nothing is a coincidence, and as per the mantra of this book 'everything happens for a reason'!

James has even developed a coincidence face. It involves

saying coincidence in a questioning way with a high-pitched lilt at the end, whilst cocking the head to the side, wide eyed and with one questioning eyebrow raised. I love it! It really does say it all!

I am convinced that coincidences are not accidental at all and are in fact part of the natural push and pull of the greater scheme of things. They are synchronicities that shed light on our lives. They are the higher-self working with the higher self of others to give us signs, to light the way and to visit us with crazy opportunities and learning. They are serendipitous gifts of cosmic wondrousness that show how intimately connected we are in often unseen and mysterious ways.

I have devised a new turn of phrase to describe such incidents. I will now refer to them as non-coincidences, as I have done throughout the pages of this book. Coincidence as a phrase does not cut it; it tends to mean happy or bizarre accident. Whilst I love happy accidents, I truly believe that they are in fact the workings of a design-led spiritual universe. A non-coincidence is no accident. A non-coincidence is a purposeful and tangible act of spiritual guidance.

First, a word of warning. Just because something seems fated, does not mean that it is a good thing. Non-coincidence can pit you up against the enemy on occasion to see how you fare. You may stumble across an ex-partner on the street, suddenly and out of the blue, but this does not mean that you should jump into bed with them immediately. It may be a chance to catch up, to see how much you have grown, or even an opportunity not to succumb to your previous passions and to walk away the stronger woman that you are.

Non-coincidence might throw a cart of chocolate cakes at you, just when you have gotten used to your healthy eating regime. This happened to me when I had first undertaken my healthy eating lifestyle. I was doing so well. No sooner had I remarked to the world via Twitter that my vegetable intake was going fabulously, than somebody offered me an array of cakes; chocolate cakes. Now this really was a non-coincidence too far! But rather than see it as an opportunity to break with my healthy ways and treat myself for having done so well, I saw it for what it was, a non-coincidence that would allow me to overcome the urge and to carry on in a place of pride and self respect.

Non-coincidence has shown me so many times what it is that I do not want. Non-coincidence can sometimes feel like a test. But as it reappears in your life with the same old lessons, its meaning becomes more apparent. If something keeps happening, or you keep coming up against the same kind of people, or the same brick walls, do not get mad, have a little think about what it is that you need to learn. What is it in you that needs to change so that the same old same old stops occurring?

Some time ago I had a marvelous offer from an apparently fabulous book promoter in the United States. He stated he wanted to work with *The High Heeled Guide to Enlightenment* and he sent me a list of his bestsellers, it was impressive. I am not overly enamored with publicity people; my experiences of success through them have been negligible and expensive. Yet, when this man's email came in I felt so flattered and happy that he wanted to help me.

Of course, I came back down to earth when I saw his prices. Whilst I could have saved up and handed over the booty, something in me knew it was not quite right.

This to me was a non-coincidence showing me my own light, and making me examine my own self. I was forced to put my values and my wants under the microscope. Of course I would love to have a bestselling book. But to do so would mean embracing a world of marketing that I can neither afford nor really approve of. I have since found out that the man is known as a conman, duping new authors to part with their hard earned cash. Had I have gone down the path of signing on the dotted line for this marketing, I would have learned a very big lesson. Either way I would have won in terms of learning, but I much prefer the inexpensive route I chose!

Non-coincidence is a complex gift. It gives you great things and it also gives you puzzles to make sense of. It can throw your whole life into chaos, because what you thought was 'meant to be' does not work out how you thought it would. But maybe that is because it was never supposed to. Non-coincidence can tempt us and leave us in a state of folly. Trick you once, shame on you, but allow it to happen twice and you can blame only yourself. Non-coincidence is not the enemy here. It is our own failings, and our interpretation of that non-coincidence that is at fault. We must learn from our failings or else we will continue to be tripped up by them until the day that we eventually decide to take the lesson on-board.

I have focused here mainly on the lessons and potential hardships that non-coincidence can bring. But believe me, there are a hundred other ways it can light up your life for the better. It can connect you through a series of apparently random but synchronous events to a person or people who are just right for you and your growth at any given stage of life. It can drop information your way that is desperately needed. Non-coincidence can play a song that means the very world to you, at the very moment that you needed to hear it.

Non-Coincidence is part and parcel of the signs I asked you to look out for at the start of the book. It is your lighthouse in the gloom, and whilst sometimes the non-coincidences are laden with meaning, depth and lessons, other times they are simply perfect meetings, happy education and wondrous 'wow I can not believe that just happened' moments!

Non-coincidence can be a funny thing. It can visit a whole boatload of crazy scenarios upon us. It is for us to work out the meaning and for us to take forward in the best way possible for our future development. Whatever you do, be certain that you will experience something from all non-coincidences. That something is sometimes profound, sometimes unique, and other times just plain old crazy! The lessons range from the infinitely miraculous to the more intense personal lessons about your self. Employing your intuition to such scenarios is the best way to get a happy result for yourself, and hopefully avoid any painstaking self-examination later. Noticing non-coincidence and paying attention to your intuition are your fast track ways to contact your guiding spirits, your higher self and to access your spiritual potential.

Intuition

Always, always, always listen to your inner voice. Whether you choose to label this inner voice as 'gut instinct', 'guardian angels', 'God', 'spirit' or your 'higher self', the advice this little voice has is invaluable. Excuse this shallow shopping related example, however, if I had listened to the voice I would have saved myself a substantial amount of money on my wedding dress. Of course I allowed the louder, day-to-day greedy voice to overrule. The quiet little voice was saying – 'wait a few weeks, it will be reduced'. The louder ego voice of my main brain was saying – 'buy it now, buy it now!' I knew I was making a mistake but, of course, I bought it now! Three weeks later the darned thing was in the sale and I missed out on a massive bargain.

Again even more recently I wrote an article and sent it to an editor at a magazine. When I was writing it I had an inkling to swap some of the paragraphs round so that the article started entirely differently. For whatever reason I ignored this inkling. I sent the article off and the editor got back to me asking me to alter the piece in the exact way my intuition had hinted at me. I had to laugh because I really should know better. It was not the worst hardship, but I could have saved myself some work by trusting my gut!

Your inner voice is valuable not only for money saving and

copy editing tips, although it is through these little examples that we can see the value intuition can have on a daily life. Intuition has greater value too, when employed full time and conscientiously it can help keep you safe and instruct you on wiser life choices. It also helps you make sense of all those non-coincidences that life will throw your way!

So how do you recognize your intuition? Well, I am sure you hear her often, however, you may not be listening. She tends to sound a little like this....

Have you ever felt sure you should not do something, but you've gone ahead and done it anyway only to feel regret later? Or have you felt you should do something, and not done it, and then wished you had?

Have you ever had a strong bad or good feeling about a person or situation, and this feeling has been proven right?

Have you ever just known something with no explanation why, but in your heart and soul you just knew it?

Have you ever had a passing thought and then a little while later that thought is reflected in real life events?

If these are familiar then that is the voice you need to listen to. Your intuition is the voice that you so often turn off, only to wish you had listened to your own smart self. I recommend that you start to listen to that little voice and do what it says. She is the sound of your truest, purest self. She always has your best interests at heart and can sense things that you are oblivious to. Be true to that little voice and see your life improve.

I follow my intuition daily. Sometimes the reasons behind an intuitive hunch are obvious, more often they are not. Recently I met with my mother for lunch and my intuition told me to walk a different way back to the car park. Everything went well, I got in my car and I drove home. I have no idea what may or may not have happened if I had gone the other way. I simply did as I was told, I trusted my little voice and as ever she saw me safe. This happens all the time. I will get a little prompt and I will follow it. Other times the prompts are louder and more insistent. Intuition is you own voice, in your own mind, only clearer and somehow wiser. Ignore her at your peril. It's when you ignore her that you know why you should have listened.

My most recent brush with ignoring my intuition was a hard one. I had joined a friend's spiritual group that lasted for several months. Even before the first session, I knew the group was wrong for me. But friends being friends I felt I had to go. I did attend, and whilst what my friend was doing was wonderful, it just was not right for me. It was no longer my version of spirituality.

I went to three sessions in all, and on the very last day I felt so full of anxiety about attending the fourth session that I literally just could not do it. I had to quit, there was no way around it, and my gut instinct was ripping my solar plexus apart with the feeling of stress. So I quit, and immediately I felt fine. If I had been listening, I would not have gone in the first place and saved myself a lot of anxiety.

Again though it is important to realize that there are no mistakes. Every time you fail to follow your intuition and end up in a pickle, you will learn something. Hopefully you will learn to listen to your intuition next time!

Intuition is a powerful ally to us. To listen to your intuition though you must first have faith in your own spiritual nature and the fact that you are right. We all, so often turn to other people for advice. It can be very hard to trust our own instinct. The more you listen, the more helpful that little voice inside will be. The more she is right, the more you will feel safe to rely on her. In time you will find the advice of others to be at odds with your own inner knowing. This does not make them wrong, but it does make their advice wrong for you. Your higher self knows what she is talking about, but you must listen! You are your own best advisor, believe it.

If you are speaking for yourself you are right. If you speak from an honest heart and a whole hunk of love then you are utterly right. Scrap ego, scrap image, scrap neurosis, worry and fear of what others might think. Be an individual. Accepting your individuality is key to this because you must be confident enough to express your truth without apology or compromise.

When you get there you will know. It is not self-righteous, it is not self-satisfied, it is a personal achievement, and it is truth, plain, simple and beautiful truth. Speak and listen to your truth, act on it freely and your life will benefit. Be your own guru, sweetie, you are the best placed person for it!

Your Thoughts

Your thoughts are powerful. There are many books informing you how you can conjure up the life you wish to live through changing the way you think. Whether you read up on cosmic ordering, or the law of attraction, it all links to the same concept. This concept in essence is that your thoughts and desires are powerful. What you think can easily come true. So be careful what you wish for!

I have found that my uncensored and unrestricted thoughts have a tendency of wreaking havoc. When I think back to my life prior to spirituality becoming my main focus, I was a disaster zone. Whatever I thought, more or less I would receive. Things happened both good and bad. And yes, I blame myself, totally and unreservedly. I made all kinds of things happen. That is not to say I was the only one doing so, we all have our thoughts, and we can all send messages out to the universe simply by fleetingly entertaining them.

Careless thoughts can lead to careless actions and events. My life has had its ups and downs and I totally blame my own thinking for that. I used to have a tendency to go off into a dark place in my head and think badly of situations. I am not as dark as I used to be, but should I slip and this occurs, well then, it is reflected in my world, in my relationships, in my attitude and in what happens to me. But should I be feeling happier, positive and I think only fabulous thoughts, then fabulous things happen. This is a simple equation; the only thing that stands in your way is your own mind.

I read an article recently which was not spiritual, but which is a great metaphor for this. A woman was speaking about doing the washing up (classic couple flashpoint). She said that she could sit around and watch for days as her husband and children did not do the washing up. It stayed piled up on the side. She could get angrier and more aggrieved about this failure to help her out. She would no doubt feel rotten inside. However she learned that if she filled the sink up with warm soapy water and left the room, she would often come back to find her husband elbow deep in suds and happily doing his duties.

This reflects how the workings of our minds can lead to very different results. Stale, angry, obnoxious thoughts lead to nothing but bad feeling. But if we open ourselves to having a little positive thought, and make the effort to put some love into things ourselves, then good will come of it. Negative thoughts turn situations off, and conflict arises. Positive, hopeful and loving thoughts makes things move, they help the tide flow, and more often than not, it flows in our favor.

Without a doubt thinking negatively about life will beget more negativity. Examine your life, because this life counts and it's not a rehearsal. Examine how you think and how you react. Perhaps in your stance of hurt feelings or anger, you are simply spreading the negative vibe. We must learn to trust that happy feelings lead to happy events. It is truly that simple.

I have found myself of late in a situation where in the past I most definitely would have felt badly and as a result I would have wreaked emotional havoc. Instead I chose to be happy for all involved, to think joyously about it and to be a ray of sunshine. I was astounded by the results of this selfless thinking. Everybody involved was super happy too. This made me feel happy for them and it was one great big love soup of happiness. Whilst at first I was purposefully being happy, by the end the happiness was all natural! It was ridiculous. I swear I did not expect such a happy result. But I got it. Try it for yourself and see. Just decide to be happy about something and really commit to that mindset. It may just rock your world too!

Do not get caught in a spiral of dark thoughts, it is too easily done. Thoughts like 'oh, he's always late' will invariably lead to you feeling angry about him being late. Change the way you think so that when he does arrive, you are happy to see him. Turn his lateness into an opportunity to grab a coffee, read a book or snatch a quick phone conversation with your girlfriends. Then when he arrives, give him a great big hug and forget about it. I am talking from experience on this one. His lateness is your opportunity! Our negative feelings make everything worse. Know this, change this and see your cool, calm happy spiritual self start to emerge.

I believe that you think your life into existence. As a human organic being you are very much the centre of your universe, and how you see things is the tone you set for your experience here. We all have a tendency to blame other people or situations when life goes wrong. But I have learnt that nine times out of ten the way we feel about something is entirely our own responsibility. The way we choose to handle a situation, can very much transform our happiness levels. By altering the way we think and making extreme efforts to stop negative, angry, blame thinking we can conjure up a more pleasant existence.

Thinking in the positive, will not necessarily bring you riches, job promotions and new partners overnight. I believe that is where so many of the positive thinking theories go wrong. So many theories tend to focus on the gain of material abundance, love and money. Wishing for such things is quite natural, but they will not come to you, until you are ready. A positive mindset might mean that you see opportunities and follow them up. Your positive attitude might even create more opportunities and draw people to you.

I have a few outstanding universal requests that I have been waiting years to be delivered. This does not mean that my positive thinking is not working, but that sometimes, when seeking things for personal gain, the universe will make you wait. So go ahead and think positive for a new home, new lover or new job, but until you transform the crucial aspects of your life, such as attitude, reaction and the basic way you think, then you will not make huge spiritual progress and your order may be delayed.

Always remember that you can make things happen with your thoughts. Sometimes you may have to wait, and sometimes your thoughts might be a bit too ambitious, but trust me, if your wishes are meant to be, they will happen. But only when the universe decides you are good and ready for them! You may really want a new boyfriend or girlfriend, but if the time is not right, you will not get one. You may get a whole bunch of unsuccessful dates and brief relationships that tell you more about yourself as a person, and more about what you do not want in a partner. While this may not be what you initially hoped for, it is certainly taking you down the correct path.

These days my interest in ordering up new material objects is minimal. At the time of writing I am looking to sell my house. Rather than placing a request with the universe, I simply keep my thoughts positive and expect it to happen. All the signs have led me in this direction, and so the spiritual intent is already there. I expect the house to sell, so I will put my energy into that and follow my intuition. That said, it is not coming easy, and a few lessons are being learned along the house-selling path, but all in all I am taking it as an experience that is getting me, eventually, to where I need to be.

As I have more fully embraced my spiritual nature I have found that my thinking tends to beget wonderful coincidence. I do not have to do this purposefully, but because I seem to be on the right spiritual path, incredible things occur with no effort at all on my part. It definitely beats having to ask the universe for something. The difference being that when the universe really, really wants you to have something, then it happily chucks it in your direction without making you jump through a single fiery hoop!

Here are some examples of how my thoughts have led to a coincidence that my intuition says a big 'yes' to. These are an example of spiritual living in practice, and when these three things all happened in one week I knew that finally I must be on the right track. All this spiritual living can be hard work, but the pay off can be very rewarding indeed.

The first example was that I was looking into a shamanism course in London. I really wanted to attend, but the cost was too much and it was too far from home. I sat down to my computer and thought to myself how great it would be if there were courses more local to me. I opened my emails and the first message that popped up was about a shamanism course that was local, cheaper and on a weekend when I have no other plans.

Soon after this I was whiling away the time at work one day, I had several random and unconnected thoughts. I thought about a guy I had once met briefly, he had invited me to a spiritual event previously, and I wondered if he would invite me again. I went on to think about how nice it would be to meet up with some new spiritual people and expand my mind a little more. I then thought about the fact James was going away and that I should find something spiritual to do in his absence. Later that day I had an email from the guy I had thought of, inviting me to a spiritual networking event, bang in the middle of the time of James's trip away.

The final non-coincidence brought about by my thinking was that I was contemplating how much I would like to get a nice professional photo done for publicity purposes. Later that day... yes you guessed it. Somebody emailed me. I was to appear in their magazine and they wanted to send a photographer around to take a nice professional portrait shot.

None of these things I purposefully thought about, nor did I order them. I believe these have come true so quickly because I have been indulged totally in my spiritual path. I have been living it full on and as a result things are moving quickly. I think it and before I can blink it happens. I love this. I have not harnessed it yet, but it sure as anything is making me think more happily. I figure that with the speed in which my thoughts materialize I dare not think anything bad.

Your thoughts are alive. That as far as I am concerned is a very simple truth. You can give birth to a whole set of happy non-coincidences or total disasters depending on where you allow your minds travels to journey.

Positive happy thoughts will help you to get to where you want to be eventually. Positive thinking is spiritual magic, but it is not a genie in a bottle. To get where you want to go, you may first have to jump through some flaming hoops and swim a personal ocean. As is life...

With a dose of faith filled intuition, positive thinking and an understanding of the coincidences that visit you, you will start to craft a more satisfying and well thought out spiritual existence for yourself. Take control, practice understanding why things happen, listen to your gut and then sit back and flow with it.

Love, love, love

In all my spiritual journeying it always comes back to this very simple point. Love, in fact, unconditional love is at the very heart of most, if not all spiritual beliefs. Love is so very important that it has two sections in this book. Indeed let me express the following, love is all you need, the Beatles got it right. Love, love, love.

Now I have embraced love and I can verify that it has extraordinary results. You do not have to go around your office declaring undying love for your colleagues and potted plants. Rather you can conjure the love inside you and then project that in all your dealings with people.

When you feel love for all people then compassion is easy to come by. Love allows you to be hugely empathic to people. In love you realize that they are simply human and that we all have faults. It becomes simple to replace any anger or frustration that you feel toward your fellow mankind with love. In love you forgive people as quickly as you can, excuse them for their misbehaviors and recognize that none of us are perfect.

This may sound challenging but I found it came remarkably naturally. And the benefits? Well it makes you a kinder person to be around, and in turn people are kinder back. It helps you view your little world from a very optimistic stance, and whilst it does not make you immune from being hurt or angered, it makes these pitfalls far easier to handle.

Love is one of the most powerful and cleansing acts you can indulge. When you radiate love and feel it deep inside, nothing can really harm you. Loving people and events, no matter what, is transformative for the soul. Love can underline your life in such an incredible way that it keeps you sane.

Above and beyond all the other advice I have issued in the past chapter, love is the one thing that is going to have the most impact on your life. Living spiritually is about recognizing the spirit in everything and everyone. So that even when things are difficult, you have the empowering resource that is love at your back. If you can learn to feel love towards all people and all situations, then darling you have cracked it.

Love absolutely diffuses all pessimism. It takes away anger, jealousy, stress and worry. If you can look at your life with a deep love, and a trust that everything happens for a reason then baby doll, you may as well just stop reading now and get on with it.

If you take nothing else from this lesson then please, please open yourself to the feeling that is love. If you can manage that, then everything else follows naturally. Really it does. If you can look at your enemy, or your ex-partner, and see them in a loving light, then hey presto all your problems are solved. Love makes things look so very different. Rather than anger, you have empathy, you have understanding, and you will feel close to people, even if those people have hurt you. Love allows you to sense their fallibility; it helps you to know why they act as they do. And when you act from a place of love, then you know deep inside that if people turn against you, they do so not because of a fault in you, but because of something within them. You will automatically forgive them their trespasses, and all harsh emotions will cease to exist inside your heart.

If you can feel love and really, intensely mean it, then you are ahead of your spiritual game. Have a go. It may sound like a difficult task, but it is easier than you think. Do it this week, do not hesitate, you can get started right now. When confronted with people or events that try your patience or hurt your heart, look to the soul of the people causing the trouble.

Remember that they are divinely linked to you, and that whilst in their ignorance and humanity they might hurt you, they only do so because of their own issues, their fears, their worries and their jealousies. Treat these people with utmost respect and love. Be kind, be calm, be cool, be a loving soul and just see what happens back.

Love is a drug and it is one that should not be on prescription only. It is free and it is accessible to you at all times, and it is your gift to all others around you. You need not walk around like a doped up and loving sycophant. All you need to do is to feel the love inside and let it guide your actions. Let love rule your thoughts and conquer any internal quarrels you might have. Express your love not through roses, romance and touchy feelies, but through respect, warmth and patience for all the people you meet.

I could write about this all day long but I would rather you went out and experienced this for yourself. I trust that you will have a go, starting from as soon as you put this book down. Maybe you are in a library or at home, or on a beach on holiday. Whether your next meeting is with a librarian, your child or the beach masseuse, let your interaction come from a flowing, loving place. Check out what happens and note how it makes you feel. Smile your love through your eyes, be generous and kind to all people, and in the words of my spiritual comedic hero, Mr. Bill Hicks, 'Love all the people all the time'. Underpin your life with love and watch everything else fall into place.

Release

Once you are embracing a spiritual life fully you will begin to see the lack of meaning in some of the things you used to build your world around. Our possessions, worldviews and love of handbags are all very well and good, but we can often get enmeshed within them and become isolated from our divine state. It is important not to become too entrenched within the belief that you are the sum of all your material possessions and accessories. The true you is invisible to the eye and is not in any way reliant upon her teeth whitening, her designer handbag or her love of Pilates for her self esteem.

In the western world we all come with dozens of add-ons and

accessories that we feel makes us individual and add expression to our spirit. None of these things are the true you. They may be ways of creating a persona of the true you, but they are not you. They may well be indicators to the outside world of the color of your soul and the make of your character, but they are not you. They are a skewed version of you, seen through the eyes of somebody else's labels and vision.

I recommend you relinquish your dependence on anything and everything that you believe represents yourself. Of course you may still enjoy reading your favorite newspaper, supporting your causes, or brandishing your glossy red lips everywhere you go, but you must be aware that these things, whilst important to you as a human, are not a patch on your true soul.

We often marginalize and box ourselves in by our attachments. We become painfully, emotionally and mentally dependent upon these. We may feel that if they are taken away, we will be nothing. But it is in this space of nothingness, where no attachments exist, that you will find your genuine reality. Not one of us came to the planet with anything other than our physical form and a great deal of potential. The materialistic society then asks us to get into bed with different products and services. We become everyday cheerleaders and publicity people for a thousand and one types of purchasable items. We are fragmented, torn and swiftly losing track of what really makes us tick.

To an extent even our spirituality can be an accessory if we become reliant on it as a definition of who we are. So aim to let your spirituality sit within you. Do not feel inclined to bring it out of your mind or heart to become something that labels and defines you. We are all spiritual, but if you use that as a tagline, which we all do from time to time, then it becomes an observation rather than a truth. You are spiritual whether you like it or not, and so to repeat this to score brownie points or to allow yourself to be interpreted by another is disarmingly bizarre.

I challenge you for a week to just simply be. Do not pepper your conversation with your achievements, your contacts or your love of high power motor vehicles. Instead exist from your inner sanctum, from your intuition and from the very sensible voice you hear in your head that tells you that you are good enough as you are, without the requirement to live through what you own, or via the politics you espouse. So for this week be nothing and in that space become all that you really are.

Beyond releasing your attachments, I ask you to release your worries and fears. Early on in the book I asked you have faith. By now that faith will, I hope, have been proven in a myriad of magnificent ways. Now it is time to release your fears and worries to that faith. Our fears tend to represent us as much as our attachments do. Our fears can take over our souls if we allow them to do so. Fear can become the crux of our life as we become tied up in circumnavigating the things that scare us. Worry can push us to control life and others in ways that are unhealthy for everyone involved.

We must drop our attachments to these emotions. We must remember that all harsh things are sent to test us, and that worrying about them will change nothing. In a place of worry we can achieve naught but a heavy heart. A heavy heart is not one that is easily accessed by the soul. I ask you to have faith that you will be loved, and guided and divinely inspired when the time is right. Whatever it is that makes your heart ache, is serving to disable your spiritual senses because you are too strongly linked in to it.

So let people do what they will. Do not try to stop them or encourage them otherwise. It affects you only because you allow it to, because you take it personally. Release their hold on you and sit calmly in the aftermath. Others will always do what they want to in the end. Release your need to be so avidly concerned for them and their behavior. Let them go... Release them and their ways and have faith that all will come right in the end. Know that no matter what happens your desire to restrict a person is causing you nothing but upset.

Sometimes we need to compromise with ourselves and open our hearts. The compromise being that we allow ourselves to worry a little less and make space in our hearts for our higher self to grow and breathe.

For this week live naturally and unheeded by those things that normally cause you stress. Approve of yourself and walk out into the world with your head held high. Do not judge yourself; release any negative thoughts you have about your life, your past, your future, your looks, your weight, your clothes and your bad hair day.

Acknowledge that you are an everlasting, ever growing creature, and that the ties that bind will bind no longer. I assure you that this is your choice. Living spiritually and dropping all that binds you is your choice. I urge you to make that choice now.

For those ready to make a choice, and to enable all that this book has taught you so far then I have devised a short exercise to help. Sit is a quiet space and follow this exercise...

Take deep breathes, calm and centre yourself. Set your mind toward your spiritual living and toward making a commitment to follow your faith from this day forward.

Envisage the vines of self-doubt and anxiety that wrap around your heart and mind. Imagine these vines breaking away and releasing all the sad feelings from your heart and soul.

Whenever a vine starts to creep back in, chop it up, melt it away, centre yourself in silence and remember that you are not your worries, your cares, your desires or your property, you are spiritual wondrousness made physical for a short time on earth. Know that and embrace it.

Put a smile on your face and feel it in your heart. Smiling makes your heart feel large and when the heart feels large the vines pop right off. Remember that and use it.

Next I want you to think or say this or something similar from your own heart...

"Guides, angels, higher-self, God and Goddess. I am ready to live my spiritual path. I am ready to become the one true soul that I am. I ask for your assistance and your guidance in this. I will listen to my intuition, please guide me. I will offer love up to all people and things, please guide me, I will release my attachments, my worries and my fear, please guide me. I will use my mind optimistically and with the faith that you will always guide me. I offer you my faith, my love and my trust. I am ready for my spiritual awakening to begin, please guide me."

To help put this into practice, and all the other learning from this lesson, drop all your worries, all your fears and all your attachments; I want you to try this for one week. Be a soul amongst many, existing and letting the day flow over you. When thoughts of possessions, or concerns try to consume you, let them drop away, meditate, breathe deeply and do nothing. Find your inner space again, align to it and exist from a pure place. When anxiety builds tap your body gently in the place where you feel it. Ask it to leave and have faith that your higher self, your guides, angels and maybe even the Goddess herself will step in to make the feelings subside.

For this week let your mantra be this, sing it chant it, live it breathe it. Whatever you do be sure to try it out and see...

"Release and Let me Be. Release and Set me Free."

Now that you have released your fears and your attachments you are ready to find your everyday spiritual space in the world. You are ready to allow divinity in and transform your life from the inside out.

Spiritual Space

Finding my spiritual space keeps me sane in a world that would otherwise drive me mad. Before I realized quite how crazy the world made me feel, I had alcohol and weekends to distract me. I flung myself into that madness with great abandon. Now I am a total hermit from that kind of lifestyle. Intoxicants are no longer my style and only make things seem worse, I need to ground myself to mother earth these days rather than flying as high as a drunken kite.

It is essential for me to recharge my spiritual batteries to enable me to cope with a world that, often, seems totally mad. Backbiting, disorder, panic, upset, cruelty and an array of other things that I am a witness to leave me drained. I am far too sensitive; psychically and emotionally to not give myself a sanctuary. If I do not allow myself some spiritual space, at least once a week, I start to feel disconnected from my spiritual source and myself.

This is a terrible, ungrounded feeling, and many of you will have experienced this. When this occurs I have to stop it in its tracks and pursue some spiritual undertaking. I also give myself moments of spiritual peace at other random times, these are my spiritual snacks that keep me going until I have time for something more significant and filling.

Never underestimate the restorative power and the importance of your very own spiritual space. Living spiritually leaves you open to all kinds of emotional junk and mental attacks from the world around you. Nobody means to target his or her issues and emotions onto you, yet despite this, you may find that you become an emotional sponge. I for one am far more sensitive to people's emotions than I used to be, and it can take its toll. A temper tantrum over something as benign as a remote control can leave me reeling and feeling as though I have been assaulted.

The number of conflicting emotions flying around can

sometimes make me feel like I am living in the fallout of a nuclear winter. I may sound as though I am exaggerating; maybe I am, a little. But I do not exaggerate when I say that I am sensitive, and that being sensitive to other people's feelings can leave me feeling battered, stressed and bruised.

I find myself longing for my bed, for alone time or being overly emotional myself. My stress tolerance lowers and little things start to really grate. When this happens I know it is time to take some spiritual space for myself.

It is still easy to lose your spiritual shape in one bad day or following one horrid argument. But not to worry, you can soon spiritualize your ailing soul. On the days where you feel all too human, then embracing your own enlightened comfort zone is hugely important

Spiritual space is about making a time and place to celebrate your spirituality. It is vital that you enjoy your spirituality, otherwise there is a danger it may become a chore. Spirituality is a precious gift and it will treat you well, in return you can create some awesome Goddess style habits that ensure that your spiritual life has staying power and longevity.

Consider your spiritual space as a reflective gift to you, one that reaffirms your faith in your own spirituality. This can include time and activities that are specifically dedicated to your favourite spiritual pursuits and other activities that you personally find life enhancing.

As spiritual seekers we have no church, no temple and no cathedral. Whilst some of us adhere to the philosophy of books, gurus and spiritual meditation groups, and many of these are helpful and lovely, they are not always what the soul needs. It is wonderful to find your own independent spiritual place in the world. Your group or guru will not always be with you, and so to seek your spirituality inside, then you must make it your practice, your art and your love. You must create your own space and recuperate, worship, breathe, exist and be simply you, a little spiritual soul.

I have experimented with making my spiritual space in a number of ways; it is a fun and creative task. I can do everything else I recommend in this book, but if I do not make spiritual 'me' time I start to feel like my spirituality is coming loose at the seams. I need events and practices that pull me like invisible spiritual strings through my life. These give my life a spiritual structure and substance. They help ground me and make me better equipped to deal with work pressure and premenstrual stress. It is all very well and good living spiritually on a daily basis, as you know, I advocate it. But if you are like me, you may find you need more than that. You need your own little slice of personal spiritual heaven on earth.

Spiritual space will help maintain your energy and balance. It shakes your inner energy up, connects you to your higher self, grounds you and enhances your spiritual vibration. However you want to put it, it makes you feel happy. Be sure to tend to your spiritual garden from time to time. Give yourself spiritual fresh air. Be the spirit that you know you are, uninfluenced by the unintentional bad vibes and unhelpful opinions of loved ones.

Stop, breathe, remove yourself from life, take it all in and give yourself a spiritual spa, a treat, a healing. Build this into your month, your week, and your day. Take your space as often as you need and preferably before you need it. Be assured that this is time out for the greater good. A happy spiritual you is a great person to know. A drained spiritual drop out is no good to anyone. Find your space and take it lady.

Let's start with the small stuff. The little things you can do every day to help reconnect you with the greater spiritual universe. These little bits can be swapped around, or pick one favourite to do often. These are examples of little things that act as reminders and refreshers on your spiritual path. They inject a little much needed enlightenment dust into a dreary day, and they help you to remember that spiritual goodness can be sought whenever it is required.

Altar

Build a little altar and use it. My altar also doubles up as my work desk. On my altar I keep photos, crystals, incense, tarot cards and angel cards. I do not (as yet) pray to my altar, but it is my little piece of spiritual hippydom, in an otherwise fairly organized and neatly laid out home. Everything that is on my altar is something I can grab hold of and use should the moment take me. It is tangible, real and helpful.

My altar is a sacred space; full of my sacred bits and bobs, feathers, stones, books and precious trinkets. Depending on my mood I could grab a pack of cards, a crystal or burn some incense. Each of these is a spiritual snack in its own right. My altar is a real, tangible testament to my faith. It is the physical incarnation of all I hold true to my heart. Place photographs, flowers, mementos, postcards, letters and scrapbooks here.

Your altar may be as neat or as random as you feel it should be. Your altar is the heart of you made real. It is the metaphor of your soul's longings and it is a place to focus and remind oneself of what lies beneath the surface. Your altar is your sacred space in your home; it is your place of personal worship. Use it as you will, but be sure that you have one.

Journal

Keep a journal of your spiritual thoughts, occurrences, dreams and activities. I find doing this is so much more helpful than a normal diary. I no longer keep a normal diary, other than to help me track my appointments. Spirituality has inherent in it a great deal of personal progression and it is helpful to record this for your future reference. Indeed a spiritual journal is vital if you are to record the fleeting thoughts and ideas that are sent to you from your divine self and other angelic hosts and guides who may be trying to help you. Some thoughts are so fleeting that if I did not write them down, I would not remember them five minutes later. So when spiritual inspiration strikes – get scribbling!

A spiritual journal is also great for recording your dreams. So keep it by your bed. Then write down your dreams in the night or as soon as you wake up. The act of writing dreams down helps to solidify them in your mind and so a notebook is so handy for this.

Record your spiritual activities as you do them. Whenever I do myself a little angel card reading or tarot reading, I record it in the diary. I like to write if any unusual non-coincidences have occurred, or any other spiritually significant events happen. Record your intuitions, when you have followed them and when you have not. Jot down passing thoughts, inclinations and lovely psychic moments. Count your blessings and record your happy moments.

Use your journal to write your prayers into. Address you angels and guides and make your wishes known. Write positive affirmations and mantras. Use your diary to ask for help from the divine. Be creative; my spiritual journal contains funny little cartoons that have come to me in meditation and doodles that I just had to put to paper. I also include my spiritual ideas and plans for the future.

I find that my spiritual journal is a real pleasure to read. Often if I carry my journal out into the world with me it comes back crammed with feathers, leaves, moss and leaflets for new spiritual experiences. It becomes a living diary of your enlightening life.

Like an altar, your journal is your spiritual life made real. It helps bring something divine into our material world. It takes the spirituality from your insides and creates a little fortress where you can rest your head and seek solace. Your spiritual life is not just in your head, make it real by placing it on paper and committing that belief to the world you can touch and see.

Bless your Home

Your home is your spiritual space as much as your heart is. You might frequently turn to a healer to bless your body, or a guru to give you affirmation, so why not do the same for your living space? Whether this space is a room in your parent's home, a six-bedroom mansion or a rented trailer on a park, it is yours and it deserves to be blessed.

You do not need to have a poltergeist running rampant to warrant a blessing, just as you do not need to be sick to have a healing. Your home is an energetic space as much as anything else. It attracts moods, emotions and vibrations; it is helpful to cleanse your four walls so that your home remains your sanctuary. Nor do you need a priest or a medium to do this for you. You have the power and ability to do it for yourself.

Start off by setting your mind to what it is you wish to usher into your home. This may be peace and love, joy and abundance, happiness and harmony. Focus on the positive and keep these in your mind as you perform a little ritual on your space. Wander from room to room offering up a blessing of sound, prayer, affirmation and burnt offerings. Chant your chosen words, sing them, whisper them, or even write them on little pieces of paper and tuck them away in the corners and shelves of your place.

Sound is a very powerful space cleanser, so besides your own chanting you might wish to play some relaxing music, ding a bell, or shake a rattle all around your home. Sound adds to the ritualistic feel and helps set the right tone for getting the energy shaken up and transformed to something pleasant and energizing.

I love to use smudge sticks of sage or Palo Santo wood, or handmade incense to purify my home. You light the dried herbs with a match, tap out the flame and let them smoulder, wafting the aromatic smoke as magical incense in the air. I do this every so often, always in a ritualistic style. I waft smoke over doors windows, beds and hallways. You can also waft the smoke over yourself for a fully holistic cleansing experience.

I make my own sage sticks by growing the sage in my garden, drying it out by placing it on a sheet on top of the fridge and then bundling it up in little bunches bound with string ready to burn. It's so much more personal and far cheaper than buying sage sticks.

Palo Santo came to my rescue when my cat Molly refused to go downstairs. She had a total freak-out at nothing and was terrified of the sofa and the living room. For a whole week we pandered to her, bringing her food upstairs and feeling quite worried for her mental health. I then absentmindedly left my lump of Palo Santo wood on top of a burning candle in a glass jar. I turned away for a few moments and the wood set on fire, releasing the purifying energy into the room. Not long afterwards, Molly came back downstairs as if nothing had ever happened. Given her bizarre behaviour leading up to this, it was as though a minor miracle has occurred! Whatever the big scary 'nothing' was that was scaring her it was shooed away by the sacred smoke of Palo Santo.

When I'm blessing my home I tend to draw symbols in the air with the smoke. If you want to maximize the love in a bedroom, waft love hearts in the air. If you want peace then go for the peace sign. If you are unsure, then I find random swirls are more than adequate. Be careful not to drop hot ash of course, you may be wishing for some hot passion, but not so hot that your home burns down!

All of this can be accompanied by as much ritual and moodiness as you see fit. Incense, candles and oil burners all help add to a spiritual atmosphere. Crystals may be placed wherever your gut feeling wants them to go. On a very basic housekeeping level, making sure the house is clean and tidy helps you to feel that the blessing can take hold without the clutter and rubbish getting in the way and spoiling the mood.

Bless your home at a full moon to celebrate life and abundance, or do it at a dark moon in the last quarter before the new moon to remove negativity and usher in joy. Do it in the morning to help bring in the feeling of freshness and rebirth, or do it at dusk to say good-bye to old habits and unhelpful life patterns. Do it at night to usher sleep, peace and calm to your home after a hectic day.

Feel confident to invent your own blessings for your own reasons. You are perfectly empowered to do so. You do not need a manual or a guide, just a heart full of hope and the will to make your home your spiritual castle!

Music

Music is a powerful force. It can lift your mood or take you down; it can carry your jiggling hips to a fabulous beat and bring back long-forgotten memories. Music evokes great feeling and passion, it is used in every single religion I can think of as a means of singing praise, expressing faith or invoking the attention of the almighty. Music is universal; it crosses borders, cultures and race. The simplest, most wonderful thing about a great track is that if you like it, you like it. It does not matter where it originates from, who wrote it or even if it is totally outside your usual stable of sounds. If it catches your ear and it makes you smile, dance or simply feel, then it has succeeded.

For all these reasons, and so many more, music is the perfect instrument by which caring sprits, guides and angels can contact us with their messages. That is why music is an important addition to your spiritual space. Most of us are not overtly psychic, although we may pay attention to our gut feelings, we may not be in any other significant contact with the 'other side'.

If you want to attune yourself more tightly to the love and messages of your guides, music might be your way forward. Listening to music is perhaps the easiest way to welcome divine guidance into your life. It is as easy as switching your I-pod to shuffle and settling back to see what comes on.

The messages in music are often very simple. It may be that songs you hear bring hope, joy, fun and laughter to your life. You may find yourself singing along unexpectedly or feeling an urge to dance like a crazy lady whilst doing your ironing. Go for it is all I can say! So many other faiths believe that music and dance bring you into direct contact with the divine. So sing your heart out, do the twist, or just pump up the volume and smile at the neighbors if they knock on the door to see what the commotion's all about.

Now I know you have been listening to sounds and music naturally all your life. But this is more about listening from your gut, from your heart and from your soul. A friend of mine said that she connects to music emotionally, but she could not think of any songs that she connects to spiritually. Well my answer to that is if you connect emotionally, then it is likely that that song has spiritual resonance for you.

We are, after all, souls in human form, we experience things through an array of human feelings and thoughts, therefore if your gut churns and your lower lip wobbles when you listen to a beautiful track, yes that is emotional, but I also believe it to be spiritual. If you have a track in mind, go back to it now, listen to it again, try to get a feel for the emotion it creates. Next time you feel that again for a different song then there is a good chance you are experiencing a song with a special message just for you.

We are the lucky audience to that heavenly channeling. The musicians may be the hosts, the co-creators and the recipients of large royalties, but we are the beneficiaries in so many deeper ways. The messages that music contains for our everyday lives, and for the bigger matters such as death, birth, breakdowns and love are infinite.

The caress of the angels is inherent in every chord, lyric and plucked guitar string that ever existed and it is really rather rude of us not to open our ears and hear precisely what it is they want us to.

Music allows us to access the entire human experience. It helps us to feel that we are not alone and that worldwide people love and suffer just like us. Your mission if you choose to accept it is as follows.

For a one week trial period change your radio station, swap I-pods with your friend, buy a random CD that attracts your attention and listen, listen, listen. Keep notes in your journal, be fervently aware of what you hear. Let music into your heart and soul, and if this works well for you then keep the tunes turned up permanently! Music is food for the soul... so eat.

Spiritual Spa

I like to check in with my spirituality every week by giving myself a spiritual spa evening. Rather than indulging in a self-administered manicure, facemask and hot bath, I have a spa with a soul based inclination.

Here are my tips on running your personal spiritual spa for your happiest benefit and soul soaking relaxation.

Find a space to make your own for the evening. My bed often plays this part for me. I will sit myself on there with a pack of tarot cards, maybe some animal cards and a handful of crystals, and I will give myself a reading. You might wish to keep your spiritual journal handy and perhaps bless the room you will use beforehand with an herbal smudge stick.

Ambience is always important so burn some incense or scented candles, play some soulful music and give yourself the luxury of un-interrupted time. Sometimes I like to meditate briefly; other times I just go straight to doing the reading. The relaxation part, as you will see, is for later in the night.

Whilst I am an experienced tarot card reader, I am terrible at doing any kind of card reading for myself as I lack the much-needed objectivity to discern what the cards are saying to me. So to help me along I use a tarot guidance book. I might ask a few questions and draw a few cards, or I may just do a spread to represent my life at the current time. A favourite is always past, present and future style spreads; as these help get some perspective on where I am and where my life is going.

I write down all the answers in my journal so that I can check up on this the next time I indulge in my spiritual spa. I then take some time to commune in my mind with the divine. I will say a little prayer, count my blessings, ask for guidance or I simply let divinity know that I want to strengthen my connection to them. Whatever you choose to say is going to be reliant on what is occurring in your life, and what you want. Make that moment with the divine your very own. Enjoy it and be assured that you are being heard.

Then comes the best bit... I follow all this up with a nice long hot bath. I burn incense, lock the door and relax with no company except the cat. I may read a spiritual book in the bath, or I may just find a little bit of peace there. I like to place crystals in the bath with me to help fuse their unique energies into me while I rest. I envisage my body surrounded by white light and I take a well-deserved break in that very familiar sanctuary.

Having a spiritual spa evening is my way of feeling some true divine relaxation. Feel free to team this with facemasks, hot chocolate and a good chick flick! Your spiritual spa will be a very blissful space that's unique to you so fluff it up and make it your own.

Meditation

Meditation is one of my favourite things. For a long time I did it as though I were doing a necessary service. But suddenly it has me in its gentle grip and I cannot get enough of it. Meditation can be taken as a small spiritual snack or if you love it, then it can be an everyday pursuit. Who knew that closing your eyes and thinking of nothing could be such a mission, and yet a mission that is so well worth pursuing.

Meditation is high up on the list of spiritual things to do. Meditation is about striving to find a still point inside your own mind and soul. It is about trying to shut out the worries, stresses and thoughts of everyday life so that something more magnificent can flood in. Meditation, for this reason can be very difficult. In this undertaking it is definitely the taking part that counts.

Do not give up on meditation because of perceived past failures; keep going in spite of your overactive mind. Think of this as your stillness time, focus on breathing in and out and see where your mind takes you. Observe your own thoughts and then try to find the stillness. Perhaps try a guided mediation or listening to restful music, whale song, or your favourite chill out style downloads on your I-pod.

You may find that a particular place or activity is more conducive to a meditative state. You might be pleased to hear that meditation is not confined to sitting cross-legged on a mat whilst doing nothing other than avoiding falling to sleep. Some people who struggle with meditation may find that setting time aside to lose yourself in an activity is equally worthwhile. I find a wonderful meditative state occurs when I am doing something in nature, walking or gardening. When I'm gardening, my mind goes blank. That's good enough for me. Others find meditation through walking, hiking, lying down in a grassy field under the clouds or cooking.

However you choose to meditate, make it part of your spiritual routine, five minutes is a fabulous start. The more stressed or hectic you are, the more you need it. It's even more valuable if you're maxed out and can feel your energy spiking like a porcupine around you! If meditation seems too difficult on certain days then find a couple of moments to sit in peace and watch the world. Watch life, be an observer and allow your thoughts to quieten down whilst you find peace in becoming part of the surroundings for a brief time. This can be done anywhere, in your office, in a park or sat waiting for a train.

Melting into your meditation allows you to get a feel for your true spirit. By meditating you can become a familiar friend to your own helpful voice of intuition. Meditation gives us perspective and calms us in times of drama and stress. When life becomes tough, instead of giving over to the drama and reaction, go away and meditate. In my experience the world always looks better through meditation rested eyes.

Here is a meditation I invented for myself and like to use to help me relax after a hard day and to help the sacred space within me open up.

Worry bead meditation

Start by sitting comfortably somewhere that allows you to have a straight back. Cross-legged is great but not necessary. A chair, bed, mat, your garden, or the toilet cubicles at work are all acceptable places.

Close your eyes and prepare your mind to relax, get a feel for your body and how it is. Aim to relax all your muscles one by one. Search your joints for tension and when you find it, release it. Take several deep breaths and when you breathe out release all negative energies and feelings that your heart, solar plexus and mind are holding on to.

Stay in this place for a while, focus on your in and out breath. Allow your thoughts to bubble up, but be sure not to linger on them. By concentrating on the breath you will help to dispel the mental machinations that will inevitably try to distract you.

When you feel ready imagine yourself in a place where you feel safe and loved. You may imagine yourself to be somewhere familiar, or a far-flung beach of your imagination. Know that in this space you are protected.

Feel the earth beneath your body and trust that you are firmly grounded to her.

The mind has two different habits, the negative and the positive habit. I want you to take all your hopes, desires and positive thinking and imagine placing them in a safe place. They are not to be examined now. Lock them up tight knowing that you can access them later and that you have the key. They may be thoughts of joy or desire, but they are not for now.

The second habit is your negativity, worries and concerns. Imagine feeling for these concerns within your body, where do they cluster? Perhaps they are in your mind giving you a headache, down your back, or in your gut.

Imagine all of these worries to be made up of lots of little colourful marbles. You are in charge of the marbles. One by one I want you to imagine these marbles slipping down your body and out into the earth where they will be transmuted into positive energies.

Some of them might pop up from the earth as new life, flowers and birds.

You are now in-between a place of worry and of joy. You are in a space where your minds habits cannot affect you.

Continue to breathe deeply and observe your feelings and thoughts. Observe what happens in your minds eye. Trust that this space is your sacred space and sit in it for as long as you wish.

When you feel ready to come back to the world draw your attention to your mind and your body. Take some deep breaths and prepare yourself to become more alert.

Wiggle your toes and fingers. Count to five in your mind and slowly open your eyes. Do not jump up and run around, treat yourself gently and get up in your own time. You may first wish to write in your spiritual journal about any thoughts, emotions or images that came to you.

Practice this meditation as often as you like. Explore the silence within yourself because within it you will find your true spiritual self.

Meditation can help you to change your life. I hope that you, like me, will soon become a happy meditation addict.

Read

When I started my spiritual path every book was the right book. I soaked them up like blotting paper and as a result found myself catapulted into a deeply spiritual world. What I read in the spiritual books seemed to transfer over into my actual life. The books I read were like a catalyst, prompting an array of spiritual wonderlands to open up in my everyday life. These were always the right books at the right time.

As for finding the right books, do not panic, they will come to you. The most influential of all books I have experienced are ones that have been recommended to me, and I have felt an urge to follow through on that recommendation and make a purchase. Other times they might be given to you, or stand out on a bookshelf amongst hundreds of others. Books find you. Build a bookshelf, and trust me, the right ones will come!

Be discovered

Be open to allowing spiritual space to find you for it will seek you out if you are ready and willing. I was once reading a book on shamanic rituals and I desperately wanted to do one. Except to do so I would have needed a whole set up around me that was near impossible at that moment in time. I was never going to find the time or the equipment to follow through on the urge.

So I gave up. I put the book down I was reading and closed my eyes. I was in the bath at the time, so I figured I would just relax. No sooner had I closed my eyes than I was flung into the beginnings of a shamanic journey. Rather than feel concerned that I had not done all the lead up preparation, I decided just to go with it. My shamanic journey went on for a good while and during that time I met my power animal, who turned out to be a donkey.

It was completely unexpected, but I loved it. This is an example of how spiritual space can make itself known to you. If the time is right you can be thrust into spirituality without any notice, preparation, book or guru to guide you. We are not always in control of how our spiritual space will happen. Trust that you will not be put in danger, but you could very well expand your mind. Do not be afraid, embrace it, live it, love it, then go write it down in your spiritual journal.

Borrow

I love to visit churches, cathedrals and temples. I see them as the home of my beliefs too, it is just that the people who built them and own them may not recognise that fact. Borrow other people's temples, churches, sacred sites and spiritual paraphernalia. At the end of the day all religions are set up to worship the all mighty. Whatever you believe, it is essentially the same thing under the guise of a million human interpretations.

Whenever I am in a church I am obliged by my soul to say a little prayer and give a wink to the deity in charge. Recently my friend Natalie and I visited Peterborough Cathedral. She looked at me nervously and said that she felt like she should say a prayer. Probably others would have scoffed, but me being Miss Spirituality and Light, I was more than happy to partake of that little prayer with her. We both remarked that afterward we felt so light and lovely. Whichever God was in charge that day had blessed us with his/her love and we went on our way happy.

Borrow the buildings that are set up to worship and feel your spirituality entwined with that of a thousand other souls. Goddess does not mind.

Spiritual Soiree

Mingling with other spiritual souls can be quite inspirational. I recommend that you start your own spiritual soiree evening with like-minded friends. I have done so and it is one of the best moves I ever made. I had recently been a member of a group where it simply wasn't working out for me. I needed to continue my spiritual exploration in a group format, but not one where there was a hierarchy and not one where I had to pay. So I gathered the company of two special friends and we set out getting spiritual together.

The group is an egalitarian little group, whereby we talk about the day to day spiritual occurrences we encounter, we use tarot cards and we meditate. We are still in our early days but I know already it will help us advance as friends and as spiritual beings.

Beyond this I hook up with other groups on occasion and make time for one to ones with spiritually inclined girlfriends. I love to explore my spirituality in all kinds of situations and with all kinds of people. Whilst going it solo can be nice, it is true that sometimes the more is the merrier!

Space in kindness

Acting in kindness and compassion towards others is the sign of a highly evolved and spiritual soul. Whether you feel you meet this description is irrelevant, you can begin acting this way immediately. Whilst your initial days, months and years of spirituality might be consumed with working out whom you are and what your spirituality means to you. For your spirituality to be of any real good then it must be expressed. Expressing it through helping others is probably the best way you can do this. In helping others you create a spiritual space not only for yourself, but for another person too. How you help is entirely up to you, parenting, teaching, volunteering or simply being a good friend are all excellent ways to express your compassion and offer up grace.

Give yourself unselfishly. Commit to be kind with every act you undertake. Even just the power of a kind word, a smile or some small assistance, may seem tiny, but to another they could be much-needed gifts. I have just received a bar of chocolate from my neighbors. I had left a post on Facebook saying that people were welcome to post chocolate through my door to help me with the editing of this book. Of course I did not really expect any to appear. A knock at the door sent me reeling as Mark from next door presented me with some chocolate all wrapped up and signed from him, Danielle his girlfriend, their son and the baby they gave birth to just two days ago. Clearly the last thing they should be doing is worrying about my chocolate habit, but in this small act they made me smile. What more could a person ask for?

Random kindness, whether it is giving your neighbor chocolate, or helping an elderly gent with his shopping bags are all equally brilliant. We can all indulge in kindnesses many, many times a day. We can spend years offering kindnesses to our children, our families, to colleagues and friends. We can become the person that people turn to in their hour of need, and in doing this we hold a light up high above our heads like a beacon of pure love, soulfulness and inspiration.

As you create a space of kindness you act in pure spirit. It holds a spiritual space for those around you, and through your compassion you make the world a brighter place.

I hope this chapter has given you some extra essential hints and tips on how to embrace spiritual living on a daily basis, in your lovely little life. You are highly capable and ready to start treading the spiritual path, and I hope I have given you the necessary gumption to do so with gusto.

Always remember that you are a spiritual being in a human body. You are already spiritual. How you choose to perform that spirituality and interpret it is entirely down to you and your higher self. Enjoy your spirituality, make it your very own pleasure, let it run smoothly along with the rest of your life and let it be your life raft when need be.

Keeping spirituality in your mind is, in my opinion, a vital key to a happy and well-lived life. All I have told you in this lesson is how I do it; this is how I keep my spiritual world fresh! Now it is time for you to get out there and figure out how you do it.

Lesson 11 - The Future

I must say just a few words about our future. Lesson 11 is a very brief discussion of possibilities and hope. The future could be very messy indeed, but I believe that spiritual empowerment can save our souls.

I believe that as humans we are due for an enlightenment consisting of a total revolution in our thinking and in our beliefs about our existence. If we do not have one then we will continue on unhappily, always looking for new sofas, new husbands, new cars and new ways to pay the bills. This is not a true existence. The future, I am sure, could be bright but we are standing at a crossroads. We have the chance to enlighten and lighten the whole planet or to sink beneath the seas with our hands in our purses and our eyes firmly set to the nose on our own face.

I do believe that the world is precisely where it is supposed to be. Whilst I may have ranted about a variety of topics that I find worrying and distasteful, that is only because the rant is part of the healing process. To make a change, to step toward enlightenment, we must first recognize what ails us. We must then rail and rant and educate and eventually raise ourselves above it all. This is true on a social level as much as it is on a personal one. If spirituality is a dose of self-help for you, then for society it is total soul-seeking style reformation.

Human society has already changed beyond recognition in the past few hundred years. We have ended up with a technologically miraculous existence. This is wonderful, but many humanistic values have gone out the window and we exist in a great big shopping mall. All things can be purchased, all services, all of life. This is at the expense of other people, animals, nature and our souls. In spite of this we do need to be in this place to be able to recognize that reformation is required. As to be here now, and to live in this chaos, gives us a chance of realizing that the chaos and our way of life is not working, it is not making us happy. It is from within this abyss, this spiritless, vain, shopping led limbo that we may move forward and embrace something better.

This is an interesting space in human history. We have attempted to create the world as humans thought that they would like it to be; yet many of us are deeply unhappy. We have forgotten our values and so we seek solace in possessions, technological stimulus and medication. Something is going to give. I feel it in my bones, and besides my bones it has been prophesized by many different peoples, for example the Mayans, and the Native American Hopis.

The world is going to change in our lifetimes and become a very different place. This moment as we know it now is a temporal glitch. It is a Westernized error of judgment, however this error is getting us to the place where we should truly be. It is bringing back our spirit. Slowly, slowly, slowly, we are realizing we are not happy. We are opening health food stores, we are listening to gurus, we are pouring our cash into world disaster charities and we are starting to wake up. But what is it that will greet us in the dawn? I guess only time will answer that conundrum.

The Internet

The Internet fascinates me. We are all merging together via the worldwide web in a way previously unknown to humankind. Telecommunications on all levels has brought people together in ways undreamt of even twenty years ago. Our mass media world has magnified the faults and the kindnesses of the human race. Pornography, violence and cruelty are all there to be easily accessed, at the click of a button. But so are the fabulous groups espousing world peace, good causes, charities and light working.

We have the ability to access each other immediately, across oceans. Our divides are falling as we realize that we are so very similar. We are at a massive crossing point in human existence and I believe that it is our role to now transform ourselves for the highest purposes of us all.

The web reminds me of home, of the place where our spiritual souls reside. I believe that when we die we will be returned to energy and that we will exist less as individuals and more as a feeling, wholeness and as divine love. The Internet, in particular social networking, brings our minds together in that same way. It is almost as though we miss the conglomeration of souls so much that we have created better ways for us to be instantly accessible to each other. We need to connect and to be part of one another's lives. It may materialize as curiosity, nosiness or even outright Facebook stalking, but essentially it stems from the desire to be accessible and close to our other parts... to all the other souls.

It is through the Internet that we can really have some degree of freedom of speech. The Internet to date has exposed an awful lot of hard truths about our planet and I hope it will continue to do so. At present the Internet reflects both the dark and light side of human activity, but in the future, the near future, I am sure the Internet will help push social changes and revolutions forward in a way that is unparalleled.

It is through the Internet that our better consciousness and our spiritual reality may start to proclaim itself. It is our last bastion of truth and the last place we can go to search for the voice of a mindset that has otherwise been silenced by the mainstream media. There is huge power in this. Just like the film, we may have to plug in to the Matrix, to help us to find our way out of it.

Energy

Quantum physics has proven that there is no true matter and that our existence as we perceive it is not truly true. It has shown that everything is energy that vibrates in a way that gives the appearance of reality. Your chair, your computer, your hair, your mind, your pet, your garden, absolutely everything in the universe is vibrating energy. The theory of some is that maybe this energy has a consciousness.

I believe that this consciousness and this energy is an intelligent thinking force. I believe that this consciousness creates itself, that in turn we create our lives and our existence. Indeed I am certain that we can raise our own energetic vibration so that we have a better understanding of the greater consciousness as a whole and so that we can live more wisely and more in tune with our natural energetic, spiritual selves. Indeed I hope that this book has helped you to do just that in some small ways.

We are at a point in history where instead of inventing new objects and things for our consumption and convenience, we must start to understand the invention of ourselves. We must raise our personal energetic vibrations for the improvement of life on this planet, perhaps in this whole universe, perhaps for the benefit of other unseen dimensions.

We must do this not just for ourselves but because we are one small part of a massive, gigantic energetic whole. Within that gigantic mass of souls, or energy, or vibration we each play our vital part. We each of us have the power to change the world, simply through how we think and through beginning to understand ourselves as the little frequency of energy that we are.

This book is aimed at helping you to raise your vibration, and to start to understand that you have total power over your existence. I have not mentioned it in too much detail until now because, quite frankly, it is a lot to take in. When my father first explained this to me as child it blew my tiny little mind. It scared me silly. I could not get my head around it at all. I hope that by mentioning it now, at the end of the book, you are better prepared.

This book is aimed at raising your vibration through your thoughts, through you simply reading it and through the little exercises I have proposed. Now I have hit you with the full whammy of what I am talking about, I hope you can take it with the good faith it is intended and not be too freaked out by the fact that your existence is completely at odds to how you may have previously thought it was.

You are energy, pure and simple. The things that surround you are energy too. Your spirit is perhaps the consciousness of that energy and your guides, helpers, and angels are facets of your energy and the energy of all things. We are all one, little vibrating sparks of spiritual potential. Do you feel the buzz?

What Next?

The future terrifies and thrills me. I believe that we have come to a point where our gluttony and soullessness cannot continue. I do not believe that Mother Earth or her spiritual powers will allow it for a moment longer. It is essential that we all start to purposefully raise our energetic vibrations so that we can tune in with our higher wiser selves that are infinite and experienced.

We need to move past the greedy, selfish structures of today and open our minds to something new and fabulous. We need to accept that we create our lives in the way that they currently are, and then do something about it. I believe that we need to downsize, fend for ourselves and not exhibit across the board trust in corporations and governments.

We need to learn to think for ourselves a little. We are currently captured in a lifestyle of convenience. Everything is easy for us so we do not argue with it. Everything is easy so why would a sane person question it? Well... a sane person would question it because in the easiness we become dumb, we become soulless and we live shopping trip by holiday by television show. We are entertained beyond ourselves. I do not want to be beyond myself a moment longer. I want to be myself.

I notice people are opening up all around to spiritual ideas and I see real hope for the future within them. They too, like me, want to be themselves and they are questioning the fake walls of this facade we call society. People are disillusioned with the shallow state of their lives and when the spiritual call comes, they click right in. They grasp it with two hands; they realize that this is theirs for the taking, and that in taking it they link into a forgotten truth.

My James is one of these people. He liked my first book, but I don't think he realized where my spirituality was coming from, or where it was leading. He then watched a video on energy and consciousness and suddenly he is Mr. Spirituality personified. Suddenly he 'gets it'. Spirituality is there in a million different forms, and we all have our own version of it. Your understanding is your own, whether you tune into energy, angels or fairies, or a little mix of all three, then grasp it with two hands and know that there is more to this life than what you are currently being sold.

Happily the Internet is playing a vital role in letting those various versions of spiritual truth get to the people that need them and in turn is helping to transform their lives. Thank Goddess for the Internet because I can never see spirituality being breaking news on the nightly shows that purport to report the truth of our world.

So how will massive enlightening societal change come about? Probably the same way as it always has. Through global events, inventions, science and the voices of change being heard and recognized.

Consciousness raising is part of it, this time it is not specifically about civil rights, or animal rights, or gay rights, but about the whole coalition of humanity forming together as souls, knowing we are linked and knowing that in hurting our brothers and sisters, nature and our environment we are hurting ourselves. My hope is that this knowing will ripple out like a tsunami and people will grasp at a happiness they have never before known. Work will need to be done. Issues must be conquered. True gurus, books and wise counsel will be required, but I believe that we are ready for this shift. I believe we are ready to realize our spiritual selves.

We have already started though, so perhaps the path is becoming well trodden. Those who have gone before have shown us how to be freedom fighters, how to wage a peaceful war against the institutions and outdated ideas that bind us all. The last century saw so many social improvements, so many marginal groups being accepted and so much protest, redemption and successes at sharing the love. It is my hope that this will continue, but that the next steps will be to free our own minds from their purported humanity a little bit, and show that our individual power and mass power as souls is very real, and hugely world changing.

I am sure that natural disasters, and manmade disasters will play a part in this too. They will force us to join together as a conglomeration of vibrating little souls, as opposed to individuals locked up in our own homes and turning the other cheek to world suffering. We will all be forced to support each other and to open our eyes to our intimate, inherent connections.

I believe too that science will have a spiritual breakthrough. Many people will refuse to believe anything spiritually inclined, or even energetically inclined until it is proven to them in some way. Or until their favorite newspaper tells them it is so. So I will hope for that and I will hope that the governmental powers that be will see the value in letting us know about the discovery. If they don't then I can only hope for a leak to the press! Whatever it takes I am sure that the true spiritual 'powers that be' will make it so!

Whilst it would be very convenient for the sky to open and for the Goddess to tell us how it is. I do not believe that this will happen. It is more likely that the collective spirit of us all will speak through a scientist, a politician or somebody in the mass media who is awakened and is not afraid to tell the world.

Until the day that spirituality is breaking news, then all we can aim for is to have personal spiritualized responsibility within our own lives. It is very easy to turn around and blame the government, society or the mass media for the state of the world. I have done so many times within this book. But I have also gone on to show how you can step outside of these ways of thinking and take your own responsibility for the way you see the world and the way you live within your world. It is totally up to you what you do next.

Raising your consciousness up and out of the societal gutter is a decision you must make. And that is truly all it is, a decision, a change of heart. You must simply conclude that you are ready to open your mind to alternative ways of being, and as I expressed right back at the beginning of this book, you must choose to have faith. Once this all starts to play out, then your vibration is raising and you automatically become part of the collective of souls who are starting to envision a new world, little by little.

I believe we are getting there. I believe that we can prepare ourselves now for an intriguing future, a future where spirit, consciousness and loving awareness sit at the hearts of all beings.

I am sure that this will lead to a better understanding of our place on the planet and in turn transform the systems we have become used to. I hope that things will become smaller scale, the desire for consumption and wealth will be obliterated and we will live out our humble, happy lives in the pursuit of inner happiness and dedicated to the growth of others and the us that exists in all the other souls around us. It is time for us all to start buzzing beyond ourselves and into a bright new future.

Conclusion

After I wrote *The High Heeled Guide to Enlightenment* and committed myself to a spiritual life I was expecting spiritual miracles. What I got was a couple of years of devil in the detail type issues to deal with. It felt like the exciting intensity of spirituality had deserted me.

I now know I was being made to live with my spirituality, to learn on a daily basis how to be spiritual. Living with spirituality whilst embarking upon modern life, can be difficult. Unless you are a powerful mystic it is unlikely your spiritual life will consist of angelic meetings, visions and psychic predictions. Instead spirituality will appear on a smaller scale, but with a touch of miraculous-ness nonetheless.

Spiritual living has become my path, my challenge and my pleasure. It has been my mission to become spiritual on a daily basis, but without entirely negating my humanity. This has been difficult at times and hugely rewarding at others. It was within this dichotomy that I found the will and the reason to write this book. I crafted it into lessons, because that is how my path has been, a lesson followed by living, followed by living lessons. These lessons are not the only ones I ever expect to face. These are just the beginning, the jumpstart towards revving ahead at full on spiritual speed.

On my path I have found that some people float around on an etheric spiritual cloud of otherworldliness and mystical superiority. To me that is a form of denial, liable to lead to hypocrisy and a resounding crash back down to earth. As spiritual beings we must embrace our humanity, whilst as human beings we should embrace our spirituality. It is about living to a potential that is only fulfilled when the sacred spiritual is allowed to dwell within a fallible human.

It is our faults as human beings that make life on this planet unique. We are not here to become models of perfection whose proverbial shit does not stink. We are here to get stinky, dirty and mess things up once in a while. Because when we do we can learn hugely valuable lessons. It is the very nature of our messy lives that we must embrace. We must learn to forgive others and ourselves for all our trespasses, then learn and move on as a wiser being.

It is in doing this that we truly embrace our spirituality. As time passes then hopefully we will make fewer mistakes, but in this learning we must accept that on occasion we may be prone to an occasional wild and crazy slip up. Every so often we will feel all too human. That, my darlings, is the point. It is via our outright humanity that our spirituality and spiritual learning will arise.

Unlike my last book *The High Heeled Guide to Spiritual Living* has not contained a huge amount of visions, swooping angels or enormous prophetic moments. What it has contained is a basic recipe by which bog standard human life can be entwined with the divine, with the mystical and with something far beyond the status quo. Within the pages of *The High Heeled Guide to Spiritual Living* I have aimed to take the idea of enlightenment and apply it to everything you know and hold dear, perhaps even your premenstrual wildness! I have intended to make your spirituality utterly relevant to you opposed to it being an airy-fairy quite contrary concept that is always out of arms reach.

It is my dearest hope that this book has helped you to transform your approach to life. I hope you now understand that spiritual living need not mean denial, guilt or expensive retreats, but that it can be done between feeding the kids, doing the laundry and catching up on paying all those irksome bills.

Spirituality is in you my dear, it is you, irrelevant of those bills and chores, you already have it, and you can never escape it. You in all your glorious humanity are already spiritual; it is your role now to use that humanity to coax the spiritual out of you!

My hope is that people who had no real interest in spirituality will now have their eyes opened to the miraculous that exists in the mundane. I hope you will see how every event or thought or opportunity is touched by the chance for a better, more enlightened life.

Your life is no accident. It is a series of possibilities, one stacked on top of another. Every single day offers up new opportunities to get to know your spirit. Every thought that flits through your head carries the weight of potential personal transformation within it. Living spiritually is about recognising this. It is about being conscious, aware and digging deep into your spirit.

What you truly are, what I truly am, well that is anybody's guess. I believe that what makes up our true spirituality is mind bogglingly beyond our comprehension at this time.

So to start to understand it, we must start simply and with our own lives. Spirituality is a throw away word, take it or leave it. Because what I really mean is infinite and indefinable. Within this infinity is sat one certainty, and that certainty is you. In your place of certainty you can begin to burrow into that infinity and find out what it means for you.

The aim of this book has been to redirect and rediscover your infinite spirituality and to bring it home to your heart. It has been my aim to take that overwhelming, complex and slightly disturbing concept and sit it within your life, where it belongs. Because no matter what else spirituality is, it is very much deeply embedded within you.

So what are my conclusions on this little manifesto of living spiritually?

Big learning does not always come from big lessons. Some of your spiritual learning will come from events that are subtle and seemingly underwhelming. They are every day occurrences that you could easily snub should you wish, or should you not pay satisfactory attention. It is vital that you learn on a daily basis and that you learn from every single event.

Keep your faith inside you, and remember that all things happen for a reason and that there are no mistakes. This may mean accepting that whilst you are a vast and mighty spiritual soul, you are also utterly human, feeble at times and sometimes totally prone to fallibility. This is always for your highest good, even when it feels like torture. Even when you act like a prize idiot and deeply regret it, this is simply a card played by your higher self to show you a little something about yourself and catalyse whatever change is needed.

Love is the key to all things and to your personal enlightenment. Feel it at all times and life just gets better.

Reaction is the enemy of all things. If we feel love then we must sit and sweat in it, even when our very core wants to scream or throw a hissy fit. Sitting in our love and making no comment or action is the most powerful act you can perform. It is far more difficult than it looks, but that is where your development and spiritual understanding will come from.

Here is a favourite…

You are spiritual because you are already spirit.

How you choose to interpret that is down to you and nobody else. Discovering your spirit is your job if you choose to accept it, which I do believe you already have. I can give pointers and a million gurus would love you to cough up the cash to take you on a fast track. But let me tell you this. Enlightenment does not come quickly. Life gets in the way and I would not like to see you poor, penniless, chanting some ridiculous mantra and dependent on oracle cards in the hopes that it might bring God to your side quicker. Take your time; you are already spiritual.

Spiritual development is not about a class or a potion or an activity. Those are niceties, spiritual hobbies so to speak. The hard work, the challenging stuff, comes not from a hike in the Himalayas, but from living your life. Running away to a retreat may be calming for the soul, but it will not necessarily get you to grips with the habits of a lifetime that drag you down or prevent you from seeing the planet through happy eyes.

To embrace your spirituality you are required to live your life. You need to see your spirit in the day to day, in the dregs, in the drunken night out and the darling moments too.

Believe this one thing. Everything is an opportunity and until you see life in that way, then you can never live to your full capacity. You will rail against your personal Goddess and question why life is so hard, why can't you and your loved ones be spared?

Well... if we were to be spared, if we lived a perfect life, we would not be seeking enlightenment because we would be air heads floating around learning nothing and never suffering. We are incarnated on this planet in part to suffer. Not because God is torturing us, but because we signed up for the torture, the torture and the bliss. I would apologize if you do not like this, but I can't do that because I believe it is true. And the sooner you embrace it, the easier it will all become.

Spirituality may begin as a solo act, but to continue that path we cannot help but see a larger picture. Spirituality is always, eventually social. One cannot claim to be spiritual but show no consideration for the suffering of our fellow human, nor can we turn a blind eye to corporate destruction ladled onto the planet whilst proclaiming ourselves earth mothers, or star daddies. It is my utopian hope that a whole barrage of issues can be healed when glimpsed through spiritualized eyes.

Spirituality is a serious dose of introspection and self help. It is continual and just when you think you are getting good at it, you will make a step backward and have to start all over again. Frustrating yes, but for the benefits it is the only way I would ever now wish to be. Stand tall, know yourself and get on with living. That is the top and bottom of it, the rest of it is fun, frolics and learning to interpret the world with spiritually refreshed vision.

Finally I will tell you a little secret. I have learned so much writing this book. All that I have written has been prompted by my ongoing real life strife, joy and regret. I have lived this thing to the hilt, and it has been painful. Sometimes I do not learn my lesson and so it comes back time and time again.

I am not a guru, I am not a saint, and I can be a sinner. I am pretty much the same person as you, with a bunch of different energy and experience to feed off.

Your life is yours; you know your truth, look inside for your own truth before you sway to the thoughts of another on your life. Learn what you can, take what you can from every event, and have faith. Know that the reason behind everything happening for a reason, is always borne out of spiritual love, learning and personal growth.

See the opportunity in everything, you are a transforming butterfly and life will push and prod you toward your beautiful flight. Sometimes the prods and pushes will be hard to accept, but they are never, and I mean never because you are being blamed or because you are wrong. Trust me, have faith, the universe loves ya baby!

Having now written and lived this little manifesto, if I didn't know better I would now take some time off from being spiritual. But I have tried that one before and it does not do any good, it makes things worse. So I am firmly set on this spiritual roller-coaster from now until forever. Who knows, give me a few years and there is likely another book in it.

I am blessed that you have shared my journey with me, and I can only hope that in your wrangling with human life you find the same little bit of spiritual spark that I did. It will get you through a bad day and it can at times illuminate your soul. Never doubt it, no matter what drama comes your way; never doubt the potential of the ordinary, the obtuse, the crazy and the palava.

I thank you for your attention, for your patience and for being my muse. I thank you too for making all my suffering worthwhile, in the humble belief that you too might learn something from it.

So that is it. My last book was finished with a big dramatic closing that made people cry and whilst I would like to repeat that, I believe the drama queen within me is all worn out. Let's save the drama for real life and our ever-encroaching learning.

So my friend I will bid you farewell and wish you luck on your high heeled, low heeled, barefoot path to spiritual living. With all my heart I wish you love, peace and happiness, and beyond that I wish you the wisdom to know that those three things, love, peace and happiness are already yours. Feel them now.

Also by Alice Grist

The High Heeled Guide to Enlightenment

BOOKS

O is a symbol of the world, of oneness and unity. In different cultures it also means the "eye," symbolizing knowledge and insight. We aim to publish books that are accessible, constructive and that challenge accepted opinion, both that of academia and the "moral majority."

Our books are available in all good English language bookstores worldwide. If you don't see the book on the shelves ask the bookstore to order it for you, quoting the ISBN number and title. Alternatively you can order online (all major online retail sites carry our titles) or contact the distributor in the relevant country, listed on the copyright page.

See our website **www.o-books.net** for a full list of over 500 titles, growing by 100 a year.

And tune in to myspiritradio.com for our book review radio show, hosted by June-Elleni Laine, where you can listen to the authors discussing their books.

MySpiritRadio